TEN HAG
THE BIOGRAPHY

TEN HAG
THE BIOGRAPHY

Maarten Meijer

EBURY
SPOTLIGHT

EBURY SPOTLIGHT

This edition published in 2023
First published by Ebury Spotlight in 2022

Ebury Spotlight, an imprint of Ebury Publishing
20 Vauxhall Bridge Road
London SW1V 2SA

Ebury Spotlight is part of the Penguin Random House group
of companies whose addresses can be found at
global.penguinrandomhouse.com

Penguin
Random House
UK

www.penguin.co.uk

A CIP catalogue record for this book is available from the British Library

ISBN 9781529903638

Printed and bound in Great Britain by Clays Ltd, Elcograf S.p.A.
Imported into the EEA by Penguin Random House Ireland,
Morrison Chambers, 32 Nassau Street, Dublin D02 YH68.

MIX
Paper | Supporting
responsible forestry
FSC® C018179

Penguin Random House is committed to a sustainable future
for our business, our readers and our planet. This book is made
from Forest Stewardship Council® certified paper.

CONTENTS

1

FROM VELDMAAT TO MANCHESTER

'Football is a game you play with your brains.
You have to be at the right spot at the right time,
not too early, not too late.'
JOHAN CRUYFF

Mid-August 2022, the Premier League table was a sight to behold, with Manchester United in last place. After a defeat against Brighton and humiliation by Brentford, a feeling of impending doom settled among supporters. Then the resurrection came.

Erik ten Hag is the only Manchester United manager to secure his first competitive win in a match against Liverpool. Cristiano Ronaldo, Harry Maguire, Luke Shaw and Fred lost their starting positions, making room for Anthony Elanga, Raphaël Varane, Tyrell Malacia and Scott McTominay. Ten Hag's bold interventions would have faced intense scrutiny had they not been effective. They worked a treat. The manager threw new signing Tyrell Malacia in at the deep end. The 23-year-old's job was to restrain one of the fastest and most dangerous attackers in the world, Mohamed Salah. Malacia did this with gusto and had little trouble with the Egyptian. Varane, a defender who has won the lot for club and country, including four Champions Leagues and a World Cup, demonstrated how foolish it was that he had ever been considered a substitute centre back. New arrival Lisandro Martínez, ridiculed in the English media for his height, played a nearly perfect game, making next to no mistakes. He was the model centre back against Liverpool's startled attackers. He registered seven clearances and four blocked shots and interceptions.

The curious dressing room power struggle of Maguire and Ronaldo was rendered moot. The captain was benched, the Portuguese star beside him. Ten Hag went with the speed of Jadon Sancho and Marcus Rashford. That was a masterstroke. Sancho's perfect piece of composure was the result of searing early pressure, leading to the 16th-minute opener, a classy goal that got even Ronaldo to his feet applauding. Rashford appeared a man reborn, confidently bypassing Liverpool goalkeeper Alisson on a blistering counter. He ended a run of 997 minutes without a goal in all competitions. Manchester United crashed into challenges and contested every ball with a fierce competitive edge. The work ethic of the entire team was tremendous. A mixture of amazement and enthusiasm swept through Old Trafford as United arguably delivered their best performance of the last five years against Liverpool. Ten Hag proved his skill and produced just the sort of triumph he needed to make a statement of intent at Old Trafford.

• • •

In April 2022, De Veldmaat became a hive of media activity. Reporters from the *Daily Telegraph*, the *Guardian*, Sky Sports and other British news organisations were prowling the streets of the otherwise sedate neighbourhood. They were there to dig up every possible morsel of Erik ten Hag lore, after he had overnight become the most interesting man from the Continent in England. In 1977, little Erik had made his first moves on a football pitch at local amateur club Bon

Boys. Club chairman Gert-Jan Klanderman said that the locals took a moment to adapt to Ten Hag's new status as an international celebrity: 'Journalists contact us via Twitter, LinkedIn and email. We welcome them all. We are proud of Erik. A few weeks ago, we kept quiet because the news about Manchester was just rumours. Now we say: stop over! We think this may just be the beginning as England have quite a lot of media.'

The journalists trawled the municipality of Haaksbergen for information and nosed around the Bon Boys training grounds. 'They suddenly were there on the sidewalk, on a training evening. We are hospitable. They want to know everything. "What was he like as a child? Was he already a leader back then? What family is he from?" I just answer that I think it is nice that he is still so involved with us and has never forgotten his origins. He still checks what Bon Boys have done, every week. We tell our youth, "Look where you can end up if you work hard." Erik has a lot of impact. He was here recently, and in no time there were crowds at the door. The fact that he is now going to United as a sober-minded Tukker is quite a feat, we are very proud of him. We are very happy to tell the English media about that.'

What is Ten Hag's secret recipe for great coaching? What is his masterful tactical plan or exhilarating pre-game motivational speech? Journalists and coaches sometimes are on common ground when it comes to looking for fitting explanations of a team's success or failure, and both float obscure theories about 'the conditions of the day' or a 'winner's feeling'. Football is not an exact science. It's a sport that is unpredictable, and that's what makes it fascinating. At the same time, it makes the coach's task a difficult one. When the result is mediocre, he is usually the first person people complain about. When it is bad enough, he gets fired. It is hard to gauge the exact influence that the manager has on the course of a game. One coach may be more successful than another under similar circumstances. Some coaches just seem to understand better than others what makes the game tick and the players perform.

Erik ten Hag shed some light on the mystery: 'A coach can't perform magic, although some media and fans seem to think he can. Put your team out there and it'll be fine. Before you get there, you need to find the right balance. That takes time, with ups and downs. And with downs, people start to criticise. That's part of the package. You need to deal with that. Coaching is about experience. The more you do it, the more experienced you get. You keep gaining new insights, if you're open to it. If you want to learn, from your players, other coaches and other cultures, you'll develop as a coach.'

Striker and Ajax team captain Dušan Tadić, who was at the centre of Ajax Amsterdam's goal-scoring prowess during the Ten Hag years, is convinced that Ten Hag will flourish wherever he is planted. 'He is one of the best trainers in the world, and it is a privilege for any player to be able to work with him. He fits every major club. Tactically I think he is such a good trainer that we are actually ahead 1–0 before the game starts, if we carry out what he expects of us. He explains everything. He leaves nothing to chance and surprises us every time. He identifies the opposition's strengths and how to stop them. Whatever they do, he has a response. He gives us such an advantage, we always feel like we are one step ahead of the other team. I think, tactically, he is a master. But he is also very good in the way he talks to the players. He is so good because he has that combination.'

The success does not come suddenly. Wherever the taciturn tactician makes his entrance, a predictable cycle follows: surprise or shock, hesitation or resistance, and then a period of transformation followed by astonishing results and almost unanimous acclaim. This happened at Go Ahead in Deventer, at FC Utrecht and at Ajax. He was particularly maligned during his first season in Amsterdam. Patience ran out, tempers flared. Everything about him was wrong: his appearance – he was 'a conehead with a Trotsky goatee'; his speech – he sounded like 'a farmer from the sticks'; his media presence – halting, awkward, unprofessional and incomprehensible. The attacks were merciless and unrelenting. If they weighed down Ten Hag, he was able to skilfully disguise it. He did not take his detractors seriously, stood his ground on the pitch and proved sufficiently thick-skinned to stay true to his convictions. He maintained his focus and kept doing what he does best: building a winning team.

Ten Hag calmly summarised his experience in the capital city: 'All that criticism? This bullying culture suits the Netherlands, and the TV programmes that use that get good ratings. Scoring at someone else's expense. I know how opportunistic it is, and it can change from one day to the next. In the Netherlands we are good at discussing the result. People want to find the guilty, and then they focus their frustrations on one person, sometimes a player, but often the coach. They want to see their image of you confirmed. I'm not going to argue with that, it's counterproductive. You know that the moment you take on this job and things run counter to expectation, this can happen. I cannot influence that. I immediately put it aside and focus on things I can influence. I focus on my team and improving my team. I'm not really bothered by it, but you can't let everything pass you by. I do want to know what the people's sentiment is. I always look in the mirror. Do I have the right self-image? If I'm in doubt, I test it in my immediate environment.'

It often seems that the Dutch feel they invented football, perhaps because they are quite good at it. And because they think they know better than anyone else how it should be played, they also feel entitled to criticise a player or coach who does not meet their expectations. The resulting tunnel vision can be an obstacle to innovation. When someone comes along who challenges convention, there can be a problem. In particular, Dutchmen have some difficulty with acknowledging excellence. The national psychology is patterned after the local landscape: in the classless Dutch ideal everyone is on level ground, in emulation of the defining geographic characteristic of the country. A leader can never be more than a *primus inter pares*, a first among equals. On the one hand, such a philosophy guarantees equal opportunity to all and helps to keep the haughty in check. But on the other hand it also ensures that mediocrity will prevail because real leadership cannot make a full impact under those circumstances. Teamwork may be sabotaged since the views of neither the coach nor of any one team member are considered better than those of anyone else on the team. Then, when the team meets unexpected circumstances, the system breaks down. Hence, teams from the Netherlands often underperform at international competitions.

A coach experiences pressure from many quarters: supporters, sponsors, the club board, colleagues and the media. To be able to handle that stress and still be successful he needs to be smart and in control of his emotions. This is at least as important as possessing great tactical skills. When these requirements are met, a person can succeed in the coaching business. Ten Hag's sometimes pedestrian self-presentation is deceptive. He is versatile, strong-willed and resilient. He keeps his cool and does things his own way. As he said when he was appointed at Ajax: 'Stubborn is also wise.'

Ten Hag showed a remarkable mixture of class, resilience and wisdom to transcend psychological and cultural barriers to build a team that performed incredibly well. With a strong dose of Twente realism, he eliminated the inclination to self-overestimation in Amsterdam, and built a new team from the bottom up, twice.

First there was the much-vaunted Velvet Revolution of Johan Cruyff, then the colourless style of play under Frank de Boer, the game revival (without prizes) under Peter Bosz and the sad dismissal of his successor Marcel Keizer. Then Ten Hag arrived. There was his difficult start and the recognition that his team lacked mental strength, and the steep learning curve that followed – domestic championships and glorious nights in the Champions League became his crowning achievements.

In 2013, after 26 years, Manchester United manager and revered club icon Sir Alex Ferguson retired. The club has been on life support ever since. Not only did his successors prove unsuccessful in their attempts to reach similar heights, but they generally made a muddle of the structure and the strategy, so that each United team since has played in an unrecognisable style. On 21 April 2022, Manchester United announced the appointment of Erik ten Hag as the new man in charge, arriving on a three-year deal. Football director John Murtough said, 'During the past four years at Ajax, Erik has proved himself to be one of the most exciting and successful coaches in Europe, renowned for his team's attractive, attacking football and commitment to youth.' Ten Hag responded by saying, 'It is a great honour to be appointed manager of Manchester United and I am hugely excited by the challenge ahead. I know the history of this great club and the passion of the fans, and I am absolutely determined to develop a team capable of delivering the success they deserve.'

The question was posed at an Amsterdam press conference why he would be the right candidate after David Moyes, Ryan Giggs, Louis van Gaal, José Mourinho, Ole Gunnar Solskjær, Michael Carrick and Ralf Rangnick had all failed to resuscitate the troubled

Premier League club. That was the green light for Dušan Tadić to hoist his coach on a pedestal once more: 'If there is one trainer who has developed at an unimaginable pace in recent years, it is Ten Hag. Tactically he is incredibly strong and is always two steps ahead of every opponent. He has proven that for years. I know few trainers who are as intelligent. Ten Hag is someone you can always go to for advice on how to become a better player. Nobody makes you better as a footballer than this coach.'

The question on everyone's mind is, *what's next*? If Manchester United were in a period of transition after the retirement of Alex Ferguson, it now feels like a total makeover is needed. The new coach inherits a squad pathetically short on confidence and bereft of the will to win, the antithesis of what was once the backbone of the club's many triumphs. Ten Hag, however, thrives in such conditions. His curriculum vitae is vivid proof that he has an uncanny ability to build a team from scratch. In this respect he is the man of the hour for Manchester United. He started work at Old Trafford in the summer of 2022, immediately after Ajax had won their third national championship under his auspices.

How does he do it? First of all, by making his team properly uncomfortable. 'As a professional football player you have to invest yourself, your body is your toolkit. For top performances, you have to be completely fit, and as a professional you are responsible for that. They can use the staff to help. Top football is really only for a limited number of players. Many feel called, only a few are chosen. If your body is right for this and is able to handle heavier workloads, you should really do everything you can to make it to the top. That has to do with what you do on the training field, but also with what you do outside of it. Food, rest, sleep. That's what you have to teach players. Some are not aware of that. But these aspects are crucial and will decide whether or not you succeed as a professional football player and whether or not you reach the top. The first point we insist on every day: mental resilience. Winning should be the benchmark for the players, a way of life. It is not only the coaching staff who should demand this of them every day. They should also demand it of each other. We are keen on that.'

A March 2022 victory against Feyenoord saw Ajax striker Antony not only grab the winner, but be dismissed after a first yellow card for celebrating with his shirt off, then another for time-wasting. Ten Hag's post-match response was ingenious: 'Whether I was annoyed? I think you were, otherwise you wouldn't ask the question. I think: if only we had a little more of that temperament in the Netherlands! Taking off your shirt, that's not possible, that's undisciplined. That costs him the match in Groningen, but the temperament he brings also has a return. If a player is not honest, I intervene immediately. I also don't like haughty attitudes or ego trippers. In addition to their qualities, I mainly look at their character and behaviour. But also: are they married, do they have children, how is the health of their loved ones? I don't interfere unnecessarily in their private lives, but if that affects their game, I will certainly inquire about it. Football is important, but there are more important things: the birth of your child, a parent's illness, a friend who needs help. I expect complete commitment from players, but I think it's normal for them to drop everything at key moments.'

. . .

Getting close to Ten Hag is not an easy thing to do. Like others who have a certain celebrity status, he carefully guards his personal domain. But by professional football's standards, Ten Hag's reserve and reticence are exceptional. He saves his warmth for those closest to him – his family, friends and the players on his team. That does not mean he is unkind to everyone else. But the curious should not poke their noses into Ten Hag's private territory. This tough shell and don't-trespass attitude do not make the biographer's task an easy one. Consequently, it takes some digging to uncover the sources of Ten Hag's brilliance and managerial excellence. But it is well worth the trouble because he is a wise and discerning human being and a leader of vision and genius.

This biography will make Erik ten Hag – the man, the football coach, the manager – more familiar to readers and help them understand what makes him unique. Why does this quiet and driven man bring such excitement wherever he goes? Why does he succeed the way he does? The book is a portrayal of Ten Hag's life, from his boyhood in Twente to the promising start to his tenure at Manchester United. It follows him through school, his first experiments with the ball in his hometown, Haaksbergen, his career as a professional football player and from his managerial incursions in Deventer, Munich, Utrecht and Amsterdam to his current state as a top-class coach. A picture emerges of an original thinker, a keen tactician, an innovator, a disciplinarian and a motivator. In the close quarters of the dressing room and on the training ground, Ten Hag's standards are exacting. But there are many players who say that this man has made them better.

The Dutch are firm believers in *nuchterheid*, the sober-minded rationalism that was well represented in their greatest thinker, Erasmus. Dutchmen think that it is wrong to let emotions gain the upper hand. The television audience in the Netherlands gets somewhat bewildered by Brazilian exuberance, the free flow of emotion among Cameroonians and the intense patriotic passions displayed by South Koreans or Russians during World Cup or European Cup matches. Words such as 'hysteria' and 'craziness' are commonly employed to describe unmitigated outpourings of emotion. As a Tukker, Ten Hag relates well to the national predilection for rational analysis and calm reserve. 'Proud of what I do? That's not in me. I keep my feet on the ground. I like to work hard, and not keep looking in the mirror at how well I'm doing. That is simply part of the national character, so it is also part of me.'

He admits, however, 'When I party, I really celebrate. I also do that optimally and maximally. Only friends know that side of me. I have some very long and close friendships. People I can always fall back on. Everyone will have their moments when they step outside of themselves, but in this age of social media that entails risks. In order to give your maximum, you have to let your heart speak. But in the end you have to go back to the ratio [i.e., logic]. I have to guard my authority as a coach. When my authority is gone, everything is gone.'

His childhood friend Leon ten Voorde suggested that there may be another reason why Ten Hag is better on a football pitch than on a dance floor: 'It's a shame that 36 years ago he was busier checking out the ladies than listening to the dance instructor's tips. That's what messed him up at all those dances on the stage at the championship celebrations on the Museumplein in Amsterdam when he tried out some dance moves after yet another Ajax victory. I advised him to stay a safe distance away from Brazilian footballer Antony when celebrating the title. Maybe he'll listen for once.'

Ten Hag has style. Who would have thought that of a man coming from the Dutch provinces? Whereas pundits in the Netherlands pontificated about his need for language lessons – English, and Dutch – and thought he was more fit for driving a tractor over a potato field than for managing a team on a football pitch, the editors of *GiveMeSport* ruled that he was one of the best-dressed managers in international football, second only to Italian Roberto Mancini. He edged out Spaniards Pep Guardiola, Mikel Arteta and Argentinian Diego Simeone, all of whom know how to make statements of good taste in the dugout. 'Manchester United have been lacking style and substance in just about every department for as long as we can all remember. Even if Erik ten Hag is unable to change that on the pitch, he'll most definitely bring a sharp improvement to their touchline approach. Smart coats, scarves, suit pants and shirts – he's a traditionalist, but he means business.'

England and the world are eagerly waiting for, not necessarily Erik ten Hag's latest top coat, but the fruits of his interventions at the United training ground, Carrington, and a revival of performance of a reborn Manchester United. He is in the right place, at the right time.

2

SON OF TWENTE

'Wee klook is, heurt één woord en begrip der twee.'
(A smart person hears one word and understands two.)

TWENTE PROVERB

The municipality of Haaksbergen hugs the Dutch–German border and is located just south of the town of Enschede, of FC Twente fame. The big cities are at a safe distance, next to the North Sea. While Enschede is connected with the populous west by the Dutch freeway system, a visitor to Haaksbergen must make his way over narrow provincial highways, through pastures with horses and dairy cows and endless fields of corn. There is no doubt you have arrived at your destination: a large star-shaped flowerbed filled with marigolds graces the town's entrance, with the words 'Haaksbergen, star in Twente' underneath. In the central square of the town is the St Pancratius Church, still by far the highest building in the town. A sign on the church facade tells those interested that the tower is 30 metres tall and was built in 1520. Judging by the town's main architectural landmark, God still has a say in things here.

This territory is called Twente and the locals are known as Tukkers. They are often characterised as a little suspicious of strangers, frugal with money and just as sparing with words. They are also said to be a little gloomy and fatalistic, maybe because fortune did not always smile on these hinterlands. But a Twente native is proud of his heritage, without feeling the need to shout from the rooftops how great he is. Although being *nuchter*, sober-minded, is considered an essential quality in every corner of the Netherlands, Tukkers most fully embody the popular virtue. At the same time, they consume alcohol in liberal quantities, preferably with like-minded people. But you will rarely be confronted with public displays of intoxication, other than at the annual celebrations of carnival – that is, Shrove Tuesday, also known as Mardi Gras. Tukkers have self-respect, are serious people and know how to get a job done. Roll up your sleeves and get to work. No talk, but action.

The average Tukker does not really mind being underestimated because that will keep strangers guessing. He is not fooled by flashy appearances but is friendly and hospitable once he gets to know you and has decided you are alright. Although he is by nature soft-spoken that does not mean he is easily intimidated. He believes in himself and will let it be known when he thinks he is being treated unfairly. Erik ten Hag is, in many ways, a typical Tukker, never effusive, but steady and calm under pressure.

'The media like to label people. I'm fine with that. I am proud of my heritage. Tukker, bald, my accent, purple or red, you name it. I am who I am, and I'm undisturbed. I don't care about what they say. Yes, Twente is home for me. As soon as you cross the River IJssel near Deventer, you are almost home. We used to say to the outside players at FC Twente, "Do you have your passport with you? Otherwise you won't get in." Twente, that is something special. And it will always stay that way.'

Culture and identity are linked to language. Tukkers have their own vernacular, which often is so different from 'Standard Dutch' – the official designation for the King's Dutch – that most non-Tukkers cannot make much sense of it. 'Tweants' is spoken daily by a majority in Twente. There are jewels of folk wisdom to be found in this eastern enclave. *An de kookante bliewen* describes a cautious attitude to life that might be translated as 'don't get in over your head'. There is a certain kind of modesty, resignation and caution in the local language. Emotional experiences are presented in an understated manner. Facts are questioned, strong opinions are shunned and sensitive issues are implied in many twists and turns.

Many Dutchmen consider Twente a bit of a backwater and the local way of speaking a dialect. But Tukkers are proud of their regional traditions. Columnist Nathalie Baartman on the Visit Twente website eloquently introduces non-natives to the mysteries of the local culture and language:

Sometimes I'm glad I'm a Tukker. Something from grandmother to grandmother with *kruudmoos* [a farmers' dish of various meats and herbs immersed in a buttermilk porridge], *krentenwegge* [a festive bread brimful of currants, traditionally baked to celebrate new births] and *midwinterhoorn* [a wooden valveless trumpet, blown during the Christmas season]. The only sound on earth that makes me still. The wooden pinnacle of folklore. The call of reflection. When her December voice resounds through the streets from eternity, I feel sheltered in Twente … The true Twentenaar reveals himself at times and places when you least expect him. In sounds … The language of swallowing complete letters. Sometimes even complete conversations. Everything my grandmother didn't say to my grandfather.

In Ten Hag some of these Tukker qualities stand out. In the often noisy landscape of professional football and the more select fraternity of successful football managers, he is a bit unusual. While in the technical area he may be shouting instructions and waving his arms, off the pitch he is rather terse – a man of understatements. Although those who know him well say that he lets go at private celebrations, you will not see outpourings of emotion from this composed Dutchman in the football stadium. A goal scored by his side rarely elicits more than a fist pump. You do not see Klopp grins, Mourinho frowns or Conte antics. If he does get angry, he channels his feeling into expressions of controlled power rather than sudden outbursts. He is reticent about everything other than football, fiercely protective of the privacy of his family and intensely loyal to his long-term friends.

The Ten Hag clan is Roman Catholic. In the Netherlands, religious affiliation is largely determined by geography: if you live south of 'the big rivers', the Rhine and its branches, you most likely are Catholic. If you live north, you probably are Protestant. The notable exception is the eastern segment of the province Overijssel. Twente is the largest Roman Catholic enclave above the major rivers. The fact that Catholicism managed to survive here long after the Reformation is due to the odd twists and turns in the sixteenth- and seventeenth-century revolt against Catholic Spanish rule. So the religious background of the Ten Hag family is not an anomaly. The elder Ten Hags implicitly connected the lives of their sons to their Catholic faith, not only through church attendance, but at school and in sports. Young Erik was an altar boy. Though the information about how he executed his duties at the Haaksbergen parish church is a little sketchy, according to Leon ten Voorde there was some room for improvement in his pastoral job performance. 'The Erik I knew then still had hair and was the cockiest and boldest of the bunch. He had the biggest mouth and also got in the most fights. My relationship with him goes back about 46, 47 years, to primary school. We were in the same class. Looking back on those younger years, I remember that he only allowed himself to be led by me in one place, and that was around the altar of the Boniface parish, where we assisted Pastor Hulleman with the distribution of wafers and incense as altar boys. Erik was not a very skilled altar boy.'

Erik ten Hag comes from Veldmaat, in Haaksbergen-Noord, a middle-class neighbourhood of which there are so many in the Netherlands, mostly consisting of rows of terraced houses with small gardens. An orderly community of neat people, with a church, a bakery, a supermarket and a barber shop. The streets are named after birds, types of shrubs and classical composers. The Ten Hag family lived on the Reigerstraat – Heron street – in a larger-than-average house on a corner. Erik's childhood home features a traditional Twente wooden facade sign on the ridge of the roof of the house, in this case 'Waving Ears of Wheat', the symbol of a good harvest and prosperity. The sign evidently worked its wonders for Erik and for the Ten Hag family as a whole. The house is very conveniently located between the elementary school and the amateur football club, both at a comfortable walking distance.

Little Erik began his footballing life at the Haaksbergen RKSV Bonifatius Boys (Roman Catholic Sports Association Boniface Boys), which eventually morphed into a secularised incarnation, the SV Bon Boys (Sports Association Bon Boys). In 1977 he put on the red-green strip for the first time as a boy in the F-youth. Soon he was a team captain. One day, when he was just seven years old, he came home after a long day of football barely able to stand on his feet, according to his mother, and vomited with fatigue. He had played three games in a row because they were always one player short. Erik ten Hag raised his hand to volunteer every time. Some people have labelled him a football fanatic or maniac, but Ten Hag's motives seem quite sane. 'I am driven. If you aren't, you will never be successful in this sport – nor in the rest of your life. But I played football as a boy because I thought it was the most beautiful thing there is. That care-free feeling … wonderful. I can still vividly picture the coaches and players of my childhood – which way we sat in the dressing room, stood on the training pitch, behaved in games. I have had many happy moments in life, but I have never been happier than in my childhood playing football.'

Erik attended the Ludgerus Elementary School. St Ludger was an eighth-century missionary to the Frisians and Saxons, and the first Bishop of Münster, in German Westphalia, 40 miles east of Haaksbergen. The school has since been renamed after it merged with the St Bonifatius school, which had been uprooted to make space for a Plus Supermarket. Confessional schools were not nearly as strict in the 1970s as they had been in the 1950s, but traditional morality was well reflected at the school when Ten Hag attended. These experiences made a lasting impression on him and nurtured his moral disposition. Had he not become a manager, he could have become a prosecutor. When Jac Schenkels refereed the match between Willem II and FC Twente in December 2001, in which Ten Hag played in defence, Ten Hag's sense of justice was offended because Schenkels once was part of the Willem II youth team. He gets angry about individuals on probation who are caught violating traffic laws and people who abuse animals. Order, discipline and principles of fair play are of paramount importance to him. The mature coach continues to be respected for his integrity and fairness, something that is not equally the case with all power brokers in top sport.

Erik routinely got together with his friends for kickabouts in the school playground. Cyril Holtkamp was one of them. He recalls, 'Initially, there was a climbing frame and two trees growing in the square, which we used as goal posts. But because we shattered one window per week, the school principal decided to clutter the square with poles, beams and more climbing equipment. It turned into a silent war, and we were challenged to find creative solutions.' The current school administration is certainly more liberal-minded than in Ten Hag's day – next to the jungle gym there is now an open space graced with two small blue goals. Ten Hag was regularly playing with boys two or three years older than him. He was the smallest, but he was in charge because he was the best. The seeds for his assertive style of play were sown early. In the schoolyard they always played on the attack, with three strikers, or even four or five.

The young Ten Hag was a football adept. When he watched matches on TV with his friends, he would explain the team tactics and rate the players' performance. He was a little like a junior version of Louis van Gaal, whom he just knew from his football sticker books. Ten Hag was about 12 years old and he appeared to know everything better than his friends. The annoying thing was that he usually did – like Van Gaal, who once infamously claimed, 'I am always right.' Every day a small group of the lads played football until it was either dark or one of the gang had to go home for dinner. Manager Ten Hag's advice to kids is based on the experience gained on the Haaksbergen streets. 'Practising kick-ups is good for your feeling for the ball. It is best to practice it with two legs. If you are very good at it, you can try it with a smaller ball. It's also good to dribble the ball at speed through your residential area. Then hit the ball every step. And make it difficult for yourself by slaloming past lampposts at speed and occasionally cutting and twisting. But pay attention, because you are not the only one on the street!'

Leon ten Voorde knows more about that. 'We grew up in Haaksbergen and all we did was play football, football, football, all day long. Erik and I were at the same football club. As young boys we went to the Diekman Stadium to watch FC Twente together. And when the Tour de France was on, we would race through the streets and create our local Tour de France. If there was a Wimbledon tournament, we would play tennis. We were always involved in sports and playing football. On a rare occasion, there was a European match on television on Wednesday evening. The stadium had to be sold out for the live match to be shown on TV. Then, even at that young age, Erik gave us lectures. They could be a bit tiresome, but to tell the truth, they also were good sometimes. So it didn't surprise me that one day he became a football coach. If you look at our childhood team photos – I think we were about eight then – he is wearing the captain's armband. That's no coincidence. You used to go to the training of a professional football club much later. Kids now go when they're 10 or 11, at some clubs even earlier. You go to the big city to start playing with a professional club. Erik played with his amateur club until he was 14 or 15. That was in the A1 youth team; only then he came into the picture.'

Sometimes having the opposite opinion seemed to be an end in itself for Ten Hag. At least, that is what Ten Voorde believes. 'If everyone thinks Roger Federer is the best tennis player, then Erik ten Hag will insist that Rafael Nadal is better. We never agree with each other. The funny thing is that I'm also working in football, but on the receiving end, the side of journalism. It sometimes causes friction when I say: "It would have been better if you had done it this way, or you should have done it that way." But he usually is not open to that anyway. I have to admit that the last few years he started to listen a little more. But I still think sometimes: *Why don't you slow down a bit? Why don't you show a little more of your other side?* Because the image most people get is that of a surly Ten Hag in front of camera. That's not the Erik from my childhood. I know that other side, how loose he can be. I know how he could be at the Oldenzaal carnival, in the past. Occasionally, you still see that: he wins the league cup and he jumps up and down. Then people do a double-take: hey, is that the coach who always so coolly and meticulously analyses the match? Yes, that's him, too. If he didn't have that, we would not have been friends.'

Bon Boys, created 90 years ago and named after Saint Boniface – Sint Bonifatius to the Dutch – is an organisation with strong local ties, a hub of the community. Since 1970 the club has been playing its matches at the De Greune Sports Park. In 2019 the name was changed to Meeting Park De Greune to reflect the expanded range of sports and social activities taking place at the venue. The amateur club is a lot bigger today than it was in Ten Hag's youth. It no longer is just Bon boys but Bon girls as well. They have 1,000 members, approximately 800 of whom are active players, across 54 teams for men, women, girls and boys of all ages. The club has four competition pitches and three training fields. Since 2009 the main field has artificial turf. The main building was expanded in 2006. There is a clubhouse, a bar, large changing rooms and a boardroom. Bon Boys has several alumni who became professionals in Dutch football, but none as famous as Ten Hag.

In 2020 the club decided to honour Ten Hag with a 6-metre-wide wall pictorial. The image was created by Theo Tulp, whose company specialises in this type of decorative art. With his 100-kilogram wall-Pen printer, Tulp worked for seven hours to transfer the oversized image to the trainers' lounge wall, millimetre by millimetre. In a video, the muralist explains that this was not just an elaborate wallpaper job. The costly computer-steered machine injected the colours of the image into the spotlessly white plaster of the wall, creating an indelible twenty-first-century fresco. Visitors will forever see a smiling Ten Hag, with his arms outstretched and his thumbs up in triumph. Underneath is written in large letters, 'Van Veldmaat tot Heldendaad.' The rhyme is lost in translation: 'From Veldmaat to Heroic Deed.' The text of the Bon Boys club song is also printed on the wall. On the opposite wall there are several large photos of the club's most famous player. Under a framed Ajax shirt is a picture of him with his Bon Boys teammates from the early 1980s. His red FC Twente shirt – number 20 – has been given a prominent place. The trainers' room is now called the Erik ten Hag Lounge.

Ten Hag was present at the unveiling of the masterpiece. Looking at it and pointing at his bald head, he said with a grin, 'Couldn't be more handsome.' In his welcoming speech, club chairman Klanderman said that Ten Hag had been a member of Bon Boys for 40 years. 'Actually, 45 years,' Ten Hag immediately responded, not missing the opportunity to make a necessary correction. 'I played my first game in 1977.' Ten Hag recalled that the announcements were made on the Geukerdijk where the cyclocross track is located today. 'Opposite the church, at café Ter Huurne, there was a box on the wall, where you could read every week where and at what time you had to play. A lot has changed since then. I am very proud that the club where I started in 1977 is doing this for me. You should never forget your roots. I have very nice memories with the players, trainers and all the people who make the club what it is today. That always remains in your heart. This is beautiful. Bon Boys is thriving, and I hope to be a worthy ambassador of the club. I hope to give something back by inspiring the young players. If that is done this way, then I think that is wonderful.'

Next to the wrought-iron gate of De Greune is a large banner introducing the Erik ten Hag International U12 Tournament. Bon Boys is evidently pleased that Ajax, Borussia Dortmund and other big-name clubs are coming to the Meeting Park with their youth teams. The tournament website announces, 'It's something to be proud of. The first Erik ten Hag Tournament immediately has a great field of participants, with well-known names, familiar faces and promising talent. On Saturday, 15 October, during the Dutch autumn school break, De Greune will host a tournament for players under the age of 12. These are young players who are just not ready for the big field, so that the technical aspect plays a greater role than the physical component.' The participating clubs are Ajax, Borussia Dortmund, FC Twente/Heracles Academy, Borussia Mönchengladbach, Fortuna Düsseldorf, Beerschot, KV Mechelen, NEC Nijmegen, Volendam, FC Antwerp, ATC'65 and of course Bon Boys themselves. 'Right away at the first edition, the organisation has already succeeded in presenting a field with which the current manager of Manchester United can be very pleased,' says Bon Boys. Entrance to the international youth tournament will be free.

In 1984 Erik ten Hag met Johan Cruyff. He got the chance to ask questions to the great man on the children's programme *Cruyff & Co.* The programme was an idea of Cruyff himself. After he had signed a lucrative deal with the Los Angeles Aztecs, he had presented a similar programme in the United States. He thought it would be good to do a version in the Netherlands. The by now retired world star wanted to share his football wisdom with the Dutch youth. The children received some football training, in which Cruyff taught each of them a certain skill. Then they were invited to the studio with the entire team to talk with him about it. Ten Hag had never seen Cruyff play live, the 23-year age difference prevented that. But he was a big fan. Through the stories of his uncles he knew that he was going to meet a living legend. The 13-year-old Ten Hag was not intimidated and constantly had his hand up to ask a question. He wasn't troubled about monopolising the show and preventing the others asking questions themselves. 'How can you best develop your technique?' Ten Hag asks, in an unmistakable Twente accent. Cruyff, sitting between the children, with his legs casually crossed, answers in his inimitable and characteristic Amsterdam way, 'Developing technique is actually simple. You have to do it. So train, train, train. You really don't need any other advice than that.'

When Cruyff speaks, the children listen attentively, but the star also makes space for them to contribute something. Ten Hag again is the most vocal of the bunch. He clearly expresses his ideas about how a coach should behave with young players. 'Especially with the youth you have to be careful that you don't shout too much, because then a football player will break. But I think that a trainer of the higher teams, the first of Ajax or Twente, for example, can say something. Those guys train very often during the week. If they make the same mistake over and over again, then something can be said about it.' Sadly, this meeting would be their one and only. Cruyff had always been a heavy smoker. When he had emergency bypass surgery in the early 1990s, he immediately gave up smoking, but was diagnosed with lung cancer in 2015. He died in 2016, just before Ten Hag started working at Ajax.

Ten Hag would later reflect on the episode: 'It was a long time ago. It was great. Johan Cruyff had such an impact on footballers like Pelé, Beckenbauer and Maradona. That was my character, obviously – that is who I am. I think I was brave and I wanted to be a good football player and I wanted to learn. When you have a moment with

Johan Cruyff, you take the moment. He's a big inspiration on how you have to play football. Cruyff was not only about winning games – he was obviously a great winner and he won a lot in his career, but also in a certain way, in an adventurous way, in an attacking way and also with great solutions. I think he is a big inspiration for many footballers and definitely for me.'

At age 14, Ten Hag joined the academy of FC Twente, 10 miles from home. He was an eager learner. When his family went on a ski holiday, Erik did not join: suppose he would be put on a side track by the Twentse Voetbalbond – the former regional subdivision of the KNVB (Koninklijke Nederlandse Voetbalbond; the Royal Netherlands Football Association, the Dutch FA) – because of a shortage of training sessions? Young Erik was a big fan of FC Twente's first team and travelled on one of the supporters' buses when they were promoted to the Eredivisie (Honour Division, the Dutch premier league) in 1984. He also was one of the 6,600 fans who went to the Diekman Stadium on 17 April 1985. FC Twente played against Sparta Rotterdam, and he was looking forward to the game. FC Twente striker Billy Ashcroft scored, but that goal only came after conceding six goals to Sparta. Ten Hag said, 'Sparta had a very good team, with John de Wolf, Danny Blind, Bas van Noortwijk, Wout Holverda, Roelf-Jan Tiktak. But Louis van Gaal was the strategist. He scored twice as well. That hurt. It was an early memory.'

He gradually worked his way through the ranks while continuing to develop his idiosyncratic ideas about football. Not everyone appreciated the young Ten Hag's interference and unsolicited advice. FC Twente coach Rob Baan once suspended him for three matches because of his big mouth. Baan later commented, 'Now that he's a trainer himself, he will doubtlessly understand why I did that. He is driven and comes from a good background. He is serious and articulate.'

Ten Hag was an admirer of 'Mister FC Twente' Epi Drost and trained under him for some time. 'At the age of 13, 14, every boy who can play a little football dreams of becoming a professional,' Ten Hag says. 'For me there was only one club and that was FC Twente. My family had a connection with Arend van der Wel. He was a scout and for many years a team leader at FC Twente. Arend sometimes took us to the game and then I was allowed to get close to the players. My big favourite was Epi Drost. *Mit dem Epi ist immer Zirkus* [with Epi it's always a circus] is the famous quote of František Fadrhonc. That's what made Epi so interesting. He always offered spectacle. Taking risks was part of his game, and he also encouraged that with young players. He stimulated creativity because that was the most important aspect of the game to him. He was a mega fan of skilful and adventurous football. Epi had a soft spot for me because I was by far the youngest in the squad. He let me play in the U23s as a 15-year-old. I learned so much from him. Epi died suddenly due to a cardiac arrest during a match. That was a massive blow for me.'

· · ·

Suriname is a swath of jungle between the Orinoco and Amazon Rivers four times the size of the Netherlands. The territory was colonised in the seventeenth century by the Dutch West India Company. As other European powers moved to grant autonomy to their colonies, so did the Netherlands. At the time of the 1975 transition to national independence, the Surinamese were given a choice of Dutch or Surinamese citizenship. Some 150,000 out of the population of 450,000 left Suriname for the Netherlands – a migration staggering in scope for the sparsely populated South American nation. Today, some 350,000 people in the Netherlands trace their ancestry to Suriname. The early Surinamese experience in the Netherlands was difficult, with high rates of poverty, crime, drug use and unemployment plaguing inner-city communities. Nowhere was that truer than in Bijlmermeer, an enclave of large, monotonous and inexpensive high-rises southeast of Amsterdam. The natural talent for playing football of many Surinamese boys was cultivated on the streets, and a good number eventually made it into professional teams.

The fluidity and incisiveness of Dutch football is, to a large degree, dependent on the skill and speed of players of Surinamese decent. The Surinamese connect the Latin American style to the cooler Dutch qualities. They bring an element of flair and daring resembling the Brazilian *joga bonito* to the meticulously tactical Dutch game. It is the mentality and capacity to do things in a more casual and relaxed manner, without the stress. Although Great Britain remains well-connected to its former Caribbean colonies through the Commonwealth system, the influence of Black Central American players on English football is limited. There is a more natural kinship between the Dutch and the Surinamese. Both highly prize freedom, so the Surinamese adapt relatively easily to Dutch football. They have a similar philosophy. The main difference is that the Dutch players tend to think in terms of concepts and solutions, whereas the Surinamese are more intuitive and spontaneous. The Dutch always feel the need to talk things through, whereas the Surinamese play a more visceral game, for the sheer joy of it. In Ajax's successful 1995 Champions League final against AC Milan, the club fielded no fewer than eight Black players, six of whom traced their heritage to Suriname.

Mohamed Rafiek 'Sonny' Hasnoe was a social worker who worked with disadvantaged children in Amsterdam neighbourhoods. He soon recognised the positive effect that football had on the young Surinamese. He also found he could engage the youngsters if they saw positive role models of the same ethnic background. He came up with the bright idea to create the so-called Colourful Eleven. From 1986 this team of Dutch professionals with Surinamese roots played matches in the Netherlands against top Surinamese clubs after the league's end. They had fun, created community solidarity and inspired the youth. In 1989 the tradition was reversed: the men would go to Suriname to play some charity matches there.

6 June 1989. The Colourful Eleven were to play in Paramaribo, the Surinamese capital. A number of players were denied permission to travel by their professional clubs, among them Ruud Gullit, Frank Rijkaard, Aron Winter, Bryan Roy and Henk Fraser, so a group of second stringers went instead. The passengers had to wait at Amsterdam Schiphol Airport. The flight was supposed to leave in the morning, but the plane, a DC-8-62, was late arriving from Miami. It was an old plane: there were problems with the fuel gauge and with the ILS, the Instrument Landing System. Some of the passengers felt that the late departure was a bad omen. After an uneventful cross-Atlantic journey, flight PY 764 tried to land four times at Paramaribo-Zanderij International Airport, but was obstructed by dense fog. On the final attempt, disaster struck. The plane of the Surinamese Aviation Company hit two trees at a height of 25 metres and crashed, landing upside down near the village of Zanderij. It was the deadliest aviation disaster in Surinamese history: 178 of the 187 passengers were killed, including 15 of the 18 members of the Colourful Eleven on board. Among the dead was a young player named Andy Scharmin.

Dutch freelance journalist Iwan Tol immortalized the episode in his book *Destination Zanderij*. 'Everything that could go wrong, did go wrong. Forward Sigi Lens [one of the three players to survive the crash] said that when he stepped on the plane, he could see it was very old. Some things were just held together with tape.' A 66-year-old American pilot was in charge of the flight. This was against Surinamese law, which stipulates that no one over 60 should captain a commercial airplane. Tol says, 'In Holland, they say it was a disaster that happened far away. We don't have a culture of thinking of our heroes like they do in England. The only thing we knew was a few pictures on television of the crashed airplane. It's known to football fans, but it's nothing like the Busby Babes.'

There was someone who did take the tragedy very seriously. The death of Erik ten Hag's friend Andy Scharmin marked a low point in Ten Hag's life. Ten Hag was a central defender just six months away from following Scharmin into the first team of FC Twente when the 21-year-old left back lost his life. Scharmin had rejected a call-up from Holland's Under-21 squad for that summer's Toulon Tournament (an annual meeting of national teams composed of youth players in Provence) so he could join the Colourful Eleven's charity game in Suriname. He was killed together with his mother and aunt. Ten Hag recalled, 'Andy Scharmin was an incredible athlete and my friend. Like me, he came from Haaksbergen and, although he was a bit older than me, we travelled to FC Twente together for years, by bus, bicycle or car. I will never forget my teammate Edwin Hilgerink standing on my doorstep to tell me that a plane had crashed with Andy and his mother on board. That was a huge blow. At his funeral I carried Andy's coffin with other teammates. It happened on 7 June 1989 – and every year on that date I have a day of mourning. The solidarity of that generation of FC Twente professionals is there to this day. Close friendships have arisen and we still meet regularly.'

Ten Hag continues: 'I often think back to my youth at FC Twente. We had a really good group. Three boys from that team were so good that they could have made it to the national team. But one of them was seriously injured at a young age and two other boys died

29

young. In Andy Scharmin, Wilfried Elzinga and Gino Weber we had three top talents. Gino was the best talent in the Netherlands at that time, an unparalleled football player with a mega technique who was completely two-footed. But he suffered from a mental illness and took his own life. Something like that puts everything into perspective. It certainly made me think about how things can go in life.' Due to long-term injuries, Elzinga's career fell into disarray from the 1991–2 season onward. In three years he played in just 19 league matches. In 1997 he signed a contract for three years with Eerste Divisie (First Division, the Dutch second-tier league) club BVO, in Emmen. But he continued to struggle with injuries and ended his career as a professional footballer in 1999. And then there was Andy. These experiences affected Erik ten Hag deeply and contributed to his drive to succeed where his friends never had the chance to.

3

TEN HAG DNA

'I think I am who I am. I am not a copy of somebody else. The main thing is that you work in a way that fits your personality.'

ERIK TEN HAG

In Hengelo, Enschede, Almelo and in other Twente towns and villages, blue-and-white signs with the name Ten Hag frequently feature in the windows of empty stores and apartments. These are not endorsements for one of Holland's most popular football managers, but indications that the properties are for sale. On any given day, there are up to 1,500 signs with the name Ten Hag along the side of the street. Often a smaller sign is superimposed – *verkocht* – sold. The Ten Hag real estate company website shows an impressive seven-floor building in Enschede with the announcement, 'Prominently located on the Koningsplein, in the centre of Enschede and right next to the new hospital Medisch Spectrum Twente, in the office building of the Ten Hag brokerage and financial services group, a total of 3,473m² of office space is available for rent.' The caveat is added that the first, fourth and seventh floors are excluded because they have been reserved for company use.

Erik ten Hag comes from a wealthy background and is a major partner in the business empire started in 1989 by his father, Hennie.

The family lived in a big house – with the claim to fame that it featured a billiard table in the basement – but the family fortune didn't come easily. The patriarch started out as a real estate agent in 1967 and grew his business into a regional hub with nine branches and more than 100 employees. Today, the company is run by Michel and Rico, Erik's older and younger brothers. Erik was not interested in the housing market. His parents were not happy to hear that he wanted to pursue a career in professional football. They would have preferred that he complete the education he was enrolled in. But once it was clear that Erik had made up his mind, they fully supported his ambitions. Hennie said, 'Football has been his thing from a young age. I remember Erik coming to tell us that he quit his studies to focus on football. That was difficult for me. My wife and I were concerned about his life after football. Of course we could not have imagined that he would have such a splendid career in coaching. Erik works day and night to achieve what he wants in football.'

Psychologists who study the influence of birth order on personality point out that the middle child often has a rebellious streak. That would apply to Erik, who was the outlier in the family and had precise ideas about what he wanted in life. 'I enjoy my job. Pleasure is the foundation of everything. When I don't have that anymore, I stop. I'm working on it 24-7. I think you should, otherwise you can't do this. You can't come to the club, train and go home in this trade. It takes a lot more, at least if you want to do it right. You have to be on top of it. I also relax sometimes when I'm at home. But even then I think about it, it always goes on. That's how I've always worked, whether I was an assistant trainer, head of training or head coach and technical manager. Playing football yourself is the best. When that is no longer possible, football coach is the best job I can imagine. I never count the hours. I like what I do, especially, getting the most out of players. But whether your name is José Mourinho, Louis van Gaal or Pep Guardiola, it's hard work. There's nothing wrong with that. Training at the top is even more difficult because of the extra pressure. That's why fun is so important, it gives you energy to keep going.'

Guus Hiddink famously said that 'football is the most important side issue in the world'. Although Erik ten Hag is at least as infatuated with the beautiful game as his eastern neighbour is, he also knows there are things in life that are more important than football. Family is one of them. Especially when considered in the context of the world of professional football, with its moral relativism, wealthy men and beautiful women, romantic dalliances and frequent divorces, he is a traditionalist. He is faithful to his wife and devoted to his children. They are central in his life. He keeps his work and private lives strictly separated, not just socially, but geographically as well. That requires, for a man who is so much in the stadium limelight, some effort and sacrifice. He spends most of his time with his team in one town, while his family lives at some distance in another.

When working for Ajax, Ten Hag confessed, 'I get energy from my work, but sometimes you have to flip the switch. Then I drive to Oldenzaal to see my family. I find peace with them. My family lives in Twente, I live in Amsterdam. Of course that's a sacrifice. But our family is strong and close enough to cope with that. It was the same when I worked at PSV and FC Utrecht. They have built up their social life in Twente. I don't think dragging your kids from one place to another is a good idea. When I worked at Bayern Munich for two years, they did come along. My youngest daughter does horseback riding, and she had to do without her horse for two years. But it also was good for their development. It was an enrichment of their lives to live in a different culture. They really liked it there. Munich is a great city because people know how to live there. Great food and the mountains are close. We went on skiing trips five times a year. I love life. Good, healthy food, with a good glass of wine, or a beer.'

That Ten Hag's family did not make the move to Amsterdam with him was, he says, 'a conscious choice. I don't expect them to live their lives in service to mine.' Also, 'football coaching is an uncertain profession, and things can change quickly. So I did not want to drag them everywhere with me. On top of that, this profession is so intensive. As a football coach you are busy, preoccupied 24-7. So I would be home, but also not really there. I have also said that I don't want to put my children through the experience of growing up in the Randstad [the metropolitan west of the Netherlands]. It means that I live by myself most days of the week, on the Zuidas [Amsterdam's financial district, with upscale eateries and cocktail bars]. I usually eat at the club during the day and prepare something myself in the evening.'

He preferred driving to Oldenzaal the evening before a day off. He says, 'My wife is not a football fan. We talk about it and she's supportive of it. By now, our three children already have left home, but they are always closely connected to us. They also don't miss an Ajax match. During the season I am not at home much. I come home once a week, sometimes twice. During international breaks I am home a bit longer. That's our family life. The children have their own lives. They have to sacrifice something, I'm sure of that. The talk is very often about me, about Ajax, about football. Everywhere they go. I understand that this is not always easy for them. You do this with 100 per cent commitment, or you don't do it at all. I think every trainer is busy with his team every minute of the day.'

Ten Hag relaxes on the golf course and enjoys watching the equestrian performances at the Military Boekelo, in the countryside near Enschede. 'I golf, run, bike, walk. When I was young I used to play a lot of board games. Stratego, for example. And Risk. The game Thirty Seconds is popular with my family. I get a lot of energy from my family. My wife and children are the most important to me. The children still visit very often and we share a family app. If things go well with them, they go well for me. My wife is a good listener and I can speak my mind to her. She is not fond of football. She only watches my games, but can understand certain aspects well. Whenever possible, we take the dog for a walk together. Unfortunately, that doesn't happen often enough. A trainer is never really free during the season. It all just goes on in my head. I think about our next opponent, for example.'

Erik was born with a silver spoon in his mouth but he worked for everything himself. His older brother Michel sheds some light on the family culture. 'We had a good home, but there were rules. We had to do the cooking twice a week, that was one of them. And do the shopping. This is how our work ethic was instilled. There was no time for laziness. If you wanted something, you had to earn it yourself. As a teenager I wanted a road bike; it cost 350 guilders. My father said, "How do you plan to pay for it?" He could have pulled out his wallet, but he didn't. I borrowed the money and paid back everything. You had to work for your money. It is satisfying when you accomplish something on your own. We are real entrepreneurs, each of us has enormous perseverance. Our work ethic is very strong, we are creative and always see opportunities that we dare to seize.'

In 1978, 'around the time of the World Cup, we founded our own club: the Veldmaatse Voetbal Vereniging, after the neighbourhood where we grew up in the Reigerstraat. I was about ten years old and chairman, Erik was treasurer together with his friend Leon. In the village you had more of those street associations. In the winter, when it was freezing, I went to the town hall to ask what it cost to rent the sports hall De Els for an hour or so. The entrepreneurial spirit was there early on.'

Loyalty and reliability are essential family values: 'We are a real family business, specialised in residential and commercial real estate and real estate management. And we have expertise in the field of mortgages, insurance and pensions. We are a reliable part-ner, well-known in the east of the Netherlands. We take good care of our employees and together we take care of our customers. What is striking is that we have very long employment contracts. Recently we celebrated anniversaries of people who have been employed for 25 years and even 40 years. That is special.'

Michel took his first steps in the company in 1996; his brother Rico, four years younger, followed in 2000. That was after their father had impressed upon both to first complete their education and gain hands-on experience. Michel worked for Unilever for a while; Rico spent time with a large estate agent in North Holland. Their father was proud and happy to have them as partners in the family business. 'Once they joined the company, it was a dream come true. Of course, this company feels like my baby, and I was only too happy to hand it over to them in 2007. Reliability is the greatest good, I've always insisted on that. Our industry, real estate, is often under fire. One evil genius can ruin it for a thousand others who do well for their custom-ers. I am very annoyed by that. I always tell my sons: make sure you have nothing to hide from customers, and that everything is right.' Rico thinks that his father's people skills greatly contributed to the company's success. 'I think we are very social and customer-oriented. My father was known as the largest networker in the Twente region. "Knowledge and acquaintances" has been his motto. We have bene-fited greatly from that in later years.'

The middle son and most famous scion of the family never felt drawn to join the company. He was not interested in business, but in football. According to Rico, that had some advantages: 'That is great for us. We are all crazy about football and regularly go to Amsterdam for a match with the whole family. Or at least a delegation. Sometimes there are not enough tickets!' It was clear early on that Erik would never become a co-owner. In Hennie's opinion, a shareholder of a service company must be employed in the company. 'But we wanted to divide everything as fairly as possible among our three sons. Then I came up with the idea to set up a private limited company, which means there are now four of us. It's nice to work together with Erik in a company. And the funny thing is that in my old age, that's what I'm most concerned with. We're in real estate, make investments, invest in start-ups, scale-ups and social projects. We're pretty busy with that. It's not for nothing that my wife says: "You'll never stop."' The third-generation Ten Hags are thriving, but it is still too early to judge whether there is a candidate who can lead the company. A grandson or granddaughter will get the chance in due time. Michel said, 'We got that too. My father has slowly let go of the business. Today he is always available for advice and assistance, but the best compliment we could give him is that he was able to let go of the company.'

The company website introduces the family business in a spirited manner.

If we tell you that we have more than 50 years of experience and that Ten Hag now has nine branches, it is almost need-less to say that we are a household name in the region. We are very proud that we are known in the eastern Netherlands region as the number one service provider in brokerage and financial services. We now have 100 enthusiastic and motivated employees. We enjoy continuing growth, both physically and in the expertise of our employees. What distinguishes Ten Hag is the total package of services and the fact that we attach just as much value to personal attention as to professional knowledge. We combine those two things in everything we do, so that you can rely on us for a long time. With a sober look at things and a proactive attitude, we are always 100 per cent committed. This is how we work on sustainable relationships. Over the years we have built up an extensive professional network and clientele and we cherish that.

The subprime mortgage crisis of 2007–10 hit the company hard. On business platform TwenteVisie, Michel Ten Hag explained, 'We lost about 20 per cent of our turnover during the crisis. Then we had to say goodbye to eight people. In 2015, the turning point came, when we regained that lost revenue. We did not need to immediately panic about the disappointing years for Ten Hag, because in the good times the family had saved up in the investment vehicle Deltaborgh Investments.' The earnings in recent years were mainly due to the invested family capital. Michel is part owner of the Haaksberger restaurant De Blanckenborgh, located in a beautiful mansion dating from the end of the nineteenth century, surrounded by century-old trees in the rustic park by the same name. 'We tackled this with nine entrepreneurs in order to preserve the building for the village.' Deltaborgh is also co-owner of a water-pumping station near the football stadium. 'My father bought it so that parking spaces could be created for FC Twente on that site.'

The Ten Hag family is socially engaged. One example is their involvement in the advancement of cycling in the Netherlands.

The TwenteVisie website claims the eastern province of Overijssel is the cradle of Dutch cycling. The first Dutch bicycle manufacturer, Burgers Rijwielen (Citizens Bicycles), was founded in Deventer in 1869. This was followed by the establishment of the bicycle association Immer Weiter (Always Farther, in German) in 1871. Michel Ten Hag, amateur cyclist, is the organisation's chairman. Former professional cyclists Hennie Kuiper, Rob Harmeling, Theo de Rooij and other bicycling luminaries united in Immer Weiter to advocate the healthy pastime and champion Twente as the heartland of cycling. The Ten Hag Achievement Prize is awarded annually to a person or organisation that has made a special contribution to the development of the eastern Netherlands. Recipients include Prof. Anne van der Meiden, gymnastics sisters Sanne and Lieke Wevers, football club De Graafschap, museum directors Arnoud Odding and Ralph Keuning, comedian Herman Finkers, TV presenter Erik Dijkstra and road racing cyclist Hennie Kuiper.

• • •

Hennie ten Hag noted how sensitively his middle son responded when he was diagnosed with bladder and prostate cancer in the early 2010s. Hennie was in and out of hospital with ongoing infections. 'Erik was training Bayern's second team at the time. He often called and drove up from Munich to Haaksbergen when possible. I could tell it didn't leave him untouched.' Maybe his son is more emotional than he is letting on. 'Erik just wants to be treated fairly by people, and when they don't treat him fairly, that is difficult for him. His urge to prove that he is right is very strong. When people belittle him, he thinks: *just wait and see. I'll show you.*' His mother, Joke (pronounced Yo-kuh), understands the heart of her son. 'Erik is quite capable of controlling his feelings with his mind.'

Erik ten Hag has a wide range of interests and is well-read. *A Thousand Splendid Suns* by Khaled Hosseini is on his bookshelf next to work by the founding father of Dutch sports psychology, Peter Blitz. He has read *Effect* by Norwegian skater Johann Olav Koss, along with classics from professional sports literature. Economic issues may not be his primary concern, but he does read some business magazines in addition to *Voetbal International*. His taste in music runs from Dutch rock band De Dijk – named for the Zeedijk, an old street at the heart of Amsterdam – to Bon Jovi and Eric Clapton.

The real Erik ten Hag is not the one-dimensional cartoon character the media have dreamed up: control freak, autocrat, dictator. He sees himself as a tolerant global citizen with an aversion to people who discriminate on the basis of origin. He was able to reach players like Quincy Promes and Memphis Depay with his involved people management. 'I hate power,' he has confessed. 'I am someone who guides players. I've been fortunate enough to have been in many beautiful places. That has enriched my life and it has allowed me to develop. But at the core I'm still the same driven boy who enjoys life. A lot of it revolves around football, but I'm also interested in other things. I follow politics and come from an entrepreneurial family. That entrepreneurship is in me. During my holidays I like to read books about commerce, marketing and psychology, and I use that in my profession. An entrepreneur must also think about his philosophy, his strategy, the quality of his product and how you motivate people.'

4

ERIK ON THE PITCH

'Haggie's a nice guy, but he's very stubborn.
A slab of concrete is more flexible.'

SIMON KISTEMAKER, FORMER DE GRAAFSCHAP MANAGER

On 13 December 1989, Erik ten Hag made his professional debut at FC Twente. He came on as a substitute for Robin Schmidt in the 66th minute of the match against FC Groningen. The game is not a collector's item: Twente lost 5–0 and the third was an own goal by Schmidt. In young Erik's defence, it should be noted that four of the five goals were scored before he came on the pitch.

Clemens Zwijnenberg, who was on Ten Hag's team, recalls, 'We used to play against each other in the youth teams, he at Bon Boys, I at KVV Losser. Then we were invited to the Twente youth section in Enschede, and we just clicked. A friendship has grown from that. Erik is a real friend, through thick and thin. We went on vacation to Mallorca and Crete together, when we were about 16 or 17 years old. When he unpacked his suitcase in Mallorca what came out first? A rubber mat. I said, "What are you up to?" Erik, dead serious, "Exercising my abs." That's how he is, someone of boundless commitment. We always had a lot of fun together, also outside of football. We drank some beers and chased after the girls. Erik is a very nice guy. I think a lot of people don't know that because he does not always come across that way. Later we also went on vacation together with our families. We just say half a word, then we know where the other is at. Some time ago, he had arranged tickets for Bayern away for us. The next day he called to check if the seats had been good enough. That typifies him. He continues to make time for everyone he knows.'

Zwijnenberg, speaking about Ten Hag's career, says that, if you ask any youth player with whom he played at Twente, it came as no surprise that Erik became a coach. 'That was just part of him; he always had his own opinions about football. There was a bit of bravado in him. He grew up in an enterpreneur's family, so he had that natural confidence. He wasn't afraid of anyone. One of the trainers would hold a pre-match discussion and ask, "Guys, who has a question?" Then Erik's hand usually would go up to ask, "Trainer, why are you doing this?" In the beginning you feel it's fun and interesting that a young player does that. But when the novelty wears off you think, *Stop it, man, we want to play football!* Then another question of "Trainer, why this or that?" We knew that he would become head coach one day.'

Despite this, Zwijnenberg admits, 'Erik had some catching up to do because he was not a great player. He has had a good career in football, but he wasn't a big-name player who could get by on reputation. I think he needed to invest more to get where he wanted to go than another trainer might have had to. When I see how he manages to do that now, it seems he has succeeded cum laude. Is he getting the credit he deserves? That is finally beginning to come. In the beginning they bullied him a lot, about how he came across on camera, about his accent, that he was just a country bumpkin. But gradually the negative things disappeared. And people started to think: *We really ought to judge him on his performance on the pitch.*

If you look at all of Erik's interviews, there is always some take-away that makes you think: *That lad really has insight into the game.'* Zwijnenberg is now a trainer at EMOS, a fourth-division Dutch club based in Enschede. On a visit, Ten Hag surveyed what was happening on the pitch and gave his approval. 'He came to look twice. "You've got it right," he told me.'

The underdog role motivates rather than discourages Ten Hag. As a footballer, he reacted with incredible doggedness when he was underestimated. Trainers like Theo Vonk and Eddy Achterberg used that to their advantage and gave him a boost by taking him down a few notches first. Once, when he wasn't quite pleased with his opin-iated midfielder, Vonk set up a tall ladder in his office to make a point. 'You are on the bottom rung, so you still have a lot of distance to cover.' Vonk ignored Ten Hag for a week, then put him on the team sheet – Erik was raring to get on the pitch. He could also get an adrenaline rush if the opponent's programme booklet suggested that FC Twente had a defensive team, or if Achterberg told him during the warm-up, 'You won't be able to do anything today.'

In the summer of 1990, Erik still lived with his parents in Haaksbergen while studying at the HEAO (Higher Economic and Administrative Education) in Deventer. It was a tough course and he endured it for a year and a half before dropping out in favour of more time on the training ground. He signed a two-year contract with De Graafschap in Doetinchem – the club name means 'county' or 'shire'. There is a special atmosphere at the provincial club. At the club's stadium, De Vijverberg, the light poles are hidden between the trees. The stadium is comparatively large for a club mostly playing in the Eerste Divisie (the second tier of the Dutch leagues). Fathers go to the games with their sons seated on the luggage carriers of their bicy-cles. The club is known for its fanatical supporters in the Spinnekop stand; sections 15 and 16 behind the goal are standing only and most of the noise is produced from this side. A clever supporter coined the term *superboeren*, super farmers, and it stuck. Ten Hag's first year at De Graafschap proved to be an eventful one, with memorable games and a happy end.

Like other teams, VVV-Venlo wasn't able to stop De Graafschap's advance to the Eredivisie. VVV not only lacked routine and decisiveness, but physical strength in the duels. However, De Graafschap committed 32 fouls against eight on the Venlo side. The decisive goal was characteristic of the difference between the two teams. De Graafschap was allowed to take a free kick. Before the VVV defence could put things in order, Erik ten Hag reached his teammate Peter Hofstede with a deep pass. The entire VVV fanbase watched powerlessly as Hofstede then outplayed goalkeeper Roox and recorded his 25th league goal: 1–0.

In the 1990–1 season, De Graafschap became undefeated champions of the Eerste Divisie under the leadership of trainer Simon Kistemaker. It was their first Eerste Divisie title. The season is so famous that the team's alumni still have a reunion every March. Life in the Eerste Divisie was not glamorous back then. Most of the players had full-time jobs and trained in the evenings. Ten Hag had one advantage in that respect. The family business was flourishing and with financial support from his father he could concentrate on playing football.

Ten Hag was not a top player, but a good midfielder who made up for his shortcomings with character and strategic insight. During De Graafschap's 1990–1 season, Ten Hag played in nearly all their matches and helped his team win promotion to the Eredivisie. He spent another season at the club, but this time only played half of the matches. Coach Simon Kistemaker saw him as a colourful character and a good team player. 'Haggie', Kistemaker called the determined young man who commuted in a Citroën provided by the French carmaker sponsoring the club. Because he was attending school, the back seat was sometimes full of textbooks. Kistemaker recalled, 'Once he was not part of the starting eleven. Haggie was in my office right away. "Why am I not playing?" he asked. I told him that he could play at right back, because we had an injury there. He was very resolute. "I won't." "Well, go sit in the stands then," I said. The next day he had reconsidered. "Can I try anyway?" That's how he was: a stubborn character who had the guts to express his opinions, but not someone who thrived on conflict.'

Hans Kraay Jr., heir to a footballing family, played with Ten Hag at De Graafschap. Now an ESPN journalist, Kraay said, 'I had a lot of talks with Erik about how we execute the plan on the field. I was 31 and raised by my father to think a lot about the game, but for a 21-year-old son of a real estate agent that was very striking. He once told me, "When I sleep, I think about football and tactics."' Kraay only once saw Ten Hag at a loss for words, when Kistemaker erroneously assumed that he had started a romance with his daughter. 'After matches, we had short, intense reviews. Kistemaker got on everyone's back: "Olyslager, you were goalkeeping like a slacker. But the second half was fantastic." And so on. The meetings weren't designed to ask questions, but of course, Erik thought otherwise. He asked Kistemaker if we couldn't do things differently next time. Kistemaker reacted. "You can only ask a question if you keep your hands off my daughter." Erik does not easily shut up, but he was quiet then.'

Ten Hag displayed the same intensity as a player on the pitch as he shows on the training field as coach. He injured his right leg in a game against Ajax when he collided with defender Michel Kreek. De Graafschap had to manage without him for two months. He was operated on by club doctor Pieter Vierhout of FC Twente. He got a plastic knee band, pieces of cartilage were removed and an edge was removed from his meniscus.

There were some frayed nerves at the Vijverberg as the 1992 season drew to a close. After Ten Hag had given his team the lead against MVV Maastricht, the news came in that competitor Den Haag was trailing 3–1. There was a glimmer of hope of retaining a place in the Eredivisie. Ten Hag's goal had been a beautiful one, but then a team-wide nervousness set in, and MVV midfielder Roberto Lanckohr equalised a few minutes later. De Graafschap tried to breach the MVV defensive wall but was unable to. Then it turned out that Den Haag had implausibly come back to win 5–3. Due to the loss of points, De Graafschap landed in the relegation zone. In theory, the deficit of one point in the race with Den Haag could still be made up. In practice it proved impossible in a duel against PSV. The Eindhoven club demolished De Graafschap 5–0 and relegation became a reality. The disappointing end to the season was sad for celebrated trainer Kistemaker, who saw three years of his hard work go to waste, but it was even sadder for the loyal fans, who averaged 7,500 spectators per game.

In the summer of 1992, Erik ten Hag returned to FC Twente. The new season started well, with the team scoring 14 times in three home games. It was not always the most sparkling football, but the direct style of play that coach Rob Baan insisted on not only brought points, but more and more spectators to the Diekman Stadium. In the first half against Go Ahead Eagles, on 18 October, the opposition had created few chances. FC Twente got to 2–0 just before half-time in a very nice way. Ten Hag, who was in the starting line-up for the first time since his return to the club, entered into a combination with Ronald de Boer. The ex-Ajax player passed the ball to Cees Marbus in a smooth movement and Ghanaian striker Prince Polley completed the job skilfully. The game ended 4–0 to Twente.

About a month later, FC Twente needed only 45 minutes to send club Roda JC back to Kerkrade with a heavy defeat. Defender René Trost tried to put on the emergency brake by fouling Erik ten Hag, which led to a penalty kick for FC Twente. Trost was first shown red before Ronald de Boer put the Tukkers ahead 1–0 from the spot. In that first half FC Twente scored three more times, again excelling in a home match. Twente climbed to second place in the table behind PSV, a feat few had thought possible earlier in the season.

December 1992: spectators were singing in full voice, 'We're going on winter sports vacation!' Worse weather was unimaginable, but Ajax and Twente decided to brave the mud nonetheless and do something spectacular. Prior to the match, referee Mario van der Ende had asked a maintenance crew to fill up the puddles on the pitch with sand. He did not think it was necessary to cancel the match. As usual, Ajax started furiously and two players from Twente, Erik ten Hag and Jan van Halst, received yellow cards after using question-able means to stop their advancing opponents. But as the going got tough, the tough got going: the more the rain came down, the better FC Twente performed. On the soaked grass of the Olympic Stadium, now known as the Johan Cruyff Arena, the team from Enschede managed at least as well as the home team. The only moments of danger consisted of long shots from Ajax's Wim Jonk and Rob Alflen, which did not trouble goalkeeper Hans de Koning a great deal. Like his teammates, De Koning wasn't bothered by the downpours, thun-derclaps and sleet. Twente forward Prince Polley scored the only goal of the match. Ajax lost to Twente on its own territory for the first time in history in a strange way. The Twente players and supporters celebrated the victory as if it were a championship final.

Ten Hag has his own recollection of the episode: 'Leo Beenhakker moved from Ajax to Real Madrid, and Louis van Gaal replaced him. The first thing he did was bring back Ronald de Boer to Ajax. He was our best player by far. I was angry and blamed the FC Twente chairman. How could he possibly let our star player go when we were positioned above Ajax in the table? We had a fantastic team with Youri Mulder and Ronald like a set of Siamese twins up front. The only thing we did was defend and then quickly punt the ball to that pair. On St Nicolas Eve [5 December], we played against Ajax in the Olympic Stadium. The weather was terrible and the pitch miserable, but we won. Prince Polley scored the only goal. And who gave the assist? Yours truly. Next, we had to play the quarter-final in the cup against Ajax, right after the winter break. By that time, Ronald de Boer was no longer with us, but with Ajax. We were ahead 2–0 for much of that game, but after 90 minutes it was 2–2. In extra time Ronald really got going and Ajax won the game 4–2. That night every supporter received a Mars bar from Ronald.'

Sometimes a bad game can still be fun. The 21 February 1993 match between Sparta Rotterdam and FC Twente was exactly such a duel. That Twente finally pulled the longest straw was a small miracle. In the final phase, the team played with ten men and, ironically, thanks to former Spartan Edwin Vurens were able to engineer a 3–2 win in the race to European football. Both teams struggled with the elements in a chaotic game. It was striking that four of the five goals came indirectly from corners. It seemed that the game was over in the first half, when Nico-Jan Hoogma and Erik ten Hag successively managed to score from pinball situations. Without Sparta goalkeeper Edward Metgod having been seriously tested, Hoogma and Ten Hag helped their club to a 2–0 lead in just half an hour. Then Ron van den Berg strengthened his position as Sparta's top scorer. After a header against the crossbar, he halved the deficit before half-time by power-fully heading in from a corner from Tom Van Mol.

When Ten Hag literally and figuratively gave a hand to Twente goalkeeper De Koning, things started to look bleak. In the 70th minute Ton Pronk's header seemed to have disappeared behind the goal line, but the ball bounced off the ground against Ten Hag's hand. The barely 3,000 spectators at Sparta stadium Het Kasteel were astounded at their good fortune when referee Hans Reygwart suddenly pointed to the spot and the unwitting Ten Hag was promptly shown a red card. The penalty was expertly converted by Van den Berg, 2–2. 'An incomprehensible decision,' Ten Hag later lamented. 'I had no intention of touching the ball with my hand at all. Besides, the ball had already crossed the line.' That was hard to verify in those days before goal-line technology, but his teammate André Paus made the same suggestion.

In the hailstorm battering Rotterdam, Vurens saved the day when he managed to break the 2–2 deadlock eight minutes before time. The vexed Sparta spectators starting throwing snowballs onto the pitch. The winning goal and Erik ten Hag's red card caused more excitement than the match itself. 'Because it was just like the wind: it blew in all directions, except the right one,' said coach Baan. In a written report, the KNVB's disciplinary committee determined that Ten Hag was guilty as charged, because he had intentionally turned away an attempt on goal with his hand. The appeals committee of the KNVB thought otherwise and waived his suspension.

After that match, things did not go quite as smoothly. FC Twente suffered a significant loss in the battle for European football in April when, in the last ten minutes of the away match against Roda JC, the team gave up a 2–0 advantage. Twente had taken the lead after 15 minutes and then seemed to think they would win with minimal effort. That seemed to work when Jan van Halst made the second goal with a long shot in the 80th minute. But in the counter-attack, Max Huiberts skilfully fell over the outstretched leg of substitute Edwin Hilgerink and persuaded referee Dick Jol to award Roda a penalty. Erik van der Luer narrowed the margin to one goal. Seven minutes later, Ten Hag stuck out a leg and Huiberts dived on the grass once more. Jol gave another penalty. A furious Ten Hag wanted to give the referee a piece of his mind. He had to be restrained by goalkeeper De Koning before he was sent to the dressing room following his second yellow card. Van der Luer saw his second penalty stopped, but Peter Hofstede reacted promptly on the rebound: 2–2.

The young Ten Hag was as expressive off the pitch as he was on it. His spirited engagement was not always appreciated by trainer Rob Baan. After training during the second half of the 1993–4 season, the 24-year-old expressed disagreement to his manager, who then disciplined him for running his mouth. Ten Hag was banned from the A-team and had to train with the B-team. As a result, he was not on the team roster for the home matches against MVV Maastricht and Willem II, and the away game at Sparta. He eventually apologised and was allowed to make another appearance after a suspension of four weeks. Despite his return to the team, cloudless happiness did not return to the Diekman Stadium. He was frustrated that he was not a regular starter and, in July 1994, he signed a one-year contract with RKC Waalwijk. He explained his decision in characteristically forward manner. 'I would rather be a base player at RKC than 12th or 13th man at FC Twente.'

Ten Hag has fond memories of the 1994–5 season, his only year in service of the Waalwijk club. 'It was hot that summer. RKC had put me up in a hotel with a flat roof. It was actually way too hot to sleep there. [Senior player and fellow defender] Hans Werdekker realised that I was having a hard time with that. He said, "Being alone in a hotel, that's no fun at all." I lived with him at his home in Oisterwijk for a few months.' The atmosphere in the team was good and there was a lot of laughter. 'In the run-up to a home game, we always ate spaghetti. Then our trainer, Bert Jacobs, did his tactical discussion in front of a large board. He was quite long-winded with his explanations. Romeo van Aerde, the right back from Zeeland, sat in the front row. He had been trying to raise his hand for minutes but failed to get Jacobs's attention. The coach went on and on. Finally, Jacobs says, "Romeo, I see you've been wanting to ask something for a long time." Van Aerde says, "Yes, trainer. There are only 12 names on the board …" And what does Jacobs answer? "So, that means you don't play."'

Under Jacobs, there was a lot of philosophising about football between training sessions. Jacobs wasn't the best trainer Ten Hag experienced. 'I also worked with Kees Rijvers. Then you are talking about a completely different level. Rijvers was fantastic. He already was in his late sixties when he was my trainer with the under-21s, but he was still training with us. He had great technique, fantastic insight into the game and still was fast on the first metres with those short legs of his. But Jacobs was really good. He had vision, worked with triangles on the field, played a positional game. He gave players a lot of confidence. Jacobs was an inspiring personality.' That was proven in the aftermath of Ten Hag's stint in Waalwijk. RKC players Hans Vonk, Marcel Brands and Marco Boogers became technical directors, and eight players from the team, including Ten Hag himself, followed in Jacobs's footsteps and became coaches.

Although his contract gave him the option to stay a second year at RKC, Ten Hag moved to FC Utrecht in May 1995. On 17 September, the approximately 13,000 spectators in Stadium Galgenwaard watched one of the early home games of the new season. Defender Ronald Koeman had recently returned from his triumphs with FC Barcelona and taken a prominent position in the Feyenoord defence. 'Het Kanon' (the Cannon), as he is known in the Netherlands, is the world's top-scoring defender of all time. As a welcome for his return home, he received a bouquet of flowers, but despite the presence of the famous sweeper, Feyenoord met with its first defeat of the season, 1–0.

As nice as it was to see Koeman playing football in the Netherlands again, the 32-year-old defender was unable to influence the game in a meaningful way. Utrecht had adapted its tactics to neutralise Koeman, who had been given a central role in the attacking build-up. His fellow defenders sought him out as much as possible, but he got little of the ball in the first half. After half-time, he had 24 touches, five of which were free kicks, a Koeman speciality. The Utrecht defence functioned well. In Erik ten Hag, Koeman found a worthy opponent, and the Utrecht player turned into the star of the match during the second half. Ten Hag was very effective in disrupting Feyenoord's offensive efforts. He was the only Utrecht player who had not been given an exclusively defensive task. Five minutes before the end of regulation time, substitute Raymond Graanoogst passed from the left. Peter Hofstede headed on and Hans Visser somehow managed to finish while falling over. FC Utrecht does not often beat Feyenoord, so this was a cause for some celebration.

Things did not always go well for Ten Hag in Utrecht. Although he was happily reunited with manager Simon Kistemaker, the coach was not impressed with his defender's performance in the away match against RKC Waalwijk. The home team was especially dangerous with free kicks, of which midfielders Danny Muller and Marcel Brands were the specialists. FC Utrecht's goalkeeper Jan Willem van Ede was forced into making some good saves. In the 72nd minute,

Ten Hag thought he could do some unhurried defending but made an error that led to a goal by Muller, the best man on the pitch for Waalwijk. The RKC player skilfully captured the ball and passed goalkeeper Van Ede with a nice looping shot. When Ten Hag and Muller met again four minutes later, the defender fouled the attacker by stepping on his Achilles tendon. Referee Hugo Luijten immediately drew out the red card. FC Utrecht could not find a way back into the match and RKC won the game 1–0.

During the 1996–7 season, Ten Hag returned for his third spell as a player with FC Twente. He got his European debut during the following season, 1997–8, when Twente made it to the round of 16 of the UEFA Cup (now the UEFA Europa League). In that match, FC Twente was knocked out by AJ Auxerre, by first losing 1–0 at home and then 2–0 away.

Ten Hag could play in several positions: controlling midfielder, central right half, central defender and libero. His real strength was his tactical insight. Ten Hag was captain and an essential part of Fred Rutten's plan for the team. As a new arrival, young winger Ellery Cairo was unsure of his new teammate after their first encounter at Twente. Cairo finished last in their pre-season running drills and Ten Hag couldn't resist making a comment: 'Don't they run at Feyenoord?' According to Cairo, Ten Hag was laughing. Cairo thought, *I'm going to hate this guy!* Eventually, though, Cairo discovered that 'he was a great captain. As a player he was OK, but he really knew his craft as a leader on the pitch. He knew where all of us had to run, where we had to stand, when we had to ask for the ball. He always knew, and he always let us know as well! He wasn't that outgoing, he was quite normal away from the pitch. But when he was training or playing he always wanted to win. If you were in training and playing in small games with Erik on your team, chances were you would win. He'd be telling you to be here, go there, do this, and if you didn't listen, you had a problem. The coach was always backing him up because he knew, *Erik knows these things about football.* As younger players, we had to listen to him.'

. . .

The website introduces the organisation by saying that players come first.

> ProProf was founded at the beginning of 1999 and is affili-
> ated with the trade union De Unie. ProProf works together
> with a number of large FIFA-recognised Dutch agencies,
> including Pro Athlete, Sports Entertainment Group and
> World Soccer Consult. If you have questions about your
> contract or if you have problems with your club, we can help
> you with that. If everything is properly arranged, you can
> fully concentrate on playing football. In the end, at ProProf
> it is still the players who matter.

Only 29 at the time, Erik ten Hag became a member of the board of ProProf in its first year. The organisation had been founded by a number of brokers. 'The late Ton van Dalen – my agent at the time – was one of them. He asked me somewhere in a bar of the Twente stadium if I wanted to join the board.' It wasn't a strange request. Even then, while playing for FC Twente, the well-being of players was a concern of Ten Hag's, as it continued to be when he became a manager.

. . .

The Enschede fireworks disaster happened on 13 May 2000 at the S.E. Fireworks depot, located in the middle of the Roombeek residential area. A fire led to an enormous explosion which killed 23 people, including four firefighters, and injured nearly 1,000. A total of 200 homes were destroyed and another 1,500 were damaged. Images of the explosion were seen around the world. The first explosion had a strength equivalent to 800kg of TNT, while the strength of the final explosion was in the range of 4,000–5,000 kilograms of TNT. The biggest blast was felt up to 20 miles away. Fire crews were called in from across the border in Germany to help battle the blaze, which was brought under control by the end of the day. S.E. Fireworks was a major supplier to pop concerts and festivals in the Netherlands. Prior to the disaster the company had a good safety record and had passed all safety inspections.

At that time, FC Twente had a team with a particularly strong regional character. The coach was Fred Rutten. Players Sander Boschker, Erik ten Hag, André Karnebeek, Berthil ter Avest, Jeroen Heubach, Thijs Houwing and Jan Vennegoor of Hesselink were native to the region. The entire team was shaken by the catastrophe, but the Twente players understandably were most affected. The question was why the KNVB did not demonstrate more empathy by scrapping the next match from the competition calendar. Herman Wessels was chairman of FC Twente at the time. 'In retrospect, we shouldn't have played, but I didn't realise the impact of the disaster that night.' Annually, the flags in Enschede are at half-mast to commemorate the tragedy.

Erik ten Hag later spoke about the painful episode. 'We had just trained at the Air Base [about half a mile from the disaster area] when the blast came. Our dressing room was in a military building with very thick walls. The windows were knocked out of their frames. Of course we didn't know what had happened. We tuned into RTV Oost and soon learned what was going on in the city. We left for Rotterdam half an hour later. On our way west we encountered masses of emergency vehicles. The cloud of smoke drifted with us, we saw it as far as Amersfoort [a city 60 miles to the west of Enschede]. Many of the boys lived in Enschede and knew many people there. I called home; we already had mobile phones back then. My father-in-law was in Enschede with my son. Fortunately, I soon found out that they were alright. There was a lot of stress in the group. Everyone wanted to know if there were family, friends or acquaintances in the disaster area. It was a traumatic experience.'

Ten Hag believes that today, the match against Feyenoord would never have taken place: 'the pressure on social media would have been far too great. Rightly so, of course, because football doesn't always have to go on. We tried, there was rebellion in the group. Berthil ter Avest and Scott Booth said, "We're not going to play." The fact that it did happen is a black page in the history of football to this day. No one should have played football that day.' The game in Rotterdam was played nonetheless. Feyenoord scored after seven minutes, but from then on, the FC Twente defence, amazingly, held on. In the middle of the second half Scottish striker Scott Booth scored the equaliser, from an assist by Ten Hag. Drama was added ten minutes before time when Twente went down to ten men after Serbian defender Spira Grujić got a red card. Ten Hag said, 'I took a position in a televised interview after that game, saying that half the city was on fire, and that it had been a lack of leadership that we were required to play anyway. I was not thanked for that. I had to leave the team, away from FC Twente. Pressure was put on the trainer [Fred Rutten], political games were played. But Fred didn't give in and I still had a running contract. I shouldn't have said it on television, but what else could I have done? I never saw that interview again, but I still feel the shame of that time.'

One year and ten days later, FC Twente faced PSV Eindhoven in the KNVB Cup final on 24 May 2001. 'If it had been up to the management of the club, I would not have been there in the Cup final season. No one wanted to play football against Feyenoord the day after the fireworks disaster, but we had to. We took the bad feeling of that time with us to the following season. Things didn't go well, it wasn't good. Hardly any reinforcements had been brought in, as money was always an issue and there was a lot of criticism. I was injured frequently and didn't play in midfield, but in defence. Then Patrick Pothuizen and Sjaak Polak arrived during the winter break and things started to run better with them in the team. The only way to success was the Cup final. PSV already were national champions; they weren't really interested, neither were their fans. So there was space in the stadium, and 35,000 Tukkers came to Rotterdam. You will never see such a migration again. Fred Rutten had recorded images of all the buses and supporters that were on the way; that's the psychologist in him. We were watching them. It was emotional, we were really stimulated by it. PSV was by far the best team in the Netherlands at that time. They had players like Van Nistelrooy, Van Bommel, Bruggink, Faber, Kezman and Bouma.'

The story of that famous 2001 KNVB Cup final really starts after the regular 90 minutes and half an hour of extra time, which ended 0–0. Penalties were needed to decide the outcome. What could possibly go wrong for PSV when they led 3–1 after three penalties, Jan Vennegoor of Hesselink and Jeroen Heubach having missed on behalf of FC Twente? PSV midfielder John de Jong came up to the spot to finish the job, but he caved in under the pressure. Twente goalie Sander Boschker stopped his shot and thereafter felt invincible. PSV veteran goalkeeper Ronald Waterreus was the next to be denied by Boschker, and the teams were level again. When

Dennis Hulshoff hit the mark for FC Twente, the pressure shifted completely onto the national champions. The 50,000 spectators in De Kuip, two-thirds of which were Twente fans, held their breath when Jonas Kolkka stepped forward for PSV. The FC Twente fans greeted him with a hellish whistling concert. The Finn's shot was weak and Boschker, ruthless. He saved again and ran with a clenched fist towards his cheering teammates, the club's hero. The cup goes to Enschede.

On that day, FC Twente captain Erik ten Hag jubilantly lifted the Football Federation Cup. Reminiscing on the achievement he says, 'When I think of the cup final, I think of the euphoria, the happiness, the sensation. It is a price that is inextricably linked to the fireworks disaster. Without wanting to overestimate the importance of football, the cup win gave the city back some pride, a year after the disaster. We really wanted to do something special for the fans, but PSV was expected to win. That seemed to happen in the penalty shootout, we were dead and buried. I don't remember much of it, all I know is that André Karnebeek half kicked into the ground and hit the target for us. Booth also scored and then Sander Boschker saved Kolkka's penalty. If you still win and you see all those happy people, you'll almost say we must have had help from above. What a party! FC Twente is a big club, but it was only the second trophy in its history. In 1975, the golden generation also won the cup. We were not as good as they were, but we still won the trophy. In retrospect, it is a shame that we did not continue together the following season, the trainer and the team: we could have competed at the top. I cannot describe the feeling of euphoria of that day. As a top athlete you don't just win prizes. We overcame and succeeded that day. The day made the season special, and it returned some colour to the city.'

Left back Sjaak Polak gave his version of the episode: 'Erik was born in Twente, he knew the club very well. In the dressing room, he was a very good leader. Before the final, he wanted to say something, looked around, and knew the mood. Then he stood up, and he began to speak. He told us, "Today, we will give a present to the people from our area, in Enschede." That was the most important thing. He told everyone, "OK, we need to give them something back. We have to fight for each other and bring the cup back to Enschede." These were the most important words he said in the dressing room. When we got the cup, in the dressing room after the match, he just said, "I'm so very proud of you all that we can take this cup back." It was an amazing day. It showed he was the leader of the team, 100 per cent. He was not a guy to shout. Sometimes, when he was mad you would hear him, but he found the right words. He's just a good guy with personality and respect, and that's the most important thing in football.'

On 5 May 2002, Erik ten Hag ended his playing career with a 0–0 draw against SC Heerenveen. He told coach John van 't Schip that he would not be involved the following season. He stopped at the age of 32 because he thought he 'had nothing to prove anymore'. There had been a possibility for him to play at Go Ahead, but according to Ten Hag, 'That offer made me seriously question myself. The best thing is to play football yourself, there's no doubt about that. My feeling told me that I had to continue for a few more years. But reason triumphed.' He had a modest playing career as a right-footed midfielder and defender, with 13 seasons at clubs outside of the Dutch elite. Between 1989 and 2002, he played a total of 336 games in all competitions for clubs in the Eredivisie and Eerste Divisie. He scored 15 times. Out of those 336 matches, Ten Hag played 221 for FC Twente. He retired with a second division title with

De Graafschap and a KNVB Cup in 2001 in his third spell at FC Twente. Even though he stopped playing for Twente, he stayed at the club as the new head of training.

5

SECOND MAN AT TWENTE AND PSV

*'Ultimately, the leader is part of the process
and must be able to subordinate himself to it.'*

ERIK TEN HAG

The *poldermodel* is the name given to the Dutch way of consensus building in which employers, trade unions and government sit down to negotiate working conditions and wages. It is a pragmatic recognition of plurality and a typical Dutch form of consultation politics and economy that goes back to the Middle Ages. It gets its name from the Dutch word *polder* – a tract of land reclaimed from the sea or a lake, enclosed by dikes. The first Dutch polders were created in the eleventh century. Dikes were placed around a low-lying area, after which it was pumped dry to gain extra land. During the feared westerly storms, when the North Sea water is pushed inland, nobles and citizens were forced to work together to stop the rising tides from flooding these new territories. The hydraulics that are involved in winning such battles against the elements are a fitting metaphor for Dutch society. If the battles were lost, the polder flooded. In times of need, cooperation between different classes was necessary and unavoidable.

This piece of geography-bound heritage has been part of the Dutch mindset for centuries. Consequently, the people of the Lowlands have an innate aversion to hierarchy. The leader must be one of the team, someone who doesn't put on airs. Armani and Mercedes-Benz are not nearly as popular in the Netherlands as they are with their European neighbours. Dutchmen and women are obsessed with *overleg*, consultation, which can make decision-making a lengthy and tedious process. Everyone needs to have his or her say. This is also known as *inspraak*, participation, or better, input into the plan, the project, the policy. There are committees for everything because everyone's voice needs to be heard. Every neighbourhood has its *actiecomités*, action committees: to welcome, or deny, North African refugees; to fight against global warming; to debate the pros and cons of widening the street, or even to organise how to protect stray cats.

Some argue that the 'polder model' has been replaced with a conflict model. Where once the communal agreement was primary, now individual interest seems more important. If the number of political parties is a measure of social cohesion, then things are not moving in the right direction. The Dutch Parliament is home to no fewer than 20 political parties, roughly double that of 40 years ago. Half of these have three or fewer representatives in the 150-seat lower house. There are several socialist parties, Christian parties and populist parties. There is a party for farmers' rights and a party for animal rights. There are several independent house members who represent, well, themselves. After every election cycle there is an episode of complicated coalition building. Considerable balancing acts are performed behind the closed doors of the political conclave in order to get a new government in place. This culture affects every aspect of society, and football is no exception. It has been said that in Dutch football teams, there are 12 equally valid opinions: those of the 11 players on the pitch and the one of the coach – and often in that order.

Ten Hag believes that the KNVB, the Dutch FA, is deeply affected by this kind of thinking. He says, 'It is up to the KNVB itself. You can't change anything because of how the association is structured. I have been the head of training. I dealt with the KNVB, and when you do you learn there are no short lines of communication. Everything has to go through committees, directors and executives. The Netherlands is the country of compromises, and the KNVB is the association of compromises. But then football development comes to a halt. Meanwhile, the strangest things are happening. The KNVB has now decided not to use referees with the youngest youth. But how does that work educationally? Kids with talent must learn to accept authority and deal with the decisions of such a man, right? What I hear is that rankings are no longer being kept either because boys could get demotivated if they are at the bottom. No referee, no more rankings among the youth … How are you ever going to get a winning mentality? Who invents such things? We have gone too far with considering the social aspect and the idea that everything should be fun and cosy. The problem is that you don't grow characters that way. This is not how you create a new Mark van Bommel or Frank de Boer. In an amateur club you are educated, you learn to be social, you want to achieve something – together – so you have to overcome setbacks, push boundaries, acquire discipline. And you see it in society as well. Playing football at a club is like life itself. If you haven't developed the right way, you're lost. What kind of society are you creating then? Really, all together we have torn the winning mentality from our football in recent years.'

It may not be a surprise that Rinus Michels is one of Ten Hag's role models. Who in professional football management would not want to pick up some points from the father of 'total football' and the

FIFA 'coach of the century'? Michels is rightly credited with forever transforming the way the game is played. One of the lesser-known facts about the great man is that he was a PE teacher before he became a coach. Most people who go to university are acquainted with at least one professor who is a brilliant expert in their field but is a pedagogic amateur capable of putting the class to sleep. This problem is not limited to academia. Having great tactical insights into football is one thing, but getting them across to players is quite another. Players are just like big children, and there is a natural resemblance between being a teacher and being a coach. The difference is the objective. A good coach does not lose sight of the educational aspects of his job. Michels was not only an extraordinary architect of football, but a brilliant instructor of players.

Although Ten Hag never taught at school, he spent years teaching youth players the ins and outs of the game. On 1 June 2002, he joined FC Twente's academy. Until mid-2008, he was head of training at the football academy of FC Twente/Heracles Almelo. He did some courses to get ready for his new responsibilities and was initially supported by former Twente coach Issy ten Donkelaar. Ten Hag admitted that 'It was a difficult decision to stop playing, but this is a position that really appeals to me. The education of football players has been professionalised enormously in recent years. The FC Twente academy has a big name. I think it would be fantastic to develop it further in the future.'

His greatest success during this period was the championship of A1 juniors in the 2006–7 season. 'I really enjoy it. All those little guys with their big dreams. You see it in their eyes. The sparkle, the fun. They are having adventures together. As a player gets older, his freedoms grow, but so do his responsibilities. The bigger the club, the bigger your responsibilities.' The coach has to appeal to a professional player's sense of responsibility. He has to remind him of the privileged situation in which he lives and convince him that along with it come certain duties. In fact, he works on not only ordinary football issues, but mental conditioning, a continuous growth towards maturity. Ten Hag is expert at managing this kind of integrative approach to player development.

Ten Hag felt that some degree of educational reform would be in order, such as delaying the selection of players to the age of 12. Some clubs start at age six, seven or eight, which seems too early. As Ten Hag said, 'Everyone is afraid of missing out, but at too young an age you can't quite predict what the potential is. In Twente, we used to refer to the Bible, "Many feel called, but few are chosen." The training sessions of the pupils at Ajax are great. But if you would start training that age group in clusters, more boys would be able to receive the same training. As a result, more boys would develop. And because you take a few extra years to choose the best, the selection process becomes more thorough. I am in favour of a concentration of educational programmes. It makes no sense that all clubs have their own academies. You end up with a surplus of players and invest money into people who don't really have the talent. We are doing well in the Netherlands, but we can do much better.'

As a player, Erik ten Hag already knew that he wanted to continue as a football coach. Following his retirement in 2002, Ten Hag took on the role of FC Twente U17 manager and the following season was promoted to U19 manager. In addition to being head of training, Ten Hag joined the coaching staff on 1 February 2006 when Jan van Staa became interim head coach following the dismissal of Rini Coolen. Ten Hag continued in his post when Fred Rutten and René Eijkelkamp were appointed as head coach and assistant in the 2006–7 season. He successfully completed the KNVB Coach Professional

Football course in May 2007. After the departure of Eijkelkamp in July 2007, Ten Hag was Rutten's only assistant.

Colleague, friend and fellow Twente native René Hake has many good memories of Ten Hag: 'We often encountered each other as opponents, he as a trainer at Twente, and I as a trainer at Emmen. He also was head of the academy at Twente, and I was head of the academy at Emmen. We talked about how you organise training and other practical issues. We connected well, and as a result Erik asked me to come to Twente. I think he is very good at managing a team, both the group and the individual. He knows how to mould his team and how he can change it with small touches that make the difference. Other than that, he is very determined and sticks to his plan. There are phases when his team struggles, but he is not dissuaded from his idea and the way of working he has in mind. I think that is why his teams always bounce back. Erik has a generous dose of humour, but you don't readily see that when he is in front of camera.'

As a youth coach of FC Twente, Ten Hag was on top of every single detail. Black shoes were required. He read books on psychology, leadership and management. He kept stacks of files and documents on players and put a lot of energy into good potential. He would stay up late to fine-tune personal development plans. He spent hours on moulding difficult characters like Eljero Elia and knew how to get through to them. Coaching was a learning experience: every season he became a little better, wiser, more complete.

In the summer of 2008, FC Twente chairman Joop Munsterman appointed Steve McClaren as head coach. By the time McClaren met Ten Hag, the young midfielder with flaxen blond hair had turned into a keen strategist with a shaved head who was rapidly advancing his coaching career. McClaren coached FC Twente's first team with Ten Hag as assistant for a year. McClaren recalled that no matter how early he got to the training ground, Ten Hag was already there. 'I thought I worked hard until I met Erik. He is very disciplined and people have to buy into that and have that work ethic. He is demanding, players have to deliver what he wants. That is his great strength, but not everyone can handle it. It's football, football, football with him, to the point of eccentricity. He carried on with that work ethic after Twente, and he's a far better coach and manager now.' Wout Brama, champion with FC Twente under Steve McClaren, shared his first impression of Ten Hag. 'We were in the junior team and the first thing he said to us was that we would be getting two weeks less summer holiday. We immediately thought: *who is this dude?*'

McClaren arrived in Enschede without bringing his own staff and so was dependent on Ten Hag. 'The pre-season was due to start the next day and I said to Erik, "Have you got our first day organised?" Over the next two hours he talked me through six weeks of pre-season work. Every last detail was accounted for. Every document ready. Every drinks break planned. He would say, "There are 20 minutes here for you to do this specific session and then we do this." I never saw anything like it before or since. For both individual players and for the team the work he did was the best I had seen. The log even indicated what the coaches would be wearing each day. He had planned what equipment had to be carried out and when it had to be brought back in. I would say to Erik during a session, "We just need that goal moved to the halfway line," and he would ask every player in the squad to do it. All 22 players. Everyone goes. That's the way he likes it.'

But McClaren admits that Ten Hag's greatest strengths are not only his attention to detail and organisation. 'He has a clear philosophy of how he wants to play football and the environment he wants to create. Tailored career planning for each player was an important focus at Twente, for every player, from youth to the first team. Tactically he's outstanding. I would have to sit in the stand to analyse games, but he could do it from the touchline and make the changes. He was invaluable in my first year. I would not have survived if it hadn't been for his work and his understanding of the game. In terms of changing games he is second to none. He was way ahead of his time. Even in Holland.' Twente had a strong first season under McClaren, who led his team to second place in the Eredivisie, behind Louis van Gaal's AZ. Twente also reached the cup final, which was lost to SC Heerenveen.

McClaren attributed the national title FC Twente won in 2010 to Ten Hag. 'Without Ten Hag we would never have become champions.' What's striking about that statement is that Ten Hag no longer worked at Twente during the championship season. In the summer of 2009, he joined Rutten at PSV Eindhoven and missed out on what is still the only Eredivisie title in the history of FC Twente. McClaren suggested that the strong foundation Ten Hag had laid in the 2008–9 season was the reason they had won the title a year later.

. . .

In 2004, Joop Munsterman started as chairman of FC Twente. He had been in media management but had no prior experience with running a professional football club. Nonetheless, during his tenure as chairman trainers Fred Rutten, in 2006, and Steve McClaren, in 2008, were successively appointed, which ultimately led to the national title. On 20 January 2015, Munsterman announced that he would retire as chairman of the club at the end of that season. In the months after his announced departure, it became clear that FC Twente was in financial trouble. The club conducted an internal investigation of Munsterman's activities, eventually holding him and some other former directors personally responsible for the trouble.

On behalf of the KNVB, independent investigator Ben Knuppe reviewed financial records at FC Twente between 2013 and June 2015. According to his recommendations, the club had to revert to a proper business model and get its finances in order. The KNVB published his proposals, which stipulated that Joop Munsterman and former chairman Aldo van der Laan should not be allowed to serve in any capacity at FC Twente. It also suggested that Gerald van den Belt, Hennie ten Hag, Hein Trebbe and Joop de Winter resign from the club board. The board should keep 'sufficient distance' and completely independently monitor the club's policies. No sponsors, supporters' associations or other direct stakeholders could be represented in this body. Van der Laan and Munsterman did withdraw from the club but had a different interpretation of the events. Munsterman detailed his side of the story in a book titled *Rood Bloed – alles voor de club* (Red Blood – Everything for the Club).

KNVB director of professional football Bert van Oostveen said, 'This is a harsh but necessary step for FC Twente. The club has a large and loyal following, is socially involved and extremely popular, but a mess was made of the management these past years. Moreover, board members deliberately withheld financial information, which was detrimental. Because of this the club is on the verge of collapse. In short, FC Twente has to work hard in the coming months, and faces difficult decisions. But this is the only way to ensure that the club can come out of the current situation and move forward. The KNVB will help and support wherever it can, but the club has to do this itself.'

FC Twente was on the verge of losing its pro-football licence and on the brink of being declared bankrupt. As a prerequisite of keeping its licence, the football club needed all its creditors, which included a number of former board members, to write off some of the club's debts. According to the *Algemeen Dagblad*, four board members were part of FC Twente's 15 creditors. Together they put more than €12 million of private money into the club. In a newspaper interview, the elder Ten Hag shared his view of what happened at the club. 'I am very disappointed in Joop Munsterman. If you are on a board together, trust should be the basis. He has deeply betrayed that trust. I had sleepless nights. I don't want to be blamed for something I don't feel responsible for. Joop, in his position of director, misinformed us about the financial situation of the club and thus misled us all. Of course, as a supervisory director, I am partly responsible and I am not running away from that. But I do want to be able to make judgements on the basis of data that are correct.'

Eventually, current FC Twente director Paul van der Kraan would apologise at FC Twente's 2023 New Year's reception for the way the club dealt with Hennie ten Hag and Hein Trebbe, and the two were exonerated. Meanwhile, Hennie ten Hag, at 79, was happy with the rehabilitation. 'Besides reliability and integrity, justice is one of the most important pillars in my life. I have always experienced what happened to us as unjust, and that hurt. The club has now rectified that. We discussed this with each other in the run-up to the reception, and I am glad that people have seen that it was not justified and that the matter was not looked at objectively. It's fine this way. Everyone makes mistakes in life.' Ten Hag has been a rare presence at FC Twente home matches in recent years. 'I only went there when Ajax visited because Erik was their coach.' The barrier to visiting the FC Twente stadium was removed. 'The unpleasant feeling is no longer there. I will definitely go and watch again. But I won't be in the stadium every fortnight from now on. We are also very interested in English football these days, and Erik's mother finds that at least as important.'

FC Twente and Grolsch, Twente's most famous beer company, have been linked in a partnership for more than five decades. Tukkers are proud of their Grolsch, recognisable by the distinct flip-cap bottle and its rich taste. De Grolsch Veste replaced the old Diekman Stadium as FC Twente's home ground on 22 March 1998. In 2019 FC Twente and Koninklijke Grolsch (Royal Grolsch) extended their cooperation for another ten years. FC Twente general manager Paul van der Kraan said, 'Grolsch has been closely associated with FC Twente since the club was founded in 1965. Grolsch is deeply rooted in the region. Even in the recent difficult period, which hopefully is behind us, the club could always count on Grolsch's support.' Jacco Potkamp, Grolsch sales director, said, 'As *noabers* [neighbours, in the Twente dialect] we intend to continue to support the club – together with the fans – in good and bad times. As icons of this beautiful region, we see many opportunities to work together and strengthen each other. We do not only pay attention to football, but also to the people and the region. Cheers to many beautiful years together!'

Erik ten Hag was cautiously hopeful. 'The big, beautiful stadium will remain, but for me to be able to come back there has to be a very good organisation. Rebuilding the club will take a lot of time and energy. I once left to return as head coach one day, but it is impossible to predict what will happen. Maybe in 2030, I'll be technical manager. I have also said for fun that I want to become president of the club one day. Why not? I have a sports and entrepreneurial background. A club like FC Twente should be led by someone who is sports related. But professional football is unpredictable.'

On 23 June 2009 Ten Hag joined the coaching team at PSV Eindhoven, where he was reunited with head coach Fred Rutten. Rutten had left for Schalke 04 the previous summer, but he was fired before the end of his first season. At first, the FC Twente leadership had given Ten Hag the green light to start working for PSV, but then had second thoughts. His contract ran for three more years at Twente, but Ten Hag argued that he could move to PSV freely due to a clause in his contract. FC Twente filed an arbitration case against him. Twente chairman Munsterman said, 'We believe that Erik wrongly left for PSV for free. We made a financial proposal to PSV quite some time ago, but we have heard nothing in response. That is why we are involving the arbitration committee of the KNVB.' The lingering financial dispute eventually was settled through the mediation of the Dutch FA, which sided with Ten Hag. He was able to continue his work at PSV without further encumbrances. Erik ten Hag left FC Twente after more than twenty years as a supporter, player, head of training and assistant coach.

Friday afternoon at the PSV training complex De Herdgang was always a highlight for Ten Hag. Fred Rutten's assistant was given free rein to train players such as Memphis Depay, Jetro Willems, Jeroen Zoet, Jürgen Locadia, Zakaria Labyad, Zakaria Bakkali and Riechedly Bazoer. 'Yes, that was a nice group,' Ten Hag says. 'It was a kind of masterclass that I gave with Phillip Cocu, René Eijkelkamp and Anton Scheutjens.' Unfortunately for Ten Hag, there was little to celebrate with his colleagues in Eindhoven. PSV did not become champions during his employment. Three times the Eindhoven team finished in a disappointing third place. In the last season PSV won the KNVB Cup, after Rutten and Ten Hag had left the club.

The Moroccan goalkeeper Khalid Sinouh worked with Ten Hag during the assistant coach's last year at PSV, the 2011–12 season, and characterised him as a workaholic. 'Some players at PSV thought he was a somewhat unusual and gruff man. But if you look at how he performed, you can take your hat off to him. It all came together. Wherever he has worked, Ten Hag has created something beautiful.

He makes people think and holds on to his line even when head-winds are blowing.' In addition to being a field trainer, Ten Hag was also an analyst and scout in Eindhoven. He regularly was on the road to analyse PSV's European opponents and to assess possible reinforcements.

On 24 October 2010 Feyenoord suffered the biggest defeat in the club's history. PSV beat the Rotterdam club 10–0. Feyenoord's previous worst defeat had been an 8–2 loss to Ajax, in 1983. The shocking result was described as a 'black page in our history' by struggling manager Mario Been. Midfielder Kelvin Leerdam received his marching orders soon after PSV had taken the lead. Some resolute defending by Feyenoord kept the scoreline at a respectable 2–0 as the two teams reached half-time. Whatever Fred Rutten said during the break seemed to galvanise his players, and his team demolished Feyenoord in the second period.

Minute 49: Ola Toivonen heads the ball behind Feyenoord goal-keeper Rob van Dijk from a cross by Ibrahim Afellay, 4–0. There is chanting in the stands. 'Ten, ten, ten,' shout the 33,900 PSV supporters who are witnessing history in the making at the Philips Stadium. A hat-trick from Brazilian Jonathan Reis was the pick of the ten strikes on goal, with the 21-year-old Brazilian repaying the club for their patience over three troublesome years when he was struggling with a cocaine addition. Starting the new season, he scored nine goals in just four games. In addition to Reis's hat-trick, there were braces from Jeremain Lens and Balazs Dzsudzsak, with Ibrahim Afellay, Ola Toivonen and Orlando Engelaar joining in the rout. Ironically, PSV lost 3–1 in the return match in Rotterdam and lost its Eredivisie lead to FC Twente. On the last day of play, Ajax won the match against Twente, and became champions. PSV experienced a disappointing season, notwithstanding the historic October victory.

Fred Rutten was in his third year as head coach. After the winter break the pursuit of a domestic trophy got derailed once more. By March 2012, his resignation was non-negotiable for the PSV board, after the national title again eluded the club's grasp. With the in-form Reis leading the front line, PSV had seemed on course to win another title, but he suffered a complicated knee injury in a collision with Roda JC goalkeeper Przemyslaw Tyton during a match in December 2010. Shortly thereafter Rutten also lost star player Ibrahim Afellay, who was sold to Barcelona during the winter transfer window. New acquisitions Georginio Wijnaldum, Kevin Strootman, Dries Mertens and Tim Matavž were expected to infuse PSV with new life. The results were mixed, until the club suffered an unexpected defeat, 6–2, against FC Twente. A week later PSV lost 3–1 against NAC-Breda. In the evening, dozens of angry supporters forced the returning players' bus to a halt at the entrance of De Herdgang. PSV had made it to the semi-finals of the cup tournament and was involved in the round of 16 in the Europa League. But three Eredivisie defeats in a row were more than the supporters and the managment could bear. PSV was no longer willing to back up Rutten and decided a day after the NAC defeat to relieve the trainer of his duties.

Assistant coach Erik ten Hag decided to leave the club as well. 'I am in solidarity with the trainer. I am not in any doubt. We have come together, so I am partly responsible. I support the trainer and all his decisions,' Ten Hag said in his final statement before his departure. Anton Scheutjens, PSV's goalkeeping coach from 2008 to 2013, thought it was significant that Ten Hag backed up Rutten 100 per cent: 'It was very strong, and it says something about his loyalty. He already had quite a large role in the coaching staff and also led discussions, although Fred was of course ultimately responsible. I don't know a player from back then who wasn't enthusiastic about Fred or Erik. Just ask them: Memphis Depay, Jürgen Locadia, Georginio Wijnaldum or anyone else; they will all say they have become better players with them. Ten Hag led the talent training sessions at PSV and ensured that the connection between youth and professional sides became much better than it was before. These were not easy years, especially because PSV had to considerably cut costs and sold the best among its players. Sometimes that was forgotten in the comments that were made afterwards. Still, the results were disappointing, and there are simply no excuses for that at a club like PSV. You have to win a prize at some point. I always thought that Erik would go far as a coach, but I could not foresee how far.'

6

COACHING 'KOWET'

'The person is worth more to me than the athlete.'

ERIK TEN HAG

The presenter of the Dutch TV programme *Studio Sport* pronounces the club's name the English way, as 'Go Ahead'. But diehard supporters in Deventer pronounce it 'Ko-wet'. This curious habit has a history. At the beginning of the twentieth century, there were two football clubs in the city. Utile Dulci, 'UD' for short, was an elite club that consisted of members of good – that is, wealthy and influential – families. The elegant Latin name, derived from one of Horatius' odes, means 'the useful through the pleasurable' – get healthy while having some fun. Until the early 1900s, football was played exclusively by the privileged class. Go Ahead was founded in 1902 by and for workers, a real club for the common people. To its credit, UD made a field available to give the poor folk a chance, not knowing that this would be the start of a permanent power shift in Deventer and Dutch football. When Go Ahead achieved its first successes, UD became less cooperative: no more free fields. Go Ahead found its own way with minimal resources and soon managed to become a solid opponent of once unchallenged UD. The Deventer derbies were fierce. Go Ahead eventually surpassed UD, culminating in a first national title in 1917.

Until 1954, Dutch football was an amateur competition. The national champion was determined by means of a competition between the regional winners. Go Ahead was the first people's club to win the championship in the Netherlands, and after 1917 it won again in 1922, 1930 and 1933. Football's transition from elite pastime to popular sport was happening in the Netherlands with Go Ahead as a driving force. The UD members and supporters always referred to Go Ahead in a dignified English manner. The mostly dialect-speaking people of Deventer, on the other hand, quickly corrupted the English name into a variant that was easier to pronounce. Kowet was born.

The name went through more than one change. In 1902 the club had been founded as Be Quick. That was a problem, because up north in Groningen there was another club by that name. So the Deventer club was renamed in 1905. In 1971 the professional division of Go Ahead separated from the amateur branch. The newly professional club had to enter the new season under a new name. Several rather dull suggestions were made, including FC Deventer, Deventer Region and IJssel Rangers, after the river that runs through the city. The trainer at the time, Welshman Barry Hughes, got involved. As a native English speaker, he thought that an English addition to Go Ahead would make sense. It would also add an air of English professionalism and respectability to the organisation. 'Eagles' was attached, referring to the eagle in the Deventer city coat of arms. After the name became official, the eagle was given a place in the club's logo, and a year later the stadium was named De Adelaarshorst – the eagles' nest.

The club has had famous players throughout its history, such as Leo Halle, Paul Bosvelt, Henk ten Cate, Ruud Geels, Bert van Marwijk and Marc Overmars. There were also big-name coaches, like

František Fadrhonc, Barry Hughes, Leo Beenhakker, Wiel Coerver and Robert Maaskant. The period from 1964 to 1987 was Go Ahead Eagles's golden age, in which they played in the Eredivisie. After a few years outside the top flight, the club returned briefly from 1993 to 1996. After that, it was a long stay in the second tier, Eerste Divisie, where they reached a high of fifth place in 2010. Marc Overmars began his career as a player at Go Ahead Eagles, playing the 1990–1 season at the Deventer club before continuing the more illustrious part of his career at Ajax, Arsenal and Barcelona. He concluded his career, however, back at Go Ahead, for the 2008–9 season. He tripled for a time as the club's player, board member and shareholder. After his retirement as player, he was the club's technical director from 2009 to 2012, and he played a key role in bringing in Erik ten Hag. It was not an obvious opportunity. This was a club that had been relegated from the Eredivisie in 1996; standards had slipped, expectations had dipped.

The 2012–13 season was a curious Eerste Divisie year, with two clubs – AGOVV and SC Veendam – declaring bankruptcy and disappearing from the competition entirely. Teams in the Eerste Divisie advance to the highest league through a system of play-offs after the regular competition ends. Go Ahead landed in sixth place in the table, behind MVV, Helmond Sport, Sparta, Volendam and Cambuur. This entitled the club to participate in the play-offs. In the first round, an away draw (3–3) and a win at home (3–0) eliminated FC Dordrecht. In the second round, Go Ahead dismissed VVV, winning 1–0 in Deventer and 3–0 away in Venlo, meaning that they reached the third and final round. The home game against FC Volendam yielded a 3–0 win, with goals from Xander Houtkoop, Jarchinio Antonia and Marnix Kolder. After the game, the ecstatic supporters stormed the pitch to celebrate with their heroes, but Ten Hag intervened by pulling his players off, saying, 'Immediately go home and go to bed. We're not there yet. The prizes are decided on Sunday, not today.'

Before the decisive game against FC Volendam Ten Hag announced, with characteristic confidence, 'Deventer deserves the Eredivisie.' On 26 May 2013, Deventer got its due. At the return match in Volendam the Deventer faithful experienced some anxious moments after striker Jack Tuyp put Volendam ahead in just 15 minutes with a well-taken free kick. Nearly 10,000 fans followed the game at home in the Adelaarshorst on a giant screen. The score remained the same throughout the game, and Go Ahead was through. As a result, the club returned to the Eredivisie for the first time in 17 years. The players lifted Erik ten Hag on their shoulders in the post-match celebrations. The team returned to Deventer basked in glory. They received city-wide recognition at De Brink, the central square in the old town of Deventer, where thousands gathered, raising their trademark red-and-yellow scarves, emblazoned with 'Return of a Legend'.

• • •

It is quiet on the Vetkampstraat. A woman is walking her dog and two boys are riding their bicycles down the street, side by side. The street has just 30 homes, mostly social housing. The small houses are decorated with red-and-yellow flags and other Go Ahead Eagles insignia. One even has a full-size sculpture of an eagle attached to its facade. At first glance, the street, with its typical herringbone pattern of maroon bricks, is not remarkable. But to local football fans, this is the most beautiful place in the Netherlands, because it is the location of the De Adelaarshorst. The stadium, Go Ahead's home since 1920, is pure art for football culture lovers. No glitzy or curvacious architecture, only the straightforward functionalism of square stands at right angles. Football's Bauhaus. The stadium is located in the middle of the working-class district of Voorstad-Oost and is reminiscent of English football in terms of its atmosphere – a kind of Dutch Craven Cottage. The glow from the stadium lights shines into residents' living-rooms, and every house has an exclusive view of the old stadium wall. The wall features tiles inscribed with club slogans, 'Red-yellow, colours of a jewel' and 'Eagles till I die'. In front of the main gate is a statue of goalkeeper Leo Halle. The 'Lion of Deventer' heroically protected the Go Ahead goal during much of the interwar years.

After Erik ten Hag had gained experience at FC Twente and PSV as assistant trainer, he made his debut as head coach at Go Ahead Eagles during the 2012–13 season. After the ill-fated tenure of head coach Joop Gall, the club went through two interim coaches, Michel Boerebach and Scotsman Jimmy Calderwood. The management, under the leadership of board chairman Edwin Mulder, carefully considered its options while selecting a more effective new man in charge. They were looking for a manager who could revive the club, was innovative and could improve young players. They spoke with Dwight Lodeweges and René Hake, but eventually settled on Ten Hag, who made a big impression with his vision and organisational skills. Ten Hag was instrumental in the renewal of the team, with the coming of Jop van der Linden, Cas Peters, Nick Marsman and Deniz Türüç. Quincy Promes came from FC Twente, and during the winter break Bart Vriends and Xandro Schenk arrived. Gradually, a very young, stable team developed.

It would be a future-defining season for the club in red and yellow, a year of culture shocks and blows, but also of a sophisticated process that led to improbable achievements. Ten years later, former Go Ahead centre back Bart Vriends travelled back in time with teammates, supporters and head coach Ten Hag. The resulting documentary was a part of ESPN's series *Beeldjes Kijken*, 'Watching Images'. Vriends had joined halfway through the season, arriving on loan from Utrecht in the winter to strengthen the defence. While he was working on the documentary, every former player told him the same thing. He says, 'What really came out from those conversations with everyone involved was that Erik ten Hag changed the professionalism at the club in just a couple of weeks at the start of pre-season. This was a small mid-table second-division club in a small city in the east. It grew into something else when he was in charge. He changed the mentality at the club. He changed the mentality of the players and the people who worked there. From day one, actually.'

Adrie Steenbergen has been involved with 'Kowet' all his life. He has been the go-to man at De Adelaarshorst for more than four decades. In the positions of chief scout, board member and team manager, he has seen 17 coaches and hundreds of players come and go. He has vivid memories of his first meeting with Erik ten Hag. 'I knew he was driven, professional. So I had carefully prepared and explained my activities in print on four full A4 pages. Ten Hag organises everything down to the smallest details, leaves nothing to chance. But I am a perfectionist myself. If the bus has to be at the stadium at 2 minutes and 40 seconds after seven o'clock, I will make sure it is. The devil is in the details, and you have to keep your promises.'

Dennis Demmers was Ten Hag's assistant at Go Ahead. 'I had already known Erik for some time. His brother Rico was my assistant in amateur football. Erik brought me to the first team of Go Ahead as an assistant. When we lost a game, for whatever reason, he was able to get the focus back on the future. He did a detailed post-match review and used the video images to make players better individually. Erik would be busy taking notes and then presented his ideas to the players. If there was criticism, it was always substantiated. If a player brought too little, he heard it. If he did a great job, then he heard it too. Whether it came out positive for you or not: you knew he said it to make you better. He invested a lot of time in that. It was clear that the players appreciated it.'

Demmers says that Ten Hag 'knew everything about the culture and history of Go Ahead. He immersed himself and knew every detail. That's one of the things he taught me: Know what you're getting yourself into when you're going somewhere. At Go Ahead, Erik introduced a top sports culture, without barging in like an elephant into a china shop. We all understood that we were in a process and that it would take time. Anyone who follows Erik knows that happens everywhere he goes. He knew so well what he was doing that no one questioned his approach, but in the beginning it did not go smoothly. He had everything figured out and worked very hard, but he demanded the same from us. He was the first one to get to the club, the last to leave. The results we got were the reward for the hard work he did.'

Ten Hag's commitment was evident at all levels, as Demmers says, 'Whenever we had to go somewhere to watch a game, he always accompanied one of the assistants. He never said: "You go ahead, I'll hear about it tomorrow." No, he was always there himself. We got a lot of energy from that. He was the one who was ultimately responsible and who drew up the plans, but he also gave responsibility to the staff. I remember that he once complimented the man in charge of the grass before a match, "You have made great turf for us. That will help us a lot." Those little things are important.' The players' home henceforth was off-limits for anyone who was not part of the staff. A chain was put up at the training grounds because supporters were no longer allowed to stand along the touchline to watch. These interventions raised some eyebrows, but Ten Hag did not mind.

'Erik had the equipment storage converted into a fitness room. He did not want players to come to the club just to train, but also to individually develop themselves, and become better and stronger. Players made use of the facility both before and after training and became the owner of their own process. We had Nick Marsman in goal, and Quincy Promes joined. Sjoerd Overgoor had a difficult season, but then blossomed and became a key player. They grew together with the team. When we first came to the club, the stadium was never sold out, but after the promotion and the return to the Eredivisie after 17 years it was a completely different story. The stadium was sold out almost every game, and it has continued to be that way. Go Ahead Eagles was put back on the map that year.'

What Marnix Kolder produced wasn't always elegant, but he was very effective. His endurance became the stuff of legend and earned him nicknames such as 'Marnix Goalder' and 'Kolderator'. He scored the equaliser against Feyenoord with nine stitches in his head and a black eye. He had joined Go Ahead Eagles in 2011 and his goals had been an important part of the club's promotion. The veteran striker soon found out that despite his status, he would not get preferential treatment. 'I was made captain, so had short lines of communication with Ten Hag. I had a private situation with my wife and wanted to skip the post-match training once. I knocked on the wooden door of the trainers' room and asked: "Can I take tomorrow off?" It is not such an important training after all.' Ten Hag stuck his index finger in the air and retorted, "Marnix, with me every training is important." Kolder then had to drive two hours from his home in the northern province of Groningen to make it to the short training session in Terwolde, next to Deventer. Eventually, he learned to enjoy his 175-mile commute to be at every practice session.

Kolder recalls that one day Ten Hag 'came into the dressing room at 10am sharp to explain the training, as he always did. But he had his training pants on backwards. He had his papers in his pocket, but they stuck out awkwardly at the back. No one had the courage to say anything, until our third keeper Patrick ter Mate suddenly raised his hand and said, "Trainer, you have your pants on the wrong way." The entire dressing room burst into laughter, but Ten Hag was undeterred and continued his talk. But when he came onto the training field later we noticed that he had turned his pants around 180 degrees. He really is the best trainer I've ever had. With Erik we would definitely have finished in the top ten of the Eredivisie the following year. I'm 100 per cent sure of that.'

After his life in football, Kolder made a complete career shift. Today, he works as a counsellor in youth care and helps young men and women who struggle with social adaptation problems. During their time together at Go Ahead, Ten Hag recognised Kolder's social intelligence, and Kolder discovered how much he enjoyed working with young players and being a positive influence on them. As Kolder says, Ten Hag 'gave me the captain's armband and that gave me a sense of responsibility. I had to be an example. Because of the role Ten Hag assigned to me, I got the feeling that I wanted to work with people in the future.' Ten Hag's strict approach at Go Ahead Eagles paid off, for the team as a whole and for Marnix Kolder personally. The year with Ten Hag pushed Kolder towards a new direction in life, one where he now puts the lessons of his trainer into practice in his current work. As a counsellor, he leaves little to chance and has to be proactive. He learned a lot from Ten Hag, saying, 'Ten Hag always said that as a trainer you have to be able to improvise well, for example, if someone dropped out during training. He would say, "You should not react, but act." That is no different in my work these days.'

Free-kick specialist Jop van der Linden understood that something special was in the making at the Vetkampstraat: 'Everyone realised fairly quickly that in Ten Hag we had a passionate coach and a real professional. Our self-belief grew throughout the season. In terms of personality and communication, other trainers may be better, but when it comes to football he certainly is the best I have experienced. He was completely crazy about football and had a clear vision that matched our level. I don't remember any discussions between him and players in the early stage. He was more open to input later in the season, but he still wanted us to follow his lead. We were good at positioning, but we were equally capable of taking advantage of the organisational naivety of our opponents. Ten Hag knows his player material very well and stays ahead of the rest by implementing his vision.'

While making his debut as head coach, Ten Hag maintained a professional distance from the players and clearly communicated his expectations to his team. He asks the question, 'How do you get better players? You have to look at this per team. A team that plays in the Champions League must be programmed differently from a team that only has a game on the weekend, or an U23 team or youth team. You cannot give players who are in puberty the same incentives as adult players because they are growing and you increase the risk of injuries. Players who make the transition from youth to a first team, say from the age of 17, can be taxed to the maximum. They are in the last phase of their physiological development. Exactly then they can make great strides in coordination, in receiving passes, the way they break away. In that phase, they have to do much more in terms of workload than the first-team players. Also, the quality of the players determines the system. When a decisive player leaves, you have to play differently. I experienced it at PSV, as assistant to Fred Rutten, and as head coach of Go Ahead Eagles.'

Because he already knew him from PSV, right back Jan Kromkamp was not shocked by Ten Hag's methods. Kromkamp had experience outside of the Dutch leagues, with Liverpool and Villarreal, and training hard was nothing new him. 'I was used to a higher level, so I was able to adapt quickly. In England you were pushed to be top and top fit. Everything was squeezed out of you. In the Dutch First Division you generally don't have that type of trainer. With Co Adriaanse at AZ we also trained very hard. Erik is where he is today for a reason. We always stuck to his regimen. We did sprints of 80 metres, 100 metres. We trained for a long time and at the end of the season we really were top fit. This is part of the reason why we got promoted late in the competition.'

Periodisation is mainly about alternating between rest and exertion. It is a systematic build-up over a number of weeks, followed by a period in which the intensity and duration of the training is reduced. 'Erik's periodisation is great. With him there always was an idea behind everything. He wanted to professionalise Go Ahead and that was necessary. Erik went to a scientist in Germany with our data and had them analysed. It didn't surprise me that he brought in stretchers to let us rest between training sessions. He calmly built things up with us. In the beginning the results weren't always good, but that changed.'

An injured Kromkamp wanted to spend some time with his family. Ten Hag didn't like it and thought he'd better work towards his recovery. Kromkamp recalls, 'We had a weekend off with Go Ahead. I had been injured for two months and had booked Disneyland Paris for three days with my family. Erik was angry, he thought it was the wrong idea. I gave a bad example ... "But coach,

I'm not even allowed on the pitch yet." "Then you go cycling and work in the weight room," he said. In the end I convinced him and was allowed to go.' Kromkamp is annoyed when people call Ten Hag a dictator. 'That is nonsense. Erik is a connector, a pleasant man, who does everything for his players and is genuinely interested in the person behind the football player. A real pro, too. Of course that sometimes clashes.'

Haaksbergen neighbours Germany, from where a whiff of *Deutsche Gründlichkeit*, German thoroughness, may have blown across the border and infected Ten Hag. Go Ahead chairman Edwin Mulder said, 'He pays attention to fringe conditions. The ball storage had to be put on a slope so the balls would roll out more easily. The dugout was to be moved closer to the centre line so that he would have a better view. And for the players: no mobile phones or caps at the club. That caused some resistance, until they saw that it worked.' Playing cards during training breaks was a thing of the past as well. Talk to each other about football, communicate.

Like several other players, Sjoerd Overgoor was a local Overijssel boy. He wasn't excited when he found out Ten Hag would be his new coach. The midfielder was trying to make it at the club after being dropped by FC Twente as a teenager. Ten Hag had been one of the people responsible for that decision. Overgoor was on loan at De Graafschap when Go Ahead came for him in 2012. 'Ten Hag had been the head of the youth academy at Twente when I was told that I was not good enough and sent away. I had a contract at Go Ahead Eagles so you can imagine how I felt when the announcement was made that he was coming. But it went completely different from my expectations. The promotion was the most special day of my career. I am not a great player, but because of Erik ten Hag I played in the highest division. He was the reason. He is the best coach I have ever had. You don't see coaches that good in the second tier. He was ten years ahead of his time.'

'We played a lot of eleven against zero,' says Overgoor. The team would line up as they would for a game, but without opposition, and practice how they would move the ball around the pitch in a match. It is a favourite training session of coaches but not popular with players. 'We would always start with the goalkeeper and he would talk us through the patterns of how we could attack. He wanted diagonal balls. Every time we played a straight ball he would stop us and make us do it again. He was exacting in terms of what he wanted. After four weeks of eleven against zero,' we were thinking, *What is this? It is so boring.* But a couple of months into the season, there were matches where we knew exactly what we had to do and everyone was seeing it the same way. He put us through it because we were not that good and needed some patterns to build on. It was clear and it worked.'

Overgoor recalls that though they did a lot of ball work, a few times they would have to do runs in the woods in groups in the afternoon. Ten Hag would tell the players that they had to run a certain distance in two minutes. 'We wanted to prove ourselves to him so our group did it in one minute and 50 seconds. He said, "No. If I tell you to run for two minutes I don't want you to take two minutes and ten seconds but I also don't want you to run for one minute and 50 seconds. Two minutes is two minutes." He was like that. If you did not stick to the plan you had a problem. He was strict, with tight rules. We as players had to get used to that. I once thought that Erik was on my back too much, so I went to see him in his office. I thought that he did not like me because he was always shouting at me. Other players noticed it as well and talked about it. I asked him what I was doing wrong. He told me that I was the sort of guy who was happy with just 90 per cent. If I was angry, I would be able to improve. It was his way of motivating me. He believed in me and felt I had more to give.'

Overgoor is a wellspring of Go Ahead lore and can explain mysteries such as why Ten Hag had a window built into his office door: 'Not to keep an eye on everyone, as some people thought. He wanted to lower the threshold for us to step into his office.' The field had to be in conditions precisely specified by the coach. 'We had a man whose job it was to look after the pitch. Erik would tell him the grass had to be 20 millimetres or something like that.' After the first training, all players threw their vests together in a big heap. 'But Ten Hag wanted them in three piles: yellow with yellow, blue with blue, orange with orange.' He had noticed that the woman in charge of the kits would bring out drinks and set them out on the table inside the dressing room. But she put them down randomly. That was a problem for the coach. 'He wanted the drinks put out in straight lines. Everything had to be perfect.'

Football always comes first. 'That was Erik's credo. We sometimes got fed up with his template exercises. Never play wide or backward. Always play slanted balls forward. We did that ad nauseam. Eventually, we all started to believe in it. He was proven right.' Reviewing match footage was a routine activity. 'If you had won 3–0, he could show you so many points for improvement that it seemed you had lost 5–0. But it worked the opposite way as well. If you had lost 5–0, he showed images that proved it hadn't been all that bad after all. That was the way he helped you keep your balance. He was very clear and strict, it wasn't always easy to talk to him, but you could always tell he had your best interests at heart. He is one of my examples. I owe a lot to him. Thanks to him my career took off, and I was able to play in the Eredivisie for several more years.'

Documentary maker Vriends said Ten Hag rarely let loose. 'I did not often see him with a relaxed kind of vibe, up for a laugh or a chilled training session. He was always very serious. I saw Erik laugh out loud for the first time at the end of May, after the promotion. Beer in hand, cap backwards on head. It was clear that this man was on top, with his maxims about football. Forever critical. We had won 4–1, against Excelsior I believe, and everything was hosanna. A day later, Ten Hag opens his laptop and lambasts us with everything that had gone wrong.' More, better. Every day, again and again. That straitjacket sometimes pinched, Vriends confessed. 'There was hardly any room for relaxation under Ten Hag. A little bit of loafing, you couldn't get away with that. A regime it was, yes, but he was not authoritarian. Every single player in that squad, even the ones on the bench, were really happy with him. Erik is a warm-hearted man, with an eye for the individual. His success has not surprised me at all. He is still the best manager that I have had in my career and he has taken every right step since then. For me, that season together was huge, one to remember. For him, it was just the beginning of his coaching career.'

There was some frustration when Ten Hag decided not to continue the journey with Go Ahead Eagles in the Eredivisie. His contract in Deventer ran until the summer of 2014, but after the promotion, he left for Bayern Munich. A shame, according to Kromkamp: 'His methods and style would have helped the club rise further, and we would probably have been a stable force in the middle of the Eredivisie because Erik is a top professional. I know that Erik would have liked to have [had] a second team to allow the reserve players to make more minutes. But there was just no money for that. Perhaps he would have stayed a year or two longer if the club had been able to meet those preconditions.' Overgoor had his own take: 'I was surprised and a little bit disappointed because I knew he would have continued to make me a better player. But he was too good for us, so it was understandable he left. We were lucky because in the first year of the Eredivisie we had nine of the eleven base players we had the previous season. So in that first year without him we played exactly how Erik wanted us to play. That is why we stayed in the highest division that year, I think.'

Between the 1960s and 1980s Go Ahead Eagles Deventer was one of the best teams in the Netherlands, then it disappeared. The club's resurrection was due, according to Edwin Lugt, club president from 2013 to 2018, to the work of mostly one man. 'It is an unbelievable success story, which we owe above all to our coach Erik ten Hag.' Lugt once lived in Bavaria, 20 years earlier, but he hadn't forgotten what it was like. He could understand why someone would want to move to Munich. 'It's nice there. We really wanted Erik to stay with us. But FC Bayern is the best club in the world, and we're just a small club. We're proud that our coach went to a club like that.'

7

IN GERMANY WITH PEP

'To define a manager, just look at his team. This is a team, and this manager makes the players play.'

PEP GUARDIOLA

Before there was total football, there was the Stone Age. The Sumerians invented the wheel, the Greeks democracy, Edison the lightbulb and the Dutch (real) football. Once upon a time, Jan Reker, founding director of CBV (Coaches Betaald Voetbal, the Association of Professional Football Coaches), compared Dutch football managers with the Dutch maritime pioneers who travelled the world in the sixteenth and seventeenth centuries. One rendition of the association's website has used a different analogy:

> Football is an art form. The 'Hollandse School' is the collective name for Dutch artists. This nickname originated in the heyday of Dutch painting, nourished by the artists' distinctive style of painting. Our football trainers are the Rembrandts of today. The Dutch trainer/coach has his own, recognisable style of beautiful and attacking football with typical wingers. Worldwide, true football fans are familiar with the term 'total football'. Call us the culture bearers of Dutch football.

The Dutch have been justly proud of the foreign exploits of Dick Advocaat, Leo Beenhakker, Guus Hiddink and Louis van Gaal. They have won trophies with Zenit Saint Petersburg, Real Madrid, Chelsea and Barcelona. Sadly, these glory days are a thing of the past. There is an apparent dearth of talent in the Dutch trainers' pool. Good enough for Holland perhaps, but not for a larger stage. Frank de Boer didn't last long at Crystal Palace and Ronald Koeman was sacked at Barcelona. Jaap Stam was fired at FC Cincinnati after he won just four of 25 games. Fast forward to April 2022, when Erik ten Hag was appointed as manager of Manchester United. Expectations are high. He has won the Rinus Michels Award three times. At the initiative of football magazine *De Voetbaltrainer*, the prize is awarded annually to the best manager in Dutch professional football. The selection is made by professional football coaches associated with the CBV and the KNVB. Ten Hag is the only one to have won the award this many times. Guus Hiddink, Louis van Gaal, Frank de Boer and Phillip Cocu each received the award twice. Ronald Koeman and Steve McClaren won it once. This record, three wins, was the reward for a trainer who looked beyond the Dutch game's philosophy, who chose to work in Germany under the umbrella of tactical genius Pep Guardiola. He learned from Guardiola's experience, vision, playing style and training methods.

In the summer of 2013, Ten Hag moved to FC Bayern Munich. He signed a two-year contract after being on the touchline for numerous training sessions and three friendlies with his new team. Bayern had been looking for a new U23 coach. At the insistence of then sports director Matthias Sammer, Ten Hag became Mehmet Scholl's successor. Sammer also expected the first team to improve as a consequence of Ten Hag's work. The German connection was not new. Sammer had been following Ten Hag's path for several years. When he was sports director at the DFB (German Football Association), he invited Ten Hag several times as a speaker. Sammer said, 'I am very pleased that he has decided to join FC Bayern, even though his team was just elevated to the Dutch top division.' Michael Tarnat, sports director of FC Bayern's youth department, knew Ten Hag from the time when he was youth coach at Twente. Together with Tarnat, Ten Hag would work to develop the philosophy of the FC Bayern youth teams. 'He has a great deal of knowledge in the youth field. I am pleased that he will be at our side with advice and action,' said Tarnat.

On his relationship with the sporting director, Ten Hag said, 'When Matthias Sammer was working for the German Football Association, he showed an interest in my vision for youth academy work. We have kept in touch since. Later, Sammer became technical director at Bayern Munich and asked me to become coach of the second team, the final station of youth development. I am eager to learn, I like to gain new experiences. It was a great opportunity to work for such an internationally leading club.' Second team or not, Bayern Munich owed it to its status to always win. 'Winning is the norm, Bayern don't settle for less. Opponents were always eager to beat us. The experience of continuously performing under pressure is very useful. In terms of physicality, German clubs are groundbreaking. The bar is a lot higher than in the Netherlands. As a result, more is also asked mentally. It turns out that people can do more than they think they can.'

Sammer was *begeistert*, thrilled about the new arrival. 'Erik is obsessed with football, in a good way. I am impressed by his professional quality and his personality.' When Ten Hag was given a tour of the Bayern Munich training complex, he came across a framed saying: 'When good is no longer good enough, you have to make it better.' This piece of wisdom was produced by Dettmar Cramer, who led Bayern Munich to victory at the European Cup (renamed the UEFA Champions League in 1992) in 1975 and 1976. The idea was permanently lodged in Ten Hag's mind. It appealed to his identity as a trainer.

The second team began the first season with eight consecutive victories. They beat Viktoria Aschaffenburg 6–0 at Grünwalder Strasse, the old city stadium that Bayern II shares with TSV 1860 Munich. 'We've made another step forward,' said Ten Hag, who had made four changes after the 4–1 win against FC Ingolstadt 04 II a week earlier. The team extended its impressive run, won their division and thus reached the promotion games for the third league. Unfortunately, they were beaten in the play-offs by Fortuna Köln. After losing 1–0 in the first leg at away at Köln, they led 2–0 in the second leg at home after a goal by Ylli Sallahi in the 88th minute. But in the fourth minute of stoppage time, a serious goalkeeping error by Lukas Raeder spoiled promotion, which also had eluded Ten Hag's predecessors Andries Jonker and Mehmet Scholl.

The Bayern II players trudged from the training ground to the dressing rooms through a snow flurry. The last session of the calendar year was done. An unusual feature of the regional league is the three-month winter break. 'A long, long time,' as Ten Hag said. In order to not lose momentum, the U23 coach decided to play numerous friendly matches against strong opponents. In these games players could work on eliminating 'deficits', as Ten Hag put it. They were on Christmas break until 8 January, but Ten Hag assigned his charges some homework: 'Clear your head and recharge your batteries,' so that the big goal of promotion could be pursued with new energy. With 13 regional league games remaining, their starting position was good: FCB II was at the top of the table with 54 points, including 18 wins and five defeats, one point ahead of second-placed FV Illertissen, with a game in hand. But the Bavarians had crumbled from a far more comfortable lead they had enjoyed a few weeks earlier, of ten points, because they lost a handful of their last games of the year.

Ten Hag was satisfied, however. As he says, 'We made mistakes, we lost our strength. I hate defeats, just like my players. But it is better that we had this phase of weakness before winter because it is only in the spring that things really get serious. It is important that we draw the right conclusions and improve in the new year. We have had six good months with a lot of positive takeaways.' He was particularly pleased with the high number of goals scored, 67, the clear top in the Bavarian regional league. Defensively, they had been well organised over long stretches of the first half of the season.

Ten Hag was inspired by the superlative sports climate that he encountered in southern Germany. 'In Munich, I was amazed by the attitude of players like Manuel Neuer, Philipp Lahm and Arjen Robben. They achieved everything in their career, but when you saw the intensity with which they trained ... incredible. They literally pushed the limits of their capabilities. That is precisely the essence of top sport: constantly pushing your boundaries and exceeding them. The players who walk around there work to improve every day and have an unimaginable drive to get the most out of themselves. They make the maximum demands of each other. This is how I experience the profession myself. The club systematically stimulates and facilitates that attitude. Take the scientific centre, for example, with every conceivable piece of measuring and testing equipment. Look at how perfect the training fields are. After every training, even at the bottom youth, four men immediately are on the pitch to plug up holes and aerate the field.'

He experienced at first hand how a tough work environment shapes the character of football players. 'Talk about building up resistance. We had to go to Würzburger Kickers, a big club in a big city, with a rich sponsor behind it. There are big clubs in the Regionalliga. But then there was Buchbach, a club in a rural town. A couple of former pro players with some locals, playing on a paddock of a field, with aggressive fans close on the pitch intimidating us. Try and win there. So you need to go full throttle, battle for every metre. As a youngster, this is how you build up character. You must have certain competencies to be able to keep going in a tough *Umfeld*. This automatically increases your sense of responsibility.'

The German word *Umfeld* roughly means surroundings in a wide range of contexts. It can be a physical area around a building or a city. It can be a social circle. For most people, their *Umfeld* is all the people they interact with on a daily basis, their coworkers, friends and family. For a coach, this includes his players, the coaching and medical staff, the stadium and grounds personnel, and the fans. It also includes the stadium, the pitch, the training grounds, the dressing rooms and his office. The emphasis on the complete management of human resources and physical environment became a key element of the Ten Hag way. At Bayern, that was essential for meeting the demands. As Ten Hag tells it, 'If a trainer doesn't win three times in a row, he can get sacked in Germany in no time. Under such conditions, a coach really is not going to give a young player the chance to adjust over ten games. No, he fields his best team. That's why the training intensity is so great: every player goes to the extreme to be part of the best 11. In Germany, you are dealing with technical directors who are close to the team and staff, and who sometimes give their opinion on TV after a game. The media also play an important role in that whole process. If a player does not perform, it will be looked at very critically. The review is substantiated with data and statistics and can therefore be quite confronting. As a player you must ensure that you are armed against that.'

According to Ten Hag, the aim of the FC Bayern Munich junior team is to develop young players and introduce them to the pros. One such example was Pierre-Emile Højbjerg, who made several appearances under Pep Guardiola in Bayern's first team and also played in the 2014 DFB Cup final. Other players under Ten Hag also took the step up to the professional level: Raif Husic, Vladimir Ranković, Alessandro Schöpf, Kevin Friesenbichler, Benno Schmitz, Dennis Chessa, David Vržogić and Daniel Wein. Ten Hag saw this as substantial proof that they were 'doing a good job. We can be proud of that.'

After narrowly missing promotion to the third division, Bayern's second team started preparing for the 2014–15 season with a training camp in the northern Italian province of Trentino, at the heart of the Italian Alps. At the time, Ten Hag said, 'It is important to grow together as a team, to become a unit. That's why we'll be taking some team-building measures there. But of course it is also important to work intensively on the physical and tactical areas. Fitness must be our basis. We only have a good two weeks until the first game of the season. We have very good quality in our squad, and I'm happy about our newcomers. The players who were with the U19s last season have great potential. I am convinced that they will make the leap into the men's division. As far as our goal for the season is concerned: of course, we want to win the championship and offer attractive football. The Regionalliga Bayern is a strong league in which you should not underestimate any opponent. I firmly believe that FV Illertissen will play at the top again, but one or two other teams will certainly come along.'

Reflecting on the previous season, Ten Hag said, 'We had a great season and ended up missing promotion by a hair's breadth. We were very unlucky. But that is football. That was something we had to digest. It is behind us now and our focus is on the future. I feel great desire to get going with the new season. We have a big goal and we have been working toward it systematically from day one. It is important that we come together as a functioning team as quickly as possible. The new players have settled in very well, but now it is important to get to know each other better. We managed things well in the first test match [against Regionalliga Bayern side SV Pullach], but at the beginning of pre-season it is also clear that there still are coordination problems. There is room for improvement, but it is too early for conclusions. I think we're on the right track and am confident about the coming season.'

Nonetheless, FC Bayern II found it a little difficult to get going in the summer. It was a different squad and Ten Hag only had a few weeks to get the team ready for the new season. He admitted, 'We didn't have the time. In the first league game against Würzburg, there were nine new players. The team got better and better. How they treat each other, how they work together, how they play football – you can see clear progress. But we cannot be satisfied now. Contentment leads to negligence. We still have a lot of room for improvement. It's all about the details. Taking chances, for example. In Bayreuth [a 2–1 win] we should have won much more decisively. We also concede too many goals. In front of 5,000 spectators in Bayreuth, against a team that plays in their own city, there is a lot of emotion in the game. Winning and losing has a completely different meaning from the youth competition. Players who come to us from the U19s first have to learn to deal with that. At the same time, those who come from other clubs have to get used to the reality that it's much more difficult to play for Bayern than against Bayern. The opponents always give 120 per cent. For them even a draw is a good result. On the other hand, for us only victory counts. New Bayern players have to adopt this mentality first.'

Centre back Matthias Strohmaier spoke about his experience of working with Ten Hag: 'I was central defender under Erik. He is a very meticulous trainer and pays attention to every little detail, all the time. But he taught me things about football that I had never heard of before. I definitely have good memories. Every now and then, you would be with him on the training ground and work on tactics for three hours. As a player, you like to question that. But then there are moments in the game when you notice that the things you worked on in training came off. That was special. I improved so much as a player because of all the things I learned about football under him. No other trainer before or after has made me think about football in that way. I still exchange ideas with him from time to time, and that commitment also shows that he is someone with a strong personality.'

• • •

When Ten Hag was at Bayern Munich as the reserve-team coach, he collaborated with Pep Guardiola. Players can find it hard to work with Ten Hag because, like Guardiola, he comes across as a little obsessive. There is such a natural footballing affinity between the two that people began calling Ten Hag 'Mini Pep', but this nickname didn't stick beyond his two years at Bayern. Ten Hag explained that it would be a misconception to think that he spent his days having lengthy philosophical discussions about football with Guardiola. 'In essence, the first and second team are separate worlds. He couldn't be expected to be involved with the second team or with the ups and downs of Erik ten Hag. But I was infected with that Bayern virus of having to win everything.'

According to Ten Hag it was a very exciting time. 'I have good memories of [Twente and PSV coach] Kees Rijvers from my early years as a player. I have also learned a lot from Fred Rutten. But Pep Guardiola is of course one of the world's best trainers. His teams play the most appealing football of the moment. That is based on a plan. During my time at Bayern Munich, I was able to experience his approach up-close, and I learned a lot from that. Guardiola stands for dominant and attractive football, a way of playing that appeals to me. I remember how Pep practised moving in with the full-backs. The players always wanted more because Pep was so enthusiastic. He talked for five minutes, and then they trained with incredible intensity. Of course you should not lose sight of reality. Ultimately, the quality of the available material determines the way of playing. Football in Germany has been different since Pep. The whole league changed because of his way of playing football. I watched almost every training. I learned a lot from his methods, how he transferred his philosophy to the pitch.'

Ten Hag says that with Pep, 'winning is always number one, but it has to be done with beautiful football. It has to be offensive, attractive and with a lot of goals. The beauty of football is important. You have to be dominant, but it's more than that. It is about grabbing the opponent by the throat and not letting go. The team should be in charge of the field, always. I do not want to compare myself to Guardiola, his list of honours is unparalleled. But Guardiola certainly inspired me. Every coach wants to play attacking football like his teams do. Adventurous, fast, dynamic, technically excellent and with so much joy. Every coach who likes attractive football strives for that. Of course, I regularly talked with him about that. But most of all,

I watched very carefully. His training sessions are a joy to watch. Guardiola has the didactic ability to do his tactical training in such a way that the players are constantly going full throttle. That way the training sessions are most effective because they are similar to actual match conditions. Of course I have written things down. I have adopted certain things, and I implement them in my own way, including them in my vision and training.'

It's like being behind the wheel: you don't think about the traffic rules, shifting the gears or pressing the brake on time; it happens automatically, in a zen-like state of mind. The car becomes an extension of the driver. Everything that once was learned is now instinct; it's part of permanent memory, the hard-drive. In football the key to making it work is to get the ideas into players' heads. The player becomes a part of the team, the pitch, the system. That became a Ten Hag hallmark – in training, in match conditions, everywhere and all the time. This type of training is also the trademark of Guardiola, who, says Ten Hag, 'really drives his philosophy and his way of playing into his players. He drills them until the automatic responses are the way he wants them to be. Possession of the ball is sacred, but only to quickly create opportunities and score. When the ball is lost, it must be recaptured within a matter of seconds. His teams always do that in a very aggressive manner.' This pressing, putting pressure on the opposing team, 'is therefore one of the most important aspects of his playing style. He is uncompromising in that. His will is really the law. Sometimes that leads to clashes with players, but Guardiola has only grown in authority over the years. That's because of all the prizes he's won.'

Who creates a club's DNA? Ten Hag says, 'Cruyff and Guardiola created it at Barcelona. Guardiola is heavily inspired by Cruyff, and he readily admits that. They differ on one point, he once told me. Cruyff used man-marking and Pep uses zonal marking. Other than that, there are many similarities. Football today is different from football back then. The spaces have become smaller, teams are increasingly compact. Opponents are better organised and the players are all very fit. It becomes increasingly difficult for an attacking team to split opponents. Guardiola calls Cruyff his great teacher, but he indicated in the past that he was also inspired by Louis van Gaal. Cruyff and Van Gaal – they never wanted to admit it themselves – do not differ that much in their ideas about football. They have a lot in common and differ only in nuances. Of course Guardiola was influenced by them, but that doesn't diminish him in any way. Guardiola has a very personal style, and he has always had the right tactical response to international developments in football.'

Guardiola, Ten Hag says, 'came up with the idea of not letting the backs play on the outside, but on the inside. That's what he did at Bayern Munich with David Alaba and Phillip Lahm. That way he created an extra midfielder in possession of the ball and more space for wingers such as Arjen Robben and Franck Ribéry. Lahm was the best right-back in the world at the time, but he had the ability to play in midfield the way Guardiola wanted. Pep has guts, he dares to be groundbreaking and innovative. At Bayern, he sometimes played with his wingers Robben and Ribéry in midfield when it suited him tactically. They were his stars. Not many trainers have the audacity to do that. He does. Because of his authority, players have faith in him. Also because what he says always turns out to be right.'

Ten Hag recalls that Guardiola would 'completely shut himself off from the outside world if he thinks it is necessary. If there was a big game coming up, you'd better not disturb him. He would sit alone in his office, playing the game in his head. Then the ideas and the tactical finds came. He doesn't lose concentration for a second. He is definitely in the top five in the world. Guardiola as a trainer has permanent value. Of course, because of all the prizes he has won, but more so because of the way he lets his teams play.' And, using a chess reference, he says, 'When it comes to tactics, we don't talk about José Mourinho, who always plays with black.' For Ten Hag, what makes Guardiola's work great is that he has demonstrated his skill – and his adaptation to different cultures – not only in Spain, but in Germany and England. For instance, in his first year at City, 'Guardiola misjudged the pace and power in the Premier League. He realised that if he wanted to play football his way, it couldn't be done without a few physically strong athletes. He is rigid in his philosophy, but not about how it is implemented. That also characterises a top trainer.'

Half-spaces are the vertical strips on the pitch between the centre and the wide areas, also known as wings. The five strips are of a similar size. A player who is on the ball in the centre should be able to reach all the strips within the range of his kicking technique. The half-spaces are close by and both wings are easily reachable. The central player has several options in terms of range: a large part of the playing field is directly accessible with one pass. Google Earth showed that Pep Guardiola, during his time as coach of Bayern Munich, marked the training field with chalk lines in such a way that the half-spaces became visible. Later in his career, Ten Hag applied the lesson he learned from Pep in Germany, training on a field with vertical lines. These lines divide a field into the left wing, left half-space, central axis, right half-space and right wing. Ten Hag explained that 'the extra lines on the field are a form of communication. I rarely use the term "half-spaces" with the players, but those lines subconsciously increase their orientation. They aren't there in matches, but my experience is that players do get a better feel for certain situations. It's a result of repeating, repeating and repeating. This also improves cooperation. At the European Championship

I saw that Germany very consciously occupied the centre and the half-spaces. First "going out", then "coming in" again and forcing something there. That really appeals to me, and it is very similar to the style of play I am aiming for.'

After two years in Munich, Ten Hag chose to move to FC Utrecht when the opportunity arose. Asked about his reasons for the move, he answered, 'I thrive in a competitive environment. However, my ambition is not to train a second team for years.' His time in Germany was not an unqualified success. Between 2013 and 2015, he tried in vain to heave the reserves of Bayern into the third division. But before and since, nobody came as close as he did.

8

TEAM TEN HAG

'Developing the culture Erik wants takes time.
If he gets the time, the results will come.'
WILCO VAN SCHAIK, FORMER GENERAL MANAGER OF FC UTRECHT

FC Utrecht was stirred up in the summer of 2015 when Erik ten Hag took over as head coach. The vision and daily reality of Utrecht were transformed under the new manager. He was personally inspired by the new adventure, saying, 'This is an attractive club. The combination of trainer and technical manager also appeals to me. In this role I am not only involved with the first team, but with the entire club, including the young talent of which there is so much here. FC Utrecht has a rich history and demanding supporters. It's a great challenge.' When he took charge of the Zoudenbalch training complex, no longer were all the practice sessions open to the public. He also limited the access of youth players to first-team territory. He wanted an additional field for the first team, which meant that the youth had to make concessions. 'The priority should be the first team. That determines the success of the club. Scouting and training also serve that purpose.'

Due to financial constraints, improving the infrastructure was a slow process. He thought the training fields were too small and that their surface was of poor quality. He was worried about injuries.

He got involved with rearranging the fields, the facilities, the staffing. The dugout was moved, and he changed the organisation of the club offices. He decreed that training hours be changed and during sessions all mobile phones turned off. 'You must wonder whether the Dutch professional player really understands what top sport means these days,' Ten Hag plainly stated. 'You can only succeed in this occupation if you give yourself to the maximum every day. I think that when you're working out in the weight room, you cannot be on your phone at the same time. Facebook, text messages, apps, Twitter, all kinds of external stimuli come in through the phone. They undermine concentration, the quality of the exercise decreases and in the end the efficiency of the strength training decreases.' Utrecht staff and players thought he was a little strange. 'This Ten Hag even decides which soap and sponges our cleaners should use,' said one of the youth trainers.

During the week Ten Hag lived in an apartment between the Galgenwaard stadium and the Zoudenbalch training complex. Sometimes he was still at the club at 10pm. On his first day at the club, he received a list from the medical staff: 'So-and-so cannot train twice a day; we have to take it easy with him; we have to train with him in stages.' According to Ten Hag, 'almost everyone had some problem. But I said that in that case they weren't right for professional football. How do you think an Olympic athlete wins a medal? By training for an hour each day? You can say that you love football as much as you want, but what matters is what you do: it is a profession. That realisation hadn't sunk in yet.' The contrast to Germany was striking. Ten Hag said: 'I worked at Bayern Munich, and I sometimes still speak to those guys who now play elsewhere in Germany. If you hear how they train there ... If I did that here, they would break down one by one. I cannot work in Utrecht the

German way. But I want to convince the players that hard work will benefit them.'

By Utrecht standards Ten Hag had been offered a long contract – three seasons. That was a sign of confidence. The Utrecht bosses had been proclaiming for years that they wanted to achieve big things. But the club had created unrealistic expectations by using flashy slogans: challenger, spectacle football, attack on the top five and so on. Ten Hag did not join the chorus. With new faces in the dugout, realism would dominate. Jordy Zuidam, director of football affairs, had led the successful pursuit of Ten Hag, thinking he could fulfil the ambitions of owner Frans van Seumeren, whose motto is emblazoned outside the FC Utrecht stadium, 'NO GUTS, NO GLORY.' Ten Hag was appointed as technical director and head coach with Jean-Paul de Jong as his assistant. The new season kicked off in good spirits. Despite the bad weather and it being a Father's Day weekend, close to 2,000 fans welcomed the players and trainers at Zoudenbalch with fireworks, torches and a lot of noise.

Ten Hag and De Jong had played together at FC Utrecht 20 years earlier. De Jong explained they also worked together as coaches. 'I did an internship with Erik at Go Ahead Eagles and our visions of football are in sync. Football is top sport, which means giving 100 per cent every day. I share that with Erik. He sets the bar high and he also has the background to know how to go about it. I wouldn't do this job under anyone else. Erik gives me space. I want to contribute to the development of the players and the team.' General director Wilco van Schaik explained the reasons for selecting Ten Hag as coach: 'We want to become a stable sub-topper' – a steady mid-table team – 'but also make players better and let the team play better. That's why I had my eye on Erik for a long time. He has worked at the top at FC Twente, PSV and Bayern Munich and has been successful as head coach of Go Ahead Eagles.'

Ten Hag would also lead the scouting and youth academy and have ultimate responsibility for purchase and sales policies. He was committed to improving the club from day one, saying, 'I will be on the field every day, and Jean-Paul de Jong has a main role. I already knew him as a player and am getting to know him as a coach. He is someone of total dedication. I want to have strong people around me, people who stimulate me. A top environment challenges people to be top themselves. You should always want to improve yourself as a player. That is, of course, the responsibility of the players themselves. But this must be motivated, facilitated and structured. And you shouldn't ask too much of them either, as a trainer you have to put yourself in their shoes. It's about communication, about saying the right things to players. We have interesting players and it's up to us as staff to make a team out of them. The statistics show that FC Utrecht hovers between eighth and twelfth place. But I'm an impatient type, I want to win every game.'

Under coach Rob Alflen and advisor Co Adriaanse, the club had had a disappointing year, culminating in 11th place in the table. Initially, Ten Hag didn't do much better than his predecessors. His first season in Utrecht got off to a hesitant start. He has very specific ideas about how his team should train and compete, but players were sceptical, wondering what the new methods would yield. Some complained about endless tactical shuffling during interminable training sessions. They did not like the long days. Then strange extra lines appeared on the pitch, dividing the entire pitch into sections – Ten Hag's unorthodox way of communicating where each player should be. The players thought he spoke in a rigid and clumsy manner, in small bursts and with many 'uhs …' He also had that strong eastern accent, which made him sound to some a little like a German who'd learned Dutch as a second language, and used strange technical jargon. Some players made jokes about it. Others let these peculiarities go because they saw he was a good coach.

Van Schaik said, 'People first had to really get used to his way of working. Ten Hag is very demanding and sets high standards, also for himself. He wanted to change things. He is a very dominant presence, taking unpopular measures and meeting the necessary resistance while realising his vision. He uses all available means to achieve that. He has a definite attitude towards training: working hard, putting in many hours, drilling, and repeating. Develop, improve and win. He expects the same commitment from his team. He involves not only the first 11 players; numbers 12 to 22 get the same attention. There are always opportunities for everyone, but you do have to go along with him. Erik is a process trainer, not an ad hoc trainer. He works according to his plan and demands complete dedication. In the beginning, players and people from the staff came to me to complain. But at FC Utrecht every player increased in value under Ten Hag.'

During the first season, Sjors Ultee was another of Ten Hag's assistants. Ultee says that Ten Hag always wanted 'to know everything. I watched opponents' matches and made the analyses, but Erik always looked them over himself. Not because of a lack of trust, but because he always wanted to see everything for himself. You have people who say: he doesn't listen to anyone and is stubborn. And then you have people who say: he only listens to the players. If you are the trainer at a big club, you have to carefully monitor everything and keep the right balance. You have to sense when to include the opinion of the right players in decision-making. He mastered that skill very well. He kept focusing on details and insisting on perfecting things, even as late as May, when most trainers think everything is behind. What I learned most from him is the nagging. That's not meant negatively. Erik is not satisfied with one right and one wrong.

Not even with nine times right and one wrong. He really wants it ten times, no, one hundred times out of a hundred. And not just somewhat good, but perfectly good.'

The shrill blast of Erik ten Hag's whistle was a common sound at FC Utrecht's training ground. Especially at the start, it was impossible for training matches to get any flow before the coach intervened after spotting something he wanted to change. The sessions could go on for hours, leaving the players mentally drained. Goalkeeper Robbin Ruiter said, 'Especially in the beginning of the training matches, every 20 seconds it was "Stop!" And then he'd explain what he wanted. But a few weeks later, everyone knew and no one needed to stop any longer. Every single detail was covered, not just about our own team but the opponents as well. You could tell he was at a very high level tactically from the start. The sessions were long and intense. It wasn't physically tough, it was mentally tough and totally different from anything we'd experienced before. In the beginning a lot of players had doubts about the way we trained. It wasn't normal. We'd come from a coach who gave us a lot of freedom; we were laughing and joking around. Then we got Erik, who was putting us through three hours on the pitch, and you thought you weren't doing much. But slowly, we realised we were getting better as a team. A lot of things on the training ground came together – it gave us a big boost. From that point we all believed in the project.'

Timo Letschert played with Utrecht in the 2015–16 season. Thinking back on Ten Hag's arrival, he recalls, 'We didn't know him when he joined, but we immediately felt he was different. We weren't used to staying on the pitch that long – hours at a time. We also weren't used to making days from 9am to 5pm. He introduced all of that to Utrecht. In the beginning there was some uncertainty as we didn't get the results. But he got the younger players like me going.

They were sometimes difficult to coach, but he has a way of reaching out, talking with players and getting them to understand him. It may not happen on the first or second day, but after a while the players begin to respond to his way of thinking, and will fight for him and believe in him.'

Analysis of games was important. Letschert remembers that when reviewing clips of matches, Ten Hag was 'very, very critical', but would also notice 'the positive things in my game'. 'He was constantly looking at match footage and talking to me about how I could make steps to get better,' Letschert says. 'The key was his individual attention – sitting together with players, one-on-one, and making a plan for everyone. Even when he got angry, he never lost his sense of purpose or focus.' Behind his stern exterior, there's another side to Ten Hag. 'I remember when I was called up by the Netherlands in March 2016. Ten Hag called me into his office. He wanted to tell me personally before it got on the Internet. After he told me, he gave me a big, fat hug. Usually, he is very professional, not so affectionate, but I will always remember that.'

Some coaches present a basic idea and leave space to fill in the rest. With Ten Hag there is no room for experimentation. He gathers a number of leaders around him in the squad who understand what he wants and they pull the group along. Utrecht gradually became a team that played dynamic football, and one that gave opponents headaches. As the months passed, everyone saw that players improved individually. Bart Ramselaar also received a call-up to the national team in 2016. Ten Hag demonstrated that he could perform well with limited resources. Rico Strieder, captain of Bayern II, had come to Utrecht with Ten Hag. The inconspicuous midfielder was Ten Hag's best buy. 'He's going to be the cement between the stones,' the coach had predicted. In his last season, he brought in Zakaria Labyad, who had been written off by many, and a year later he was one of the Eredivisie's best attackers.

Ten Hag assessed the state of his team. 'We have to learn to kill a match when we have the lead. We have to become more professional in that regard, extend the lead and finish the game. It still happens too often that some players are too interested in their own success, choose the wrong moment and then we concede a goal. In away matches we have to become more mature; you can tell just by the number of penalties that are awarded against us. That's because of naivety. Some of them may have been unjustified, but usually we caused them. We have to get smarter about that. In transition moments, we have to find the way to the goal faster, more directly and with better returns. We're getting stronger, so we have to play at a faster pace. Physically, we can and should go a step further. In short, there are plenty of areas for improvement.' After a surprise defeat against Roda JC, he said, 'I saw immediately that they were always one step too late. Actually, I saw it as soon as they got onto the pitch: how they moved, how they walked. It was clear that the minimum requirement wasn't there.' When a match against FC Twente was also lost, the enthusiasm among FC Utrecht supporters waned. But then the team impressed with an unbeaten run of six matches around the winter break, five of which were won.

According to centre back Willem Janssen, 'Erik ten Hag changes your club, your team, yourself. Your perception of football, of cooperation, of the importance of new methods, of professionalism. At Utrecht, he transformed me and had the skill to make his vision a reality, even if his method was annoying at the start. You develop a different view of your own qualities. I was an attacking midfielder for a long time but under him I became a centre back, even though I was already 28. I became captain and gained much more insight into the game – a whole new world opened up. He constantly stopped the game, which was annoying at the beginning. You enjoy the game and then the whistle blows again and Erik says you were positioned wrong. But he also explained why you had to stand elsewhere. And then you thought, *Damn, he's right.* Erik has certain basic ideas about football but also looks at the players at his disposal. He is not the romantic we like in the Netherlands; he wants to win. The season before he arrived we finished eleventh but Utrecht wanted to be in the top five – and that is where we ended in his first campaign. His great class is that he knows exactly what he wants, and how to make it work. He discusses his vision extensively in meetings and then makes it trainable on the field. I've had many good coaches, including Steve McClaren and Co Adriaanse, but Ten Hag's simply the best.'

Ten Hag is Dutch enough to welcome input, but only at the right times and to a certain extent. There never is any doubt about who is in charge. 'I noticed that the players were open to my approach and ideas. Everyone does it in their own way, but as a coach you have to stick to your philosophy, looking left and right and taking into account the club culture and the situations of the players. Sometimes I have to make concessions. But if you *polder* too much, you lose the thread. Someone has to map out the way. My father used to say, "If you have something in your head, you can't get it out easily." But as a trainer I have learned more over the years, for example in the field of leadership, that there isn't just one way. The coaching profession has become so complex, that's why you constantly have to extend yourself.'

The FC Utrecht coach was certain of his methods. 'Once they see that it works, it strongly motivates them. I myself have never doubted. It was just a matter of waiting on how fast the result would come. In the beginning, the players mostly had difficulty with the many situational coaching moments during training. Now there is a certain level of acceptance within the player group, but they still don't like it. We want to master several game systems and that is possible only if you make it trainable. You can't do it in one training and with one video take. Something like that has to be fine-tuned. An 11:11 practice game may be good, but it can also be done in smaller forms. To get better at minimising mutual distances, both lengthwise as well as in the width, you can train 6:6. Whenever we use such forms, I explain to players what I expect from them when the ball is located at a certain spot on the pitch. How are you positioned relative to each other? What are the solutions? In my experience, it takes time to drive these things home.

'As a trainer you have to monitor very carefully that you keep giving space to the creativity of individual players. I know it's my pitfall to spoon-feed a lot, so that players sometimes get too little chance to make their own choices. I have to say it helps that I'm aware of that. On the other hand, a certain structure, which arises from your playing style, also offers a lot of room for creative players to excel. I have noticed that in the past with Marko Arnautovic and Quincy Promes, among others. When they feel free within the certain frameworks you give them, they are at their best. No matter what, I expect a top sports mentality from everyone. Several times a week, my players are at the club from 9am to 6pm. There is a lot of time for extra guidance, such as watching video images and working on individual points for improvement.'

Ten Hag continues: 'Of course, different times, different players. Personally, I still enjoy that video of Ruud van Nistelrooy that shows him writing down his goals in a notebook. That was completely self-motivated. Nowadays, you make a PDP with players, a personal development plan. Today we over-organise education. We arrange everything for the youth players. We regurgitate everything. What we get with that is a type of player who is not independent. When we used to play against a team that suddenly operated with three defenders, you immediately saw the players look to the side for instructions. Then I had to start organising things as a coach. At Utrecht we now have reached the point where they themselves know what to do in certain situations. But that did not happen by itself. Young players today get into a van that takes them to the club. There they can rely on tutors, dietitians and I don't know what.'

To counter this, Ten Hag says that he tries 'to include as many variations as possible in my training. The reason is simple: humans are born adapters. If you do the same thing too often, the routine gets in the way and the brain is not sufficiently stimulated. Then the development is not optimal. As a trainer you have to be creative and regularly come up with new ways of training. One reason for this may be the match problem against the next opponent. How are you going to make that trainable? Your own playing style is always the decisive factor, even with running forms. Our game requires quick action and many changes of direction, just like in international football. You have to integrate that into your match preparation.'

The media have been fond of calling Ten Hag a control freak. It suggests he does everything on his own, thinks he knows best and doesn't trust anyone. He is not that kind of manager. He has a definite vision but is open to the ideas of others. The organisation that grew at FC Utrecht was similar to what was in operation when he was at FC Twente with Fred Rutten and Steve McClaren. The division of labour in the newly composed technical staff was transparent. He intentionally worked with an assertive field trainer like Jean-Paul de Jong, while assistant trainer Sjors Ultee and assistant technical manager Jordy Zuidam played important roles in the staff. Ten Hag was head coach and technical manager, so he could exert most influence. It was all carefully planned. This could not be done by one man, but only together with a group of other strong characters who had leadership ability and expertise. That is why he talked about Team Ten Hag.

Alex Abresch, Utrecht's video analyst, compiled statistics from matches. He would review what part of the field the team had possession in, how many duels the players won and lost (and whether on the ground or in the air) and so forth. The analysis would examine how many passes a given player played forward, backward, sideways and diagonally. On this strategy of statistical analysis, Ten Hag said, 'Data are about two things. First, the correct interpretation is crucial. What exactly do certain statistics say? Next, the trick is to make what you gain from the statistics trainable or at least convey the meaning to your team. I often hear trainers say, "I had the feeling that …" But I'm not looking for a feeling, I'm after facts. In some cases, data can provide you with important information. For example, last season [2015–16] we were one of the most effective teams in converting shots into goals. That's no coincidence. I am all for shooting, but there has to be a real chance of a goal. If you shoot for the sake of shooting, you're actually missing out on a better chance. In such a case, the statistics confirm what you would like to see. You can use something like this for your team: why do we do what we do and what is the desired effect? You want to give them the confidence that what you are doing actually works. Players should not be distracted by scoreboard journalism.'

In the 2015–16 season, FC Utrecht performed very well, missing European football by a hair's breadth. Ten Hag guided FC Utrecht to the final of the KNVB Cup – in which Feyenoord prevailed, 2–1 – and reached fifth place in the table. During the Trainers' Congress, Ten Hag won the Rinus Michels Award. The head coach of FC Utrecht was preferred over Frank de Boer (Ajax), Phillip Cocu (PSV), Ron

Jans (PEC Zwolle) and John Stegeman (Heracles Almelo). It meant a lot to him. 'They are your competitors, so of course, you want to beat them. But they also inspire me. Such a selection is subjective. Why do I deserve this more than Frank de Boer, who may win a fifth title? We haven't won a tangible prize yet, but that is precisely why I appreciate this selection all the more. Nobody expected that Utrecht would be at this level. We went into the season to develop something. We now are strong performers. I see this prize as an incentive for all of FC Utrecht. We're on the way. It's not good enough yet. It could be better.'

Over the years, Ten Hag witnessed a lot of changes in football. He questioned the impact of the Bosman ruling of 1995. The decision banned restrictions on foreign EU players within national leagues and allowed players in the EU to move to another club at the end of a contract without a transfer fee being paid. Critics of the ruling have suggested that it has helped to turn players into football mercenaries who sell their services to the highest bidder. It made things financially more attractive for players, but was bad for football's team spirit. The ruling stimulated player individualism and self-interest. While he deplores these developments, Ten Hag is aware that personal circumstances matter. He knows that as the privileged son of a real estate magnate he is in a different set of circumstances than a Turkish, Moroccan or Surinamese immigrant son in the Amsterdam suburbs. The Germans have a saying that appeals to Ten Hag's pragmatism: *Geld ist nicht alles, aber ohne Geld ist alles nichts* – money isn't everything, but without money everything comes to nought.

'You can hardly blame them for the fact that today's generation is very self-centred,' Ten Hag acknowledges. 'They have to be like that to survive in modern society. Is there anyone who looks after them? But a football team only functions if everyone works together. How do you get all those individualistic characters to do that? I think that can only be done by making sure that you have a good relationship with your players and that the guys have that among themselves as well. To achieve that, you don't have to go on holiday together or go paintballing. In my experience, team building starts on the field. We do a lot of positional games, and then it's about how high you set the bar. What do you require from players? And what do they require from each other? I demand focus and quality, correct ball speed, playing in the correct leg, and everything in constant motion. You build up from less complex to very complex. If players aren't focused, if they're just doing something, the training won't work. You want to see that they are working on it, that they start to coach, stimulate, motivate and correct each other. That is team building. Through the way you work as a trainer, the exercises you do and the demands you make, you can forge an individualistic group into a team. But that requires hard work. As a trainer you have to be razor sharp every day.'

Back in Twente, Ten Hag says, 'You used to have the *noaberschap* [neighbourliness]. That was something of the farmers. If a cow was sick, a farmer would get a new one from other farmers so that he could stay in business. They also helped each other with haymaking, so they went through life together. Didn't you have neighbourhoods in the big cities where people looked after each other's children? Wasn't the door unlocked? Jan Terlouw had a story about the string that no longer hangs out of the mailbox. I totally agree; it is not possible anymore. Now, if you don't lock your door, your furniture is for sale on eBay. The world has completely changed.' Jan Terlouw, the former deputy prime minister and author, reminisced about the time after the Second World War when the Netherlands was rebuilding itself. Terlouw had said, 'At that time I lived in Utrecht with my family. Strings hung from front-door mail slots everywhere. The kids could just pull the string, unlock the front door, and walk in. They are no longer there. We no longer trust each other … The government no longer trusts citizens. Citizens no longer trust politicians. Everything is tightly controlled and regulated.'

Ten Hag says, 'In the past, teams stayed together much longer and a real bond developed between players. Now they often are at a club only for a short time and then move on. They get the opportunity to earn a lot of money quickly and they take the chance. That is not a reproach, just an observation. Players have become more individualistic and mainly choose for themselves. That makes it difficult for a trainer to "keep all the frogs in the wheelbarrow" and to form a close team where no one puts himself above the group. You have to do it together. Only when the team is right can individual players excel. Look at Bart Ramselaar and Timo Letschert. Timo earned a top transfer to Serie A. That is good for him and for the club, but also for the group of players that remains behind. They have all seen what Timo had to do for it. That really challenges the rest. The next step in their career is mainly the result of the collective efforts of the team. To get that realisation between their ears is perhaps my most important task as a coach. We are talking about a bit of awareness. What is needed to perform at the top level? Do you have the discipline to execute a plan? And are you able to make adjustments where necessary? For that you sometimes need an incentive from the trainer, but in the end players have to pick it up themselves.'

Players became better and increased in value under Ten Hag. FC Utrecht's upward mobility in the table did not go unnoticed and at the end of the season it sold its best players, Bart Ramselaar and Timo Letschert. The club could make substantial financial steps forward. Ramselaar was sold to PSV Eindhoven. The transfer of the midfielder was the best deal done since the beginning of Wilco van Schaik's five-year tenure as general manager of the club. Including bonuses and a resale percentage, Ramselaar generated more than €6 million. He was the first fully home-grown player who earned that much. A few weeks earlier, defender Letschert left for the Italian club Sassuolo for €4 million. For years FC Utrecht had been in the red. Due to these financial gains, there at last was some calm at the club. The gaps were closed, and investments were made in scouting and facilities. The medical staff was reorganised, and a nutrition assistant was hired.

Ten Hag didn't lose his nerve when things weren't going well at the start of his second season. 'I follow my own path, don't get distracted easily. And I'm critical of myself, constantly ask myself: what can be done differently, what needs to be improved? Last season's good performances have given us a lot of credit with the supporters. Even during the slow start of the competition, there was hardly any grumbling.' Ten Hag noted that, more and more, opponents adapted to Utrecht. PSV did it in the second half of their match, for example, and SC Heerenveen from the start of their game. 'We take this into account, but you can never exactly predict what the opponent will do. What I do find is that such adjustments are often to our advantage. At the end of October, the club was back in the left column [the top half of the table] and the third Cup round was reached. It's about rebuilding a team. If that works, the results will follow. I live day by day. As coach, everything revolves around the next match. And given my position as technical director, the long term for FC Utrecht matters. It is important that I can work here in an environment where I feel at ease, with people who have the same drive. There are no big egos here; everyone is committed to the club. That is a condition for maximum performance, just like on the pitch.'

Left winger Urby Emanuelson worked with Ten Hag during the coach's last season at FC Utrecht. He says Ten Hag 'is a very warm, sweet man who has a very good sense of how to deal with the players. You could tell that everyone was enthusiastic about him, even the so-called rebellious guys. He always had time for the players and was involved with them regularly, also outside of football. I think he put a lot of time into it. I don't want to say that he is a father figure, but you can certainly laugh with him. I can only be positive about the months I worked with him. About how he asserts himself in the group, how he treats players, his style of play and his tactical insight. Ten Hag thinks more internationally than many Dutch coaches. It's clear that he worked in Germany, with Bayern and with Pep Guardiola. In Holland, not playing 4-3-3 is almost blasphemy, but Ten Hag uses different systems as a weapon. He is doing what Pep is doing. He changes things, he challenges beliefs and wants players to be flexible. At Barcelona, Man City and Bayern they all do it. They play three or four different systems, sometimes in one match.'

In Utrecht, Ten Hag introduced the 5-3-2 system, considered a conservative concept in the Netherlands. He used it in combination with a 4-4-2 system and finished fifth and fourth in the Eredivisie during his two seasons in charge. 'The basic idea is actually offensive, because you try to get the best positioning in front of goal from an offensive point of view. The strikers have room to move to the side and the full-backs must have the ability to play well in midfield. Then it really becomes a 3-5-2 system. Not the name, but the execution is important. That's what matters.'

Some people seem to believe Ten Hag is a wizard. He is not. It takes time to implement the way he wants to play. But he doesn't panic when initial results are bad. Team captain Willem Janssen has his own experience with that. 'He struck the right chord with me mentally. I remember we were 2–0 down at half-time once and I had played a negative role in both goals. Erik just said, "Now you are going to show the real Willem in the second half." He sticks to what he wants, convinced that it will bring success. Then when you start winning, it strengthens the group dynamic, the belief in his plans. It was cool to see that opponents were no longer able to get a hold of us. We were the first team in the Netherlands to switch systems very easily. During matches we went from 4-4-2 with a flat midfield, to 4-4-2 with a diamond, to 5-3-2, to 3-5-2. He also has an eye for the person behind the footballer. He used a mental coach looking after the psychological side of things, Joost Leenders, but also looked for causes himself if you underperformed. He is interested and empathic when he notices something is going on in a player's private life. He even came to some guys' houses to support them.'

• • •

Erik ten Hag had a very difficult weekend. He did not want to respond publicly to what he called a 'private matter'. But he told his team just before the play-off final against AZ in May 2017 that his son had been in a serious car accident. Willem Janssen said, 'My best memory of Erik is when I saw him at his most emotional. It was the weekend we qualified for the Europa League through the play-offs. We had lost 3–0 at AZ Alkmaar in the first leg and nobody gave us a chance. A day before the return match Erik was missing and we heard he was in hospital with his son. It was uncertain whether he would be at the game. On Sunday morning he was there and he did the meeting. He gave this incredibly beautiful, intense match talk. He said, "My son has miraculously survived this accident; now it is up to you to make a miracle too." I had goosebumps the entire game. That, added to the fact that we had messed things up during the away leg and wanted to set it right, meant that we just couldn't lose. We went out roaring, determined to win for Erik. We won

3–0 and qualified on penalties. It was a sublime culmination of a fantastic collaboration.'

On 28 May 2017, Utrecht café and bar owners earned their average monthly income in one day when FC Utrecht managed to crown themselves winners in the play-offs from an almost hopeless position. They got a European ticket after a thriller of the top order, reaching the second preliminary round of the Europa League in a sensational match against AZ. Few had given Utrecht any chance, but Team Ten Hag wiped off a 3–0 defeat from the first game. After their home victory, AZ seemed on course to make it to Europe. But within half an hour of the return match, FC Utrecht was leading 2–0. First Willem Janssen hit the target, then Sébastien Haller doubled the score. The third goal did not come, although an AZ defender was shown a red card midway through the second half for taking down a player advancing on goal. A few minutes before time, Gyrano Kerk made sure that his team got extra time to decide the battle. Because no goals were scored in extra time, the decision had to come from the penalty spot. Andreas Ludwig failed on behalf of FC Utrecht, but because two AZ players also missed, the number four in the Eredivisie still entered Europe. Ecstatic players, fans running onto the pitch, and a string of sales of European tickets resulted.

Ten Hag was ecstatic, by his standards, and effusive in commentary on the improbable turnaround at Galgenwaard. 'The team won mainly because we have now shown what it takes to win trophies. Willpower. Conviction. You have to manage the pain and push boundaries, physically and mentally. In Alkmaar we were below the required minimum, and the disappointment was very deep. Of course, there was little chance that we would pull this off, but a chance is a chance. We went full throttle. I am prouder than proud. We got what we deserved.'

Ten Hag understands the psychology of failure and success. 'It starts with reading characters, knowing how the person behind the football player works. When I see someone play, I can paint a picture of what kind of person he is based on how he moves, reacts when losing the ball, conceding a goal or committing a foul. If you know that, you will adapt your guidance. I choose a separate approach for everyone. But then you're still not there. You also have to deal with the collective, how all those characters relate to each other. Before a match I size up the spirit. At AZ away, I didn't feel any charge in the dressing room; we were not on the front foot. During the warm-up I could see from the way they were passing the ball that it was going to be a difficult afternoon: how they hit the ball, no conviction, there was nothing behind it. Back in the dressing room I felt it again. Each player has his own way of preparing, one picks on his socks, the other hides under a towel. As long as things are going well, no problem, but if they're not going well, they just keep doing it. I try to break those routines before they become a form of compulsion. They start thinking they lost because they have not been under that towel. They will really believe it was because of that. This is how you create an excuse for failure.'

Ten Hag admits, 'I don't know beforehand whether we will win, but I do know if we're going to play a good game. At home against AZ, in the final of the play-offs, I felt an instinct akin to the urge to survive in the dressing room. I saw energy and excitement, and then we turned a 3–0 loss of the first game into a victory on penalties. When you talk about mindset, that was the perfect example. My best match as a coach. Tactically it was right, the execution was perfect, but especially mentally we completely broke AZ. It wasn't until the 82nd minute that they had their first shot on goal. We won that final in the mind. It's at times like these that I'm proudest of my players.'

Ten Hag had hinted he might be in Utrecht for a while, at one point saying, 'I'm not looking for a top club. You have to be content with what you have. Working at the top is of course wonderful, who would not want that? My résumé isn't bad. I've done everything; from head of training to head coach and technical manager. I want to be successful with the people here. I'm really enjoying it, this is a wonderful project. Theoretically, I can work here for another five years. But in practice, the coach does not have a long shelf life. The first half of the competition went very well, but what happens if there is a storm? You can't be successful all the time in football. So: live by the day.' His successes had not gone unnoticed. Although he still had a contract with Utrecht until mid-2020, he left for Ajax midway through the 2017–18 season.

In 2017 FC Utrecht recorded more Eredivisie victories than ever before. Ten Hag confirmed his reputation as 'crown prince' – as the monarchy-loving Dutch like to call the heir apparent in any métier – among football managers in the Netherlands. Despite the departures of key players like Sébastien Haller, Nacer Barazite and Sofyan Amrabat, he forged a team that performed well in the preliminary rounds of the Europa League, notably against Polish club Lech Poznań. Unfortunately, the club was eliminated by Russian side Zenit Saint Petersburg. Ten Hag concluded, 'Together we have taken great steps in the process of becoming a sustainable sub-topper. This is the result of the good work of many. I am proud that I have been able to lead this in collaboration with the supervisory board, the management and particularly Jordy Zuidam. I am leaving a competent staff and above all a group of players with a lot of character. I will miss everyone unimaginably and wish FC Utrecht, the supporters and especially the team a successful 2018!'

9

TUKKER IN AMSTERDAM

*'Ten Hag was long opposed and taunted in Amsterdam
by a bunch of incredible dunces, who couldn't get used
to the fact that a stammering Tukker turned out to be
smarter, more civilised and more gifted than they were.'*
SJOERD MOSSOU, *ALGEMEEN DAGBLAD*

Ajax midfielder Abdelhak 'Appie' Nouri walks, stops, drops to his knees and lies stretched out on the field during a pre-season friendly. The jolly atmosphere of the practice match has suddenly evaporated. Club doctors from both Ajax and Werder Bremen scurry around and attempt to resuscitate the 20-year-old before he is taken away by ambulance. In the intensive care unit of the hospital in Innsbruck they discover the cause of his collapse: an irregularity in his heart beat – arrhythmia is the medical term. A scan shows that a large part of Nouri's brain no longer functions, probably because of a lack of oxygen supply. Doctors say the chance of recovery is zero. A year-long investigation finds that the medical treatment Nouri received on the field was 'inadequate'. After four more years of medical and legal wrangling, Ajax announces that the club will pay the family €7,850,000 to cover all past and future medical bills. Nouri's 34 shirt is officially retired.

The tragedy happened just three weeks into Ajax coach Marcel Keizer's tenure. It cast a pall over Ajax's new season. Keizer thought that the slow start was understandable. 'It can still be very tough at times. Yesterday there was something from Appie on TV. Wonderful to see him like this, but then you immediately know how heavy it is. It's not easy. We have never used it as an excuse, but that doesn't mean you just ignore it. We are a few weeks behind; I hope everyone understands why.' After 17 games Ajax was second in the Eredivisie, five points behind leader PSV, not getting through the preliminary rounds of the Champions League and Europa League, and losing a key cup match against FC Twente on penalties. Ajax sacked Marcel Keizer and his assistants Hennie Spijkerman and Dennis Bergkamp after five months.

• • •

When The Hague native Martin Jol began playing more realistic football as Ajax coach during the 2009–10 season, Johan Cruyff was displeased with what he saw as a loss of the club's identity and stepped in. He felt Ajax had been drifting in the wrong direction for some time and in his *De Telegraaf* column he sharply criticised the state of affairs at what once was the Eredivisie's most successful club. After Ajax's lacklustre performances against a strong Real Madrid and a weak Willem II, Cruyff expressed dismay under the headline, 'THIS IS NOT AJAX ANYMORE'. 'This Ajax is worse than the team Rinus Michels joined in 1965. It is a disaster everywhere – in finances, education, scouting, purchasing and football.' The distinguished Ajax emeritus and idol of thousands took part in a technical think-tank meant to come up with ideas for a turnaround. Cruyff has never been someone shy to voice his opinions, especially where it concerns his footballing alma mater. He introduced a new development model to be implemented by Wim Jonk and Dennis Bergkamp. Both were appointed as heads of the academy over the summer. Cruyff himself took a seat on the Board of Commissioners beside Edgar Davids, Paul Römer, Marjan Olfers and chairman Steven ten Have, producing what could have been a balanced blend of two former players, a media specialist, a sports lawyer and a management consultant.

He initiated the so-called Velvet Revolution to reverse the tide. It put former Ajax players at the helm everywhere, assuring the continuation of cherished football traditions. With the addition of former Ajax icons such as Frank de Boer, Dennis Bergkamp, Wim Jonk, Marc Overmars, Bryan Roy and Edwin van der Sar, the organisational structure of the club was changed. A 'technical triangle' composed of new head coach Frank de Boer, youth coordinator Wim Jonk and bridge between senior and youth, Dennis Bergkamp, would chart the technical path of the club. Whether by conscious choice or because of personal disposition, Cruyff was a practitioner of so-called seagull management, a style in which a top executive interacts with people at the lower echelons only when a problem arises. The perception is that such a laissez-faire style of management involves hasty and ad hoc decisions. The long-term results of the revolution at Ajax were probably not the ones Cruyff envisioned.

One of Ten Hag's final matches in charge of FC Utrecht was a 2–1 victory at Ajax in November 2017. On 28 December, he signed a two-and-a-half-year contract as the new Ajax head coach. The appointment of someone without Ajax pedigree was a break with Amsterdam tradition. It signalled the informal end of the Cruyff revolution that was initiated in 2010. To release Ten Hag, the club had to pay FC Utrecht more than the initially expected €700,000. Ajax was happy. Utrecht was not. Club owner Frans van Seumeren was disappointed that Ten Hag left before his contract expired. But Ten Hag had been clear about his option of moving to a better club if the opportunity presented itself. Former footballer Clemens Zwijnenberg said, 'Erik is a man of his word. I think he struggled with his departure from Utrecht, but you can't pass up the chance to go to Ajax.'

Dedication and loyalty are of paramount importance to Ten Hag. That he was leaving FC Utrecht for Ajax, just when they were building something impressive, was atypical. 'On the one hand, it was great, but I still had a contract with FC Utrecht. I think that if you start something, you have to finish it. However, in football it doesn't always work that way, as in this case. Ajax is the only club in the Netherlands for which I was prepared to make that exception. Ajax is the leading brand in the Netherlands and gets most attention from the media and on social media. Not only in our country; the club is popular outside the Netherlands. At Ajax it is also the most difficult to be responsible for the first team. You know that when you sign here. I did it with full conviction and in the knowledge that switching midway through the season was not a guarantee for success.'

On the beautiful training fields of the Cascade Wellness and Lifestyle Resort in Lagos, Portugal, the 27 Ajax players appeared on the field at around four o'clock. Practice matches against Danish club Lyngby BK and German side Duisburg were on the programme. The winter training camp was open to the public and Ajax fans could get a close look at their team. Attention was lavished on Ten Hag, the club's third coach in just a year. In the Algarve, he had to maintain a careful balance. He wanted to extend his influence over team play, but it is hard to change things dramatically mid-season. He built rapport with the players. A little fun with Klaas-Jan Huntelaar here, an arm around Justin Kluivert's shoulder there. But every training session had a competitive element. The motto unchangingly was: win, win, win. Ten Hag admitted, 'We need to be more goal-oriented and have more variety in our attacking game. We have the qualities for that as a team and also individually. We are working hard to prepare ourselves well and we cannot look too far ahead. I maximised performance everywhere I worked. I live in the now and we are about to embark on a journey.' There had been quite a few empty seats at Ajax home matches that season, but Ten Hag was hopeful. 'The attendance at Eredivisie games has been falling. At Utrecht, the number of spectators has increased over the past two and a half years.'

Ten Hag faced a challenge of suddenly remodelling a player group halfway through a season's competition. That was not easy for a man who always speaks about the 'process' of team development. Ten Hag works towards building a mentality where everyone understands what the culture is and what he has to do to develop and sustain it. The players would need to quickly get used to their new coach and his idiosyncratic ways. Ten Hag said following his arrival, 'We have exactly two weeks until we have to beat Feyenoord. This [winter break] requires a completely different approach and management than when preparing in the summer. Then you can build things up, test players for positions and take the time to stress areas of development. Now we come into an existing situation. I train long, but not necessarily hard. Depending on the programming, phase or accent, I also train short and very intensive. But what is that anyway, hard? I'm working on my squad and that's a process that never ends. Every day there is room for improvement, and where do you do that as a player? On the field. Prizes are won on the training ground.'

Erik ten Hag is not exactly a socialite, but he immediately got involved in Ajax life, coming to Christmas drinks and other mix-and-mingle events. He commuted in his Ajax-furnished Mercedes between the Johan Cruyff Arena, his modestly furnished apartment on the Zuidas and his family home in Oldenzaal. Before accepting the job, he rang Louis van Gaal, wanting to know what coaching Ajax was like. He visited the former manager in his luxurious apartment in Résidence Helmhorst, located in the coastal town of Noordwijk aan Zee. Whether the two sat in the living-room with its heated marble floor or on one of the terraces with views of the dunes and the North Sea is not known, but the exchange was meaningful. 'While I was still coach of FC Utrecht, I spoke with Louis. That was very useful. I wanted to talk to him, and he was open to that. In my second season, I had another talk with him. How did he look at Ajax? How could you survive in the force fields at the club? What was his view of the team? He was a valuable sounding board, and it contributed to our success. He gave me pointers that we implemented. I always use my assistants as my sounding boards. I think it is a good idea to listen to people who understand the business. I think it is good to listen, to think about it, but in the end I make my own decisions. A coach does a lot of listening, but makes up his own mind. That is real leadership: work hard for a common goal, while all involved have a good feeling. I think I also listen to my players. I take them seriously, they are intelligent. As long as they remember that the team is number one.'

Van Gaal was not welcomed at Ajax with open arms in 1991, and Ten Hag had to overcome scepticism 26 years later. Did he suit Ajax? A trainer of his calibre should be able to work anywhere, but Ajax is not just anywhere. In Amsterdam's Johan Cruyff Arena you should win, but above all play attractive football. With Frank de Boer Ajax became champions four times, but the supporters were getting bored with the endless positional play. His successor, Peter Bosz, didn't win anything, but with a bit of good fortune reached the final of the Europa League, and he was highly regarded in Amsterdam. The pressing pleased the fans, and some excitement was back. With Ten Hag, Ajax got a pragmatic coach, one who looks at the players he has at his disposal and adjusts his way of playing accordingly. That could be 3-4-3, but just as well 4-4-2 or 3-5-2.

Ten Hag knows that 'ultimately, as a coach, you want to win, be successful. But you also want to do it a certain way. That's part of the Dutch national consciousness. Especially in Amsterdam the way you are playing is as important as the result. You have to master the higher art of coaching to get there, one that brings real satisfaction. But you have to work very hard to make it happen. It has to grow throughout the season. What also matters in that is how you manage expectations. Fans are whipped up by the media: they don't see what exactly is involved in all of it and that sometimes it takes time. The fans just want to win right away and it has to happen with beautiful football. Period. That is understandable. But when the media don't recognise what you are doing and begin to put you under pressure, it becomes more difficult.'

During Van Gaal's time as Ajax manager, 'Louis didn't have friends at *De Telegraaf* and *Nieuwe Revu*. With hindsight, it was a disgrace the way they covered him in his early period.' Ten Hag notes, though, that since then the 'force fields have grown exponentially. In the time of Louis van Gaal you only had two serious agents, Rob Jansen and Sigi Lens, who advised all the Ajax players. But look at how things are now: of the 11 on the pitch, every single one has his own agent. Those 11 have only one thing on their mind: the big bang, the megatransfer. They're all shouting off the rooftops: "What matters is the development of the player!" Well, that really isn't the case. All of that creates restlessness. That makes things very difficult for the coach.'

Goalkeeper Khalid Sinouh wondered whether Ten Hag was the right choice for Ajax. 'I experienced Erik as assistant coach at PSV. There is no question about his qualities. He certainly has them. He is demanding, and he has a clear vision of football. And he is a good guy besides. But his personality doesn't fit with Ajax. He can be a little stiff, a real Tukker, a bit grumpy. He doesn't always come across well in the media. He lacks the charisma of Guus Hiddink or Ronald Koeman. But there are few trainers of his quality in our country. He has a particular football paradigm and he does not deviate from that. He keeps control over everything. That is a feature all good trainers have in common. Ten Hag is a realistic coach, tactically strong, someone who has a different view of contemporary football. At Bayern Munich, he experienced Pep Guardiola. He also wants to have everything organised a certain way and nothing left to chance. A workaholic, just like Ten Hag. They say that wisdom comes from the east. Let's hope for Ajax and Ten Hag that's true.'

• • •

In a primer on the Netherlands' society and culture, *The Undutchables* by Colin White, the newcomer to Amsterdam is warned about the dangers that lie ahead in the Dutch capital. 'Upon arrival at the glorious Amsterdam Centraal Station, don't look anyone in the eye or you'll be hustled – for hashish, heroin, cocaine, a cheap hotel or botel (boat-hotel behind the station), sleep-in, left-wing newspaper, right-wing newspaper, non-affiliated newspaper, shoe shine, petition signing, joining a demonstration or a riot, recruiting squatters (*krakers*), women's liberation or gay liberation movement. Staring at the ground is good practice for the moment you exit the station and encounter the heaps of dog shit which decorate the streets of Amsterdam.'

Amsterdam is unique in more than one way. It is the only crowned city in the world. The crown, presented to the capital by Emperor Maximilian I in the late fifteenth century, can still be seen on the Blauwbrug (Blue Bridge) across the Amstel. Does that mean that Amsterdammers have reason to feel superior to people elsewhere in the Netherlands? Those in the provinces do seem to feel a bit intimidated by the brash capital inhabitants. Amsterdammers have a somewhat combative, defiant attitude and generally think they have one up on their fellow Dutchmen. Ten Hag noticed. 'Amsterdammers are direct. But that is also beautiful. The baker around the corner from where I live is a fanatical Ajax supporter. If it sucks, he says it sucks, but with a smile. I've never had any trouble on the street. Negativity mainly comes through social media, and from a certain corner, nicely anonymous and easy.'

Centuries before Amsterdam became synonymous with weed and over-tourism, it was a beloved hub of European Jewry. When Sephardic Jews were first persecuted and then expelled from Spain in the Late Middle Ages, they found a safe haven in the northern capital. Echoes of that era still drift through the canal city in the form of Yiddish-based slang, including Amsterdam's enduring nickname, 'Mokum', simply meaning 'place' in Yiddish. When the locals say *de mazzel*, they are wishing each other 'good luck' in Hebrew (*mazzel tov* is the formal Hebrew version). The Jodenbuurt, the Jewish Quarter, was the centre of Amsterdam Jews for centuries before the Second World War. It is known as the birthplace of Baruch Spinoza, the home of Rembrandt, and the Jewish ghetto during the Nazi occupation.

The Dutch pride themselves on their liberalism and tolerance. Amsterdam was probably the least antisemitic city in Europe prior to the Holocaust years. Yet, the survival rate of Dutch Jews was much lower than in neighbouring countries, including Germany. Eighty per cent of the Netherlands 140,000 Jews died in Nazi gas chambers. In Amsterdam the percentage was even higher. Some suggest that this may have been the result of a misapplication of the Dutch penchant for administrative duty. The Amsterdam police force, under the leadership of chief of police Sybren Tulp, played a particularly important role in the deportation of the Jews. The facts of the episode are not well-known and the topic is avoided in history textbooks. In his book *Dienaren van het gezag – De Amsterdamse politie tijdens de bezetting* (Servants of Authority: The Amsterdam Police during the Occupation), Guus Meershoek, a professor of governance at the University of Twente, details the dark page in Dutch history.

It was really in the 1960s and 1970s that Ajax became known as a 'Jewish club'. Some of the chairmen who led the club during that time were Jewish, while it also had successful Jewish players such as Bennie Muller and Sjaak Swart. The club's somewhat remote Jewish links regularly led to antisemitic abuse from rival supporters. A segment of fans began to fight back by calling themselves 'Super Jews'. In the 1980s, skinheads of the notorious F-side were sporting tattoos of the so-called Ajax star – the Star of David – on their shaven scalps. The extremism has since become more subdued, but the symbol still appears on T-shirts and fans can be seen waving the Israeli flag at matches. Jewish icons still are widely used in Ajax merchandising. Former Ajax chairman Michael van Praag once tried to put the urban legend to bed, saying, 'Ajax is not a Jewish club, and its fans are as Jewish as I am Chinese.' Like at Tottenham Hotspur, 'being Jewish' was seen as the best response towards rival fans who used antisemitism to attack the club's loyal support.

Whatever its worth, the abstract connection to Jewishness at the club did not directly translate to ethnic tolerance and multiculturalism. Ten Hag immediately distinguished himself from the Amsterdam natives by his Twente accent and unique diction. In an Ajax video the trainer provided a tactical analysis of a goal against PSV. He spoke about 'creating several 10s' and 'destroying an opponent by running without a ball' and 'opposite running movements that open up spaces'. Football coach Andries Jonker had a hard time getting used to Ten Hag's way of speaking. Jonker had preceded Ten Hag as the manager of Bayern Munich II. He was born in Amsterdam and said that he would never use some of the expressions that Ten Hag uses. 'Erik has his own jargon. He's not an Amsterdammer, he's not someone from the west. I am, and I don't say things like "high in concentration". It doesn't even occur to me. But I do understand what he's talking about. It is also nice that we have someone with his own language. As long as we can understand him, it's okay.' Not everyone agreed.

Compounding Ten Hag's ability to communicate was his discomfort in front of camera. He was not born with a gift for elegant rhetoric and the easy quip. Sometimes, he has difficulty getting his message across. 'Why are you talking so weird?' he snapped at *De Volkskrant* journalist Willem Vissers after Ajax's 3–2 defeat at Vitesse. He meant that he didn't think the journalist's question – 'Do you think the form has flowed away too much at Ajax in recent weeks?' – made much sense. Vissers countered on FOX Sports that this sounded strange from the mouth of a man who 'seems forever hoarse and says "uh" 27 times in half a minute'. Whereas people had taken Ten Hag's somewhat monotone presentations for granted at Go Ahead Eagles and FC Utrecht, at Ajax they expected better PR. 'As a trainer you have to have flair to succeed at Ajax and Ten Hag does not have that,' opined Aad de Mos, who coached the club from 1981 to 1985. 'The wise men may come from the east, but the football wise come from the west, they think at Ajax. Ten Hag must therefore immediately prove himself in the Arena. They sit down and say: show it to me. He does not have the credit that Frank de Boer had, for example, when he started as Ajax trainer.'

At Ajax, everything is magnified, especially with someone who is not an organic part of the tribe. Ten Hag didn't just face scepticism and criticism in his first year. Sometimes it was more like character assassination. Leading Dutch newspaper *De Telegraaf* pulled out all the stops to malign 'the peasant from the countryside'. The Twente accent was not the only thing he was mocked for. His appearance was another. The hair on his head was in the wrong place: nothing on top, everything on the bottom. He was ridiculed by football commentators Johan Derksen and René van der Gijp on the talk show *Voetbal Inside*. Derksen likened him to a 'garden gnome', the ubiquitous Dutch garden decoration. Ten Hag shrugged it off, dismissing it as part of 'cabaret'. 'You have to endure these kinds of attacks and need to have some thick skin. That also applies to people in my immediate environment, those who love me. Anyone who can't handle that is not suitable for this job. I always try to think about why someone says something, what motivates him. Football analysts aren't in a position to evaluate me personally, but it's their livelihood. And you also have to understand Dutch culture. The Dutch are very good at griping.'

The nineteenth-century poet Oscar Wilde said, 'In the old days men had the rack. Now they have the press … We are dominated by journalism.' Dissatisfaction with media behaviour is not limited to today's politicians, artists and football managers, but has been with us for a long time. Players and coaches the world over begrudge the treatment they receive at the hands of the press. These are not groundless complaints. The sports media, maybe more than any other, are expert at churning out nonsense in quantity. That sports coverage and celebrity scandal-mongering are commonly linked in a profitable but second-rate press is an international reality. Spectator sports are not generally known as an arena of measured analysis and calm reflection.

The media are, fundamentally, profit-motivated institutions. They are businesses, as are professional football clubs. However, the interests of the press and the clubs are often diametrically opposed. Whereas the manager is interested in maintaining an environment of stability where he can work on building his team, the media are interested in the opposite. Few sports magazine readers would be interested to learn that Erik ten Hag and Ajax had a pleasant after-noon of training; antagonism and conflict sell more copies and increase viewer ratings. Match outcomes of course are of particular interest. In football the results speak for themselves. If a coach wins games, he is the hero; if the team performance doesn't quite live up to expectations, he quickly becomes the villain.

Leon ten Voorde, Ten Hag's childhood friend, who'd since become a journalist, asked, 'Didn't those attacks on TV and in *De Telegraaf* mean anything to him? Of course, they did, but he finds it particularly unpleasant for those close to him: his family, his parents and the rest of his relatives. It has not affected him personally as much. And it certainly has not changed his way of working and thinking. Sometimes I think: *come on, smile, and enjoy yourself a bit more!* The other day, I had him on the phone after a game, on his way home from Amsterdam to Oldenzaal. He just continues, staying calm, and producing level-headed analyses. He can be excited for a moment, but then he has to move on because the game against Fortuna Sittard awaits him, next Sunday.' Ten Hag was portrayed as a stereotypical grumpy Tukker at Ajax. His parents didn't want to say much about it, except that they thought it affected him more than he showed. His father said, 'He has a strong sense of justice. The criticism was at odds with that. But Erik knows how to separate his thinking from his feelings very well. He suppresses his feeling with his mind because he envisions a higher goal.'

Erik ten Hag said, 'The tone when I came in here was: we are Ajax and we know how the world works. Then someone comes along and says it's another way. I was met with scepticism at first. In the dressing room, anyone can say anything, as long as it stays within those four walls. That is very difficult here. I don't run with the crowd. My different approach has brought success at my previous clubs. I don't lose any sleep over the criticisms of my media presence. In top sport you don't have a chance if you go whichever way the wind blows. You must have a vision, a sense of direction. You have to be yourself and stay the course, otherwise it won't work. My aim is to get the most out of my team. If I fail to do so, I *do* lose sleep over that. Vitesse away – what did I do wrong? PSV away – where exactly didn't we get it right? That occupies me. But not how they portray me. That is often false and unfair. Yes, I don't speak like an Amsterdammer, but Amsterdam speech also is a dialect. Yes, I am hoarse, but I am not the only one. Especially after a match in which you have to shout at the top of your lungs to be heard above the noise. There are trainers aplenty who have problems with that. You can always pick on certain aspects of someone's media presentation and ridicule them. I think that happens to many other people in football as well. You could make quite a list.'

His first ten matches had yielded 23 points: seven wins, two draws and a defeat, by no means bad. Yet the pundits decided that things weren't going well under the new trainer. In the absence of European football or obligations in the cup tournament, Ten Hag's assignment during the second half of the season was straightforward. He had to close the gap of five points with PSV in order to avoid a fourth season in sequence without any prizes. After ten matches, that gap had grown to seven points. The Eindhoven team was four victories away from the national title. With matches against NAC, ADO Den Haag, FC Groningen and Roda JC still to come, Ajax could do little else than hope.

The Tukker's limited credit ran out rapidly. Making Ajax champions again in his first season was the goal for which he had been brought in. Ten Hag's 'process' was set in motion, but the results were neither good enough nor coming fast enough. Another prizeless season was unavoidable, with fewer points per game earned under Ten Hag than under his predecessor – an average of 2.1 points compared to 2.2 points under Keizer. Ten Hag himself saw progress – he thought Ajax passed more, and that the team controlled the games better; more opportunities were created and defensively it was more stable. Aad de Mos still was not convinced: 'He can say all that, but I don't see Ten Hag's hand at Ajax yet. I don't see a specific way of playing, which I do hear him talk about. He seems to fall into the trap many Ajax trainers have fallen into. He allows himself to be taken in by the club's board, instead of sticking to his own way. Peter Bosz asserted himself, but Ten Hag is playing himself into a crisis. I see no vision.'

Ten Hag responded, 'There is a very negative sentiment and I can relate to that. We did not become champions. That is always Ajax's goal, so the moment you don't achieve it, it is unsatisfactory. Adding to that the club was quickly knocked out of the cup tournament and the European competition, and this already being the fourth year in a row without a prize, then it is logical that there is a negative feeling. Let me be clear: the coaching staff is not satisfied, the fans are not satisfied, Ajax is not satisfied, obviously. But I would like to put things in perspective. You can't just say that everything is bad. In the first half of the season, the drama surrounding Abdelhak Nouri was frequently discussed. That didn't suddenly disappear in recent months; it ran like a red thread through the entire season. Then there were other factors such as the bizarre number of long-term injuries.'

He continued: 'Nevertheless, I think there were positives in our game. We created the most chances in the Eredivisie, but the return lagged behind. We still scored more goals than any other team. We conceded the fewest chances and the fewest goals. Just some things to consider. So I want to say: it's not all that bad. But I haven't heard anything about that or read it anywhere. The trainer should always take responsibility for the result. It's like being a government minister. It doesn't matter that you don't have 100 per cent influence over something, you are responsible for it. We expect first place here, and we didn't finish there. I understand that fans are not happy with that. I am not happy with it myself.'

If a manager does not get immediate positive results, then he has a problem, particularly in Amsterdam. Former striker René Eijkelkamp worked with Ten Hag, first at FC Twente and then at PSV. Some thought that once the national title was out of reach, the new coach would get some room to work on his team-building process. But Eijkelkamp said, 'It doesn't work that way at Ajax. You have to win every week and the second place has to be secured now. I don't think it is quite as bad as the press writes it is now, but I think next season you will really see football the way he wants it. It wasn't easy for Ten Hag to come in mid-season, but in the end I see him succeeding at Ajax. He has always been so serious when it comes to his profession. You can laugh with him about things besides football, but an outsider can't see that.'

Anyone analysing a Ten Hag team sees that he makes room for outstanding players. They infuse his teams with dynamism, creativity and attractive football. He explained his thinking in an Ajax interview: 'As a coach you have to learn what players are made of. The character of the player is important and you have to adjust your leadership style accordingly. It is a process – to gain that insight. What does the group need, what does a player need individually? I am a coach who tries to give players tools and has been successful with that. With me, the creative players always crop up. Think of Marko Arnautović, Eljero Elia, Quincy Promes, Zakaria Labyad, Nacer Barazite, Yassin Ayoub, Deniz Türüç. I could go on with creative players who have all excelled under me. And take Hakim Ziyech this season at Ajax, during the last period: exceptionally good. David Neres has had a bad spell after the winter break but also regained his former level. I again heard media criticism: Ziyech, Neres and Kluivert would no longer perform. But a month later, they all had assists and goals to their name. And then I don't hear anyone anymore.'

Ten Hag only had two weeks in winter before the competition restarted. So he said to the players, 'We are going to build on what is good,' and that was the footballing ability of the team. But 'the defensive security had to be improved. I thought Ajax played too openly, the team conceded a goal too easily. I focused on creating more opportunities, coupled with more control. Control is easily interpreted as something defensive, but to me it stands for putting your stamp on the game, for being in charge of the pitch. That's what you want, and I want more and more of that. Of course, that shows in the game result: 4–0, 5–1, you name it. But if you don't use your chances and it stays at 1–0 or 2–0, that calls for criticism. Then you quickly get slogans such as: "He is a defensive coach." But if you have a lot of the ball, the opponent cannot score either. We aim to find solutions more directly and faster. I focused on creating more opportunities, coupled with more control. That worked, but I'm not satisfied yet.'

The disenchantment with the 2017–18 performance climaxed on 15 April 2018, at the away match against PSV. The Eindhoven club won the match 3–0, securing the league title for the 24th time in the club's history. Gastón Pereiro put PSV ahead after Hirving

Lozano's shot had been blocked on the line by Matthijs de Ligt. Luuk de Jong headed home Joshua Brenet's cross, and Steven Bergwijn's half-volley sealed the victory. To make matters worse, Nicolás Tagliafico and Siem de Jong were both shown red cards. Tagliafico, known for his industry on the pitch, collected a second yellow and Siem, the older brother of better-known player Luuk, was sent off for a bad foul. Torches were sent flying from the stands by angry Ajax supporters.

Later, general director Edwin van der Sar tried to calm a group of Ajax fans when the players' bus returned to the Johan Cruyff Arena. The atmosphere was bad and police officers were on hand to prevent the conflict from boiling over. Aggressive fans kicked and hit the bus until the Ajax chief executive got off to talk to the group of around 150 angry supporters. They demanded that Van der Sar resign because they felt he was responsible for the club's disappointing season. Ten Hag got off the bus to assist Van der Sar. The two spent almost two hours talking with the group before the bus was allowed to continue to the arena's parking area and the players could get off. It was a pivotal moment in the Ajax season.

Willem van Hanegem, the great former player of Feyenoord, who was known as 'De Kromme', the Crooked One, for his bandy legs, is a midfielder-turned-football commentator. In his weekly *Algemeen Dagblad* column, he wrote, 'Ajax has missed the boat for years. They sacked Marcel Keizer, and Erik ten Hag was brought in as the great saviour. That's because there are plenty of folks in this country who are always blindly running after certain people. Ten Hag played a few times with five defenders and suddenly he was proclaimed a tactical miracle. Now these same people who patted his back are bothered by his way of speaking. Of what interest is that to me? Look at his performance instead. He didn't do well – and that while Ajax had more options than PSV, with players like Onana, De Ligt, Ziyech, Frenkie de Jong, Van de Beek, Huntelaar and Kluivert.'

The 400 Ajax supporters in the away section showed what they thought of the last match of a painful season on a sweltering final day of the Eredivisie competition. Ajax was playing away against Excelsior. Ten Hag and his staff started with a 3-5-2 system. Considering that nothing was at stake in Rotterdam, the formation may not have mattered much. After half an hour Ajax defaulted to the more familiar and fan-friendly 4-3-3 when the injured Klaas-Jan Huntelaar was replaced by the Brazilian David Neres. In the 20th minute, a clumsy own goal was produced by, of all people, team captain Matthijs de Ligt. The Ajax fans sounded off, 'Erik, hit the road!' and treated goalkeeper Kostas Lamprou to a whistling concert. The slack game combined with a very slow tempo had the fans serenading the team to *Slaap Kindje, Slaap*, the Dutch version of the lullaby 'Hush, Little Baby'. Kasper Dolberg – not a fan of playing on artificial grass – fought many a battle with the equally strong defender Jurgen Mattheij. To applause, Ten Hag exchanged the Dane for Colombian Mateo Cassierra. Ajax came out of the dressing room refreshed and after Justin Kluivert's quick equaliser, Hakim Ziyech was awarded a penalty, which he expertly converted – 2–1. Ajax ended a difficult season with a lukewarm match and modest win.

The manager had his own view of the season's events at Ajax. 'I have sometimes felt like I've been sitting on a volcano, with everything going in a downward spiral. Of course, it would have been easier for me to move in the summer. That's easy to say in hindsight. But I thought: not the ideal time to get in, but I do see opportunities. PSV were on top, with a gap of five points, and if they tripped up, we could make good. But they had a great season and hardly dropped any points. I saw how those things work during my time at Bayern Munich. Every detail can be picked out for emphasis. The media, people in general, always find something if they look for it. A hundred things can go right, but if one goes wrong, you can latch on to it and highlight it. That is the football world.'

. . .

The income of a professional football club is generated mostly through broadcasting rights and merchandising. Consequently, the size of the market is of considerable importance. Unfortunately, in a small country like the Netherlands that size is very limited in comparison with other, larger countries in the European competition. The income of the major Dutch clubs, the 'big three', Ajax, Feyenoord and PSV, cannot be compared to the top clubs of countries with a much larger market. Even some provincial clubs in England, France, Spain, Germany and Italy can spend a multiple of what the treasurer in Amsterdam can spend. In a country of 17 million people, Ajax's domestic TV money is about €10 million, while the last- placed team in the Premier League gets well over €100 million per season, by a recent count. A generous money supply line is essential in modern-day top football, not only to pay for the one-time transfer fee of a real star, but to be able to cover the annually recurring expense of his salary. Financial constraints limit the possibilities of a club like Ajax in European top football.

Even the bigger Dutch clubs, which have much less financial power than clubs in larger European nations, don't go on a player shopping spree just for the sake of playing a good tournament. At Ajax, the club president might be willing to pay €15 million in transfer money for a player but only if it concerns someone with a good 'rest value'. That means that only younger or very talented players are considered: the club benefits from his sports skills in the short term and can resell him at a considerable profit later. Obviously, such players are hard to come by. If they are around, all the major European clubs will be knocking on their doors. Such policies can easily cause friction at the club between the business management and the coach. The coach is interested in the immediate improvement of the team performance, the short term, whereas the club board wants to see a good return on its investment, the long term.

Although Ajax buys players that cost little in comparison with the real big stars, they do have the potential to grow into great players. But they will have to maintain themselves consistently at the highest possible level. This was the Ajax purchase policy for years. An understandable approach from the club's business point of view, but it makes competing in a European competition very difficult. It often appears that the company philosophy is at odds with the vision of the coach, the man passing through, the man of the short term. That's where the challenge of the coach lies: performing at the maximum possible level within the limited range of possibilities of the club. Players already at the club won't continue with Ajax just because the club has qualified for the Champions League. They follow the money and not much else. If a player has the option to go to an English or Spanish side – even one that does not play in the Champions League – they will go there and not stay in Amsterdam. It is difficult for a Dutch club to become stronger through the purchase of a star, a player who can improve the team performance by 10 per cent. When a bigger wallet appears somewhere else, they move.

As the Dutch clubs inevitably are way stations for talented players to pass through, clever scouting is a necessity that has to continue. Like sharks, these clubs have to keep swimming in order not to sink. In the Champions League, the power of the Italian, Spanish, English and German participants has only increased. In order to qualify for the last 16, a team has to first successfully compete in a group with the likes of Chelsea, Barcelona and AC Milan. A group like that is very tough for Ajax. These big clubs can make investments of €100 million or more. So where does that leave a top team in the Netherlands with transfers between €5 and €20 million? Premature departures are constant at Ajax. In 2016 Davinson Sánchez arrived from Colombia for €5 million, for a five-year stay. A year later, he left for Tottenham Hotspur for €40 million. Great for the Amsterdam bank account, but the sudden departure of the strong defender left a hole in the centre of the defence that was not immediately filled. In 2019 Frenkie de Jong went to Barcelona and Matthijs de Ligt to Juventus, both for transfer fees of €75 million.

The Amsterdam club suffered a frustrating trophy drought, partly the result of the same fiscal policy. Since 2012, technical director Marc Overmars worked on putting together a championship-worthy first team. He was very skilled in the financial department, but that overflowing bank account had little value as long as there was no success on the pitch. 'So much money in the bank, when will Ajax do something with it?' It had been a frequently asked question. At the end of August, the conclusion usually was that Ajax had a good summer in terms of income, but that damage had been done in sporting terms. The mindset of fiscal conservatism did not disappear overnight. But when Ten Hag joined the club and challenged the economic tunnel vision, he was heard by the club management. They were aware that a new disaster season could be fatal for their own positions. They realised it was time for a real turnaround, with Ten Hag as a major architect. Agents, technical staff and scouts were all told that Ajax would not succumb to the same problem for another season.

Ten Hag is not naive and knows how the transfer market works. He declared, 'I have received the guarantee from the management that

Ajax will do everything they can to keep the core team together. Every club in the Netherlands, including Ajax, will have to make transfers. You can replace one or two players, but to keep the automatism, you should not let more guys go.' After an outgoing transfer, the club often opted for a replacement from its own youth. But the lack of trophies during four seasons forced the club to act rigorously in the transfer market. Ten Hag emphasised the need for a balanced composition of the team. Ajax has been famous for its academy products and for enabling its youth players to break through to the first team. Ten Hag kept an eye on home-grown talent. Ryan Gravenberch (16) and Noa Lang (19) received playing time, while Carel Eiting (20) and Noussair Mazraoui (20) were featured in the first 11. But having experience on the pitch was essential, not only to immediately improve performance, but to provide the leadership young players needed. With Zakaria Labyad (25), Daley Blind (28) and Dušan Tadić (29), Ajax's first team got a completely different face.

Considerable sums for transfers were allocated in the budget, with the performance on the pitch a priority. With the acquisition of Tadić and Blind, Ajax clearly went against the current: the two players left the paradise of the Premier League to return to the Eredivisie. Tadić, at €11 million, and Blind, at €16 million, were expensive for Ajax. The cost further increased due to bonuses. The financial position of Ajax remained comfortable, but the hoarding seemed to be a thing of the past, all with the goal of bringing the championship trophy back to Amsterdam. Overmars went a step further, suggesting that Ajax should 'become the Bayern Munich of the Eredivisie'.

Overmars and Ten Hag share common roots in the east of the country and worked together in Deventer. Clemens Zwijnenberg said, 'Marc Overmars should get credit for believing in Erik. Of course, he had seen his performance at Go Ahead: the team was promoted to the Eredivisie. I can imagine that it would take a while for a player to get used to Erik's training intensity and understand what he wants. But when you come to a club like Ajax, you have to get results from the start. If you don't, then you will quickly lose your footing and the criticism will come. I think Marc managed that very well and continued with Erik as coach.'

Leon ten Voorde said, 'It's the question whether it's smart to come in halfway through the season. Trainers regularly do it, but it often backfires. If you ask them afterwards, they say: I shouldn't have done it. I talked about that with Erik. What if Ajax comes? Would they come again six months later? Probably not. The train will not pass twice. So I understood that he decided to go. Ajax needed a trainer at that time. He did it and had a pretty tough run the first six months. He was hurt in the process. Some media didn't think he had what it takes because he came from the east of the country – the countryside – and that couldn't be right. But he pursued his path stoically. When things went really bad – losing 3–0 to PSV, the bus episode – he made a plan with Marc Overmars to do summer transfers that would give the club the edge. They both stayed calm under pressure. I think that without Overmars, he may have been fired; someone else might have lost his cool. At clubs they are very much influenced by the outside world. I think that of ten directors, eight would have fired Ten Hag after his first six months at Ajax.'

Ten Voorde said that Ten Hag not only is 'convinced that he is right', but believes completely that 'my way is the way'. Ten Voorde admits that such an attitude 'can be pretty annoying now and then, but I do think that if you want to survive as a coach at the top, you cannot let yourself be distracted by all kinds of peripheral matters, and by the media. He always says, "I do it my way." You can't say that it doesn't bring success; he's always had that in him. People easily think that with Ajax you always become champion. But if you look at the last 10, 15 years, you can see that is not so inevitable. He doesn't come from that famous, notorious Ajax culture, and he still managed to hold his own there. If you look at the season, at what has happened at Ajax and how he has managed things, I think that shows the difference between an average trainer and a top trainer. It stayed calm in the dressing room – as he usually says. You can tell that he is a real professional.'

According to Ten Hag, 'Ajax is the leading brand in the Netherlands and has international class. Ajax stands for stylish football and radiates grandeur. Not only the football, but also everything around it. There is that self-awareness in the club. You can tell that by the good youth players who moved on to the first team: Matthijs de Ligt, Frenkie de Jong, Ryan Gravenberch, you name them. They all have a certain invincible feeling. They are self-aware. I thoroughly enjoy that. On the other hand, the self-confidence in Amsterdam tends to turn into arrogance, and that immediately becomes a big liability. Having difficulty dealing with setbacks, having difficulty coping with circumstances that are different from the desired: a poor pitch, a bad referee or a defensive opponent. Sometimes you have to accept that's just the way it is and deal with it. Don't whine, and make sure you win. You have to focus on your tasks – the team tasks and the individual tasks. That's what it's all about. That resilience has been built.'

Wherever Erik ten Hag goes, there is initial resistance because things have to be changed to suit his very particular way. Everyone had to get used to the stubbornness of the new coach in Amsterdam. From daily discipline to training work, from tactical flexibility to physical development: the classic and somewhat self-satisfied club was pushed firmly in a new direction. Though still based on the conviction of dominant and attacking football, the style was repackaged into something much more dynamic, contemporary and versatile. To get what Ten Hag eventually would develop at Ajax, it takes lots of work and a group of good attacking players. When defenders are playing very high up, there is a lot of space for opponents to get in behind, with increased risks of counter-attacks. That means that every pass has to be just right, there can be no mistakes. Ten Hag knows well how to work with people, and when the Ajax players started picking up his system, they said they began learning a lot from him. That showed in the results.

In November 2019 for the magazine *EW*, Belgian sports pundit Hugo Camps summarised the Tukker's first season in Amsterdam in his own way:

> Erik ten Hag is a perfect cartoon character. He replaces speaking with gargling and his expressions of joy make one detour after another so that at the end only a pale grimace remains. Ten Hag's appointment as Ajax coach was controversial. Ten Hag was seen as a hick from the sticks who had to make his living in the provinces. But the successes dispelled that prejudice. Ten Hag became a crown jewel of Ajax.

10

FROM REVILED TO REVERED

'Greatness is not a function of circumstance.
Greatness, it turns out, is largely a matter
of conscious choice and discipline.'
JIM COLLINS, *GOOD TO GREAT*

The sign at the entrance reads, *Hotel Klosterpforte, in aller Ruhe geniessen*, 'ENJOY YOURSELF IN PEACE'. 'Monastery Gate', the name of the hotel, should convince anyone it is an oasis of tranquillity. This is not a regular tourist destination. Here, in the countryside of North Rhine-Westphalia, less than a hour's drive from the Dutch border, an impressive new sporting facility was built in 2006. With two flawless training pitches, a modern gym, a wellness centre and other luxurious amenities, Klosterpforte is a mecca for football teams. Watford FC and Turkish club Bursaspor have stayed there, so too Louis van Gaal with his team AZ Alkmaar. Klaas-Jan Huntelaar was a guest with Schalke 04, and the Portugal national team used the grounds to prepare for the 2006 World Cup. Ajax travelled to the training site in the picturesque German town of Harsewinkel for its first training camp under Ten Hag.

While training sessions at De Toekomst (The Future), the Ajax grounds, had become increasingly secretive in recent years, the training in Germany was more accessible. It was hot during Ajax's stay, but that was no reason to take it easy. As always, micromanager Ten Hag kept a very close eye on everything happening around him. He was not satisfied with the sprints and would intervene after a poorly executed exercise. 'Okay, let's do another one. Noa [Lang] does not follow the line. You have to function as a team, I said.' The division of labour was clear. Carlo l'Ami focused on the keepers, Björn Rekelhof did the physical training, while Aron Winter and Richard Witschge focused on individual players. Ten Hag and his assistant Alfred Schreuder were involved with the group every moment of the training. Schreuder led the various forms of positional play, with Ten Hag more in an observing role. During the practice games, the head coach asserted himself more. If the team in vests put pressure the wrong way, so that the other party could easily play in between, Ten Hag immediately stopped the match to make the necessary corrections.

The previous season, Ten Hag had no other option but to build on the work of his predecessor, Marcel Keizer. There was no time to introduce the players to a rigorously different system. In Harsewinkel, he reviewed his first six months at Ajax and established priorities. He said, 'We have two important focal points during this training camp. First of all, of course, the physical part. The second week of training we want to lay a good organisational foundation. Our way of playing is central to this: instilling patterns, automatisms, familiarising players with our game principles, how we want to play. Dominant and attractive. The run-up to the new season is longer now. During the past six months, we also had opportunities to make things trainable during the week, so it's not like we're starting from scratch. That is an advantage. But now we can tighten things up from the start under excellent conditions and that is important. In my opinion, in the first half of a football year the foundation is laid, and in the second part of the season you can work more on the details.'

He had to convince his players of the necessity of doing things in a completely new way. One of the aims was to accustom them to zonal marking rather than man-marking, something relatively uncommon in the Netherlands. At Bayern, Ten Hag had gained experience with zonal marking, and he worked on transferring this new knowledge and awareness to the Ajax players. 'There definitely is progress. The moments when they lose sight of it are decreasing. Zonal marking should provide us with more opportunities when we can move forward, putting on pressure that yields results. We are starting that development now, but it won't happen overnight. That needs to be instilled in the players' minds, and that's why it's important that we work on that now.'

Ajax was in Birmingham, England, from 14 to 20 July 2018 for a second training camp. Wolverhampton Wanderers and Walsall FC were their opponents on 19 July, at 3pm and 8:45pm, respectively. In what was Wolves' first pre-season friendly on English soil, they had to come from behind after Donny van de Beek had given Ajax the lead in the opening period. The game ultimately resulted in a 1–1 draw. At Walsall's Banks's Stadium in the West Midlands, Ajax were stunned in a 2–0 defeat by the League One outfit. The smattering of Ajax fans on hand were not impressed, but the Eredivisie team might be forgiven, given that they were playing with a B-team.

The training grounds of De Toekomst serve the first team of Ajax as well as the Ajax Youth Academy. Located close to the Johan Cruyff Arena, it comprises nine fields and a main pitch with an audience capacity of 2,000. On 20 June, the 2018 World Cup was still in the group stage, but the new football season had already started in Amsterdam. Nicolás Tagliafico, Lasse Schöne, Kasper Dolberg and Hakim Ziyech were still in Russia, but postponing the first day of training was not an option for Ten Hag. The games in the second qualifying round of the Champions League were looming on the horizon, and many young faces could be seen in new training kits. Ten Hag was at the training ground early on most days and would go for walks around the perimeter. According to a security guard's report the pensive coach sometimes would unwittingly pass a familiar face before doubling back to greet them.

In the new format of the Champions League, large sums of money – about €15 million – beckon for a team that qualifies for the group stage. In Amsterdam, every effort was made to be ready by the end of July. That meant short holidays. Ten Hag was uncompromising, saying, 'Even if Nicolás Tagliafico makes it to the final at the World Cup with Argentina, he will still play with us against Sturm Graz ten days later. It is very important, and Nico is fit and familiar with our system. During the season we will see when we can give him a moment of rest. We will look at that on a case-by-case basis. Lasse Schöne and Kasper Dolberg are still active in Russia as well. It also has to do with their status there, starting player or substitute.' Five weeks before the meeting with Austrian club Sturm Graz, the focus was already on their two-legged confrontation. A win in the first two official matches meant European football from then until the winter break.

At Ajax, Erik ten Hag emulated Rinus Michels, Johan Cruyff and Louis van Gaal quite openly. 'Louis is an example for me, just like Rinus Michels and Johan Cruyff. They have had the greatest influence at Ajax, but their importance transcends the club. They have influenced football in the world. The three are keys to the philosophy I also follow: attacking football that inspires. I see myself in their tradition.' He borrowed specifically from the 1995 Ajax team, which had won the Champions League under Van Gaal. 'I hesitate to say it,' Ten Hag admitted, 'but a few elements are similar. It is about possession, movement, vertical attacking patterns and pressing. The wingers move to the centre to make space for the wing defenders. The midfielders get the ball from the defence. It's about playing in the opponent's half as much as possible. All attack, all defend.' Ten Hag has his own conceptions about football and caused a small revolution by converting the 4-3-3 to a 4-2-3-1. He thought the group would split up before it could become a golden generation, but he hoped that if they could keep the same team for two years, 'maybe with two new players, we would be a candidate for the semi-finals of the Champions League'. It did not take that long.

The Netherlands don't have the four automatic Champions League spots that England, Spain, Italy and Germany are given. After finishing second in the Dutch league the previous year, Ajax had to play three games to qualify. To increase chances of Dutch involvement at the highest stage, there periodically was some talk of a joint competition with Belgium. Ten Hag was somewhat open to the idea. 'I certainly won't say no in advance. But it depends on how fast international development goes. It seems that the landscape will change in the near future, with more guarantees of European participation. In that case, a Beneliga may not be the solution. Whatever is decided, we can already start strengthening the Eredivisie, so that there is more resistance and a commercially more attractive format. Clubs then can perform better in Europe. The policy of the KNVB and the Eredivisie should be aimed at ensuring that all clubs meet the requirements of top performance sports. That's the only thing that's sustainable in the long run. Nothing else is.' Considering the limited Dutch involvement in the Champions League in recent years, qualifying via the play-offs would be an impressive achievement. In reality, the performance level soared far beyond expectations. Ajax played six matches in the preliminary round, with only the second half in Liège going in fits and starts. Otherwise, the team smoothly played around its opponents.

On 25 July, Ajax started its European campaign with the home match against Sturm Graz. The World Cup had just ended. Dušan Tadić had not yet made his debut, Daley Blind had not been reintegrated into the changed formation and Frenkie de Jong was still positioned at centre back. Despite these limitations, Ajax showed its class, with an outstanding Hakim Ziyech, winning comfortably 2–0. Over the two legs, they scored five times against Austria's second-strongest team. The productivity was as high with five goals against Standard Liège, the number-two team in Belgium. The net was found three times in the first game against Dynamo Kyiv, the runner-up in Ukraine. Ten Hag's Ajax demonstrated that it's possible to play your style in the Champions League while still getting results – four wins and a draw, something that had been considered by many impossible to achieve for a Dutch club. Ten Hag thought and acted offensively. His vision caught on with the team, and the spark of the team ignited the supporters. The atmosphere at the European home matches was electrifying: the Johan Cruyff Arena boiled from start to finish. The match against Standard Liège may have been the best home event in years.

The attack proved to be the best defence in the return match against Dynamo Kyiv. The Ukrainian team's promise to play attacking football was kept only in the first ten minutes of the game. As soon as Dynamo won the ball, both wing defenders pulled forward in an attempt to cause Ajax problems. The strategy was short-lived due to the effective Amsterdam response. Together with De Ligt and Blind, Frenkie De Jong, dropping deep, brought stability to the play and limited Dynamo's attack to the first stage of the first half. Through ball possession Ten Hag's team controlled the match and frustrated

Dynamo's hope of a comeback. The game ended 0–0, which was enough for Ajax to qualify. The supporters had to wait four years for it, but Ajax had reached the group stage of the Champions League, in bold and confident style.

The accomplishment earned the club a lot of praise in the media. Twitter commentary was, of course, first: 'Everyone complained about Overmars and especially Erik ten Hag. Nevertheless, they stuck to it, went against the grain, spent money and ensured that Ajax qualified for the Champions League with good football. Ajax, with many of its own boys, is slowly becoming Ajax again!' 'You can talk all you want, but Ajax and Ten Hag have done something that seemed almost impossible before. And the way they did it, too, was really great class.' *De Volkskrant* wrote,

> The qualification is justified and deserved. Ajax also had the class to return cachet to Dutch club football and will eagerly look forward to the draw on Thursday. It was good to see how Ajax dominated and combined, kept the ball in the team and sought the attack, thanks to depth in the game, technical ability and cleverness.

The *Algemeen Dagblad* saw that Ajax was the much better side even without taking advantage of opportunities.

> Ajax was superior even when they were sloppy. This is sporting revenge for the past season when Ajax was not active in the group stage of a European tournament, for the first time since time immemorial. It is also a huge boost for trainer Erik ten Hag who delivered a top performance with this qualification.

In the group stage, the world saw how Ajax stopped Bayern Munich in the Allianz Arena. The match was played at a time when Bayern was adrift in the Bundesliga, but Mats Hummels nevertheless managed to put his team ahead early on. Noussair Mazraoui equalised and the match stayed that way. Drawing 1–1 away at Bayern is a big accomplishment. The return match was not the cleanest, and certainly was one of the more bizarre confrontations of the Champions League campaign. The Ajax players followed their coach's instructions, out-possessing the Germans 55 to 45 per cent. After a dazzling 97-minute encounter, the counter stood at 3–3, meaning that Bayern Munich was still the group winner. During the game, after first falling behind, Ajax restored the scoreline to 2–1 by the 82nd minute. After a frenetic final phase there suddenly were six goals, three on each side. The symmetry did not end there: Robert Lewandowski and Dušan Tadić scored braces, with the second goals coming through penalties from both. Ajax's Maximilian Wöber and Bayern's Thomas Müller were both sent off within eight minutes of each other. Four of the six goals were scored when each team had only ten men on the field. The matches against Portuguese and Greek opposition were less spectacular, but yielded the required result. On aggregate, Ajax edged out Benfica 2–1 and dispatched AEK Athens decisively 5–0. Ajax reached the knockout stage in the Champions League for the first time since 2005.

Like everyone at and around Ajax, Erik ten Hag was happy, although he expressed it in his typically measured way. 'This is the most difficult job as a trainer in the Netherlands, but at the same time the most beautiful. Ajax has 4.4 million followers on social media. That's as much as the rest of the Eredivisie put together. That's huge [in a country of 17 million people]. Those people are interested and they have an opinion. The Dutch always have to have an opinion. That is part of our culture. I am not naive. Being an Ajax coach is a kind of reverse car wash: you go in clean and come out dirty. All Ajax trainers, without exception, have come under fire. You have to have a certain imperturbability to survive here. But this also is the best job: you get to work with the best players, the greatest talents, with the best facilities. And then you get to experience a series of 12 European matches like we did over the past few months. The team had to become Europe-proof. The entire European campaign was a highlight: the joy in Kyiv when the qualification for the Champions League was a fact. All the home games were a big party because of the interaction between players and fans. It is especially enjoyable to see people enjoying us. The way we played won the hearts of the people. That was probably the best thing.'

There was no lack of purpose and drive in the Champions League campaign. Ajax did very well to qualify for the round of 16, but also received a lot of cards getting there: 17 yellow and 1 red were collected in the group stage. Only Valencia got more that Champions League season. Of the clubs that were still in the race, Ajax collected the most yellow cards. The card records are not cleared until the semi-finals, so several Ajax players were on edge. Players with two yellows had to be careful, because a third card would result in a suspension.

Football intelligence and social intelligence can go well together, as was demonstrated by Ajax personnel during the Christmas break. The club got a lot of compliments about videos that appeared on social media: Erik ten Hag reading a poem and talking about the wise men from the east; the emotional message on the morning of Real Madrid–Ajax, in which Donny van de Beek's father, Kasper Dolberg's sister and Hakim Ziyech's best friend left messages for their loved ones. Prior to Ajax's Florida training camp, they created a light-hearted video series in which players were tested on their knowledge of the USA. The first episode with Nicolás Tagliafico was a hit. The footage showing a Dušan Tadić who had never heard of Michael Jackson's *Thriller* or Pharrell Williams was hilarious.

On 5 January 2019 Ten Hag and his team flew to Orlando to get in shape for the continued pursuit of their 34th national championship. Ajax played the first match of the Florida Cup against Brazilian club Flamengo, which plays its home matches at the iconic Maracanã Stadium in Rio de Janeiro. Flamengo is Brazil's most beloved team and, together with its maligned fellow Cariocan team Fluminense, holds the record for most spectators ever at a match: 194,603 was the official tally (observers at the derby said that the counters were too tired to keep track after that). Ajax played with a B-team and the match ended in a 2–2 draw. Flamengo won the penalty shootout. Ajax played its second and last match in the United States against São Paulo. That was a special day for David Neres, because the wing attacker started his senior career with the team before moving to Amsterdam. Ajax won 4–2, and Matthijs de Ligt was named man of the match. In addition to Ajax and the two Brazilian teams, Eintracht Frankfurt participated in the tournament. Flamengo won the fifth edition of the Florida Cup, with Ajax a point behind in second place.

In the Champions League round of 16, Ajax had the misfortune to draw against Real Madrid. The Champions League winner of 2016, 2017 and 2018 defeated Ajax 2–1 in the Johan Cruyff Arena. Supporters, analysts and journalists had little faith in a good outcome at the away match at the Bernabéu. Valentijn Driessen, football chief of *De Telegraaf*, was so certain of failure that he demonstratively did not travel to Spain: Ajax would not stand a chance at the Real Madrid home ground. But on 5 March 2019 Erik ten Hag and his team got sweet revenge. It was a one-in-a-million match. A perfect game, played on the biggest imaginable stage, against one of the greatest clubs in the world.

Because of the deficit, Ajax could not stay deep against Madrid but had to play an aggressive, attacking style from the opening whistle. After only a few minutes they narrowly escaped when Raphaël Varane's free header hit the crossbar. On the other side, the first Amsterdam attack was immediately on target. A slider by Hakim Ziyech made it 1–0, and the crowd sat up. David Neres made them jump to their feet by poking in the second goal. Real tried to storm the Ajax goal after the break, to no effect. Shortly after the hour came the Ajax uppercut. Noussair Mazraoui barely kept the ball in at the touchline. Moments later the ball fell for Dušan Tadić, who struck it beautifully: 3–0. Marco Asensio soon eased the tension a fraction by pulling one back. But before fans in the away section got the jitters, there was an Ajax free kick on the left. True to form, Lasse Schöne raised an arm as a signal for his teammates. Despite the scoreline, there still were eight Ajax players in the Madrid half waiting for the cross. They might as well not have been there: the Dane brilliantly swept the ball beyond the immense reach of 6ft 7in. goalkeeper Thibaut Courtois for 4–1. In Madrid, Ajax experienced the best evening of its twenty-first-century club history.

The image created by photographer Etsuo Hara tells the story of Real Madrid–Ajax most concisely. Stars Luka Modric and Vinicius Junior sit on the grass, their body language expressing disbelief. Frenkie de Jong speeds away with the ball at his feet. Next to him, David Neres dives into space. The baroque composition captures the reality of the day: Ajax as a team of lightning-fast movement, brilliantly taking advantage of the spaces, stunning Real Madrid and putting them to rout. Tactics outsmarted power, crushing an elite club in a defining match of the Champions League. If Erik ten Hag produced a masterclass of the Dutch school, it was a variation with new influences: still adventurous and technically gifted, but enriched with tempo changes and modern pressing play. Dutch, but no longer naive or otherworldly.

Euphoria reigned in footballing Netherlands. The miracle of Bernabéu marked the end of an unprecedented football crisis. After the Spanish spectacle, the Dutch armchair generals of football asked who coach Ten Hag and his players should still be afraid of. Ajax-Amsterdam was once again regarded with admiration and respect. And the equally important corollary: Dutch football regained a measure of esteem. The people of the Netherlands have grieved the loss of its golden generation and the glory days in the stadiums. It is not easy for Dutch football fans to see Belgian players outrunning, outplaying and outscoring Dutch players, and Belgium in toto outperforming the Netherlands for the better part of a decade. In Madrid, justice was done; Dutch football was resurrected, Holland's dignity restored.

On 16 April 2019, Turin's Curva Sud stand roared frantically to the final notes of the Champions League anthem, reminding the Ajax players of the grandeur of this stage. On the field a bombastic light show ushered in the evening. After a drawn first leg in Amsterdam, Juventus wanted to storm to victory, doing what they had done to Atlético Madrid in the round of 16. In the Allianz Stadium, Ajax faced its ultimate test of strength against Italy's premier football team, who in the first half were the better side. But after the break Ajax whirled, freed from doubts, playing with guts and bravado. With a small tactical tweak Ten Hag engineered Ajax's midfield dominance. De Jong and Van de Beek moved a little higher up the pitch, Lasse Schöne dropped a little deeper. The Ajax faithful sang praises of the tactical ingenuity of the coach. It turned into a merciless reckoning with an old adversary. The tables were turned: men played like boys and boys played like men. The Curva Sud became increasingly quieter as the match progressed, and the crowd in the away section sang louder and louder. Ninety blistering minutes later, it was a reality: Ajax had reached the semi-finals of the largest club tournament in the world.

It takes some doing to convince Italians that they have been properly outclassed. Ajax did just that in Turin. The morning after the 2–1 victory to the Dutch, *La Gazzetta dello Sport* published their report, zeroing in on the purchase of Cristiano Ronaldo the previous summer, declaring that one player cannot make the difference – it's all about the team and Ajax understood that.

> Cruyff's 14 rules for football players. Teamwork is number 1: 'If you want to do things well, you have to do them well together.' Number 9: 'Technique. It is the basis of every-thing.' Number 14: 'Creativity. It's the beauty of sport.' Erik ten Hag's Ajax has it all. A perfectly organised game idea, which is combined with quality, technique and courage. Cruyff's grandchildren overwhelmed Juventus, in terms of execution even more than in terms of the result. They deserved the semi-finals.

The Amsterdam-based *De Volkskrant* focused on Erik ten Hag's work on the players' fitness levels, a Ten Hag hallmark.

> Juventus–Ajax was an intense fight, a fight that had to end in bitterness for one and euphoria for the other. Ajax won, just like in Madrid against Real. It is unbelievable. Ajax knocked Cristiano Ronaldo out of the tournament, the king of the Champions League who was summoned to Turin to win the cup here too. Ajax was better, and much

fitter. Trainer Erik ten Hag almost always fields the same team, but the players are in a great flow and think they are invincible.

The Independent was not short of superlatives for the great Ajax: 'This is the greatest story in the modern history of the Champions League because it is entirely at odds with every other page of it. This is a proud historic club but a financially powerless one. David only killed one Goliath; Ajax have now killed two in six weeks.'

Edwin van der Sar, the chief executive of the Dutch club he first joined as a 20-year-old goalkeeper in 1990, won four league titles, three Dutch Cups, the UEFA Cup in 1991 and the Champions League in 1995 during his time as a player with Ajax, before leaving for Juventus, later joining Fulham and then Manchester United. When he returned to Amsterdam in an administrative capacity, he spent many afternoons watching Ajax's youth teams in training. Sitting inside the 55,000-capacity stadium named after club legend Johan Cruyff, his attention once again turned to winning trophies. Ajax had beaten Juventus, the club that proved too strong for the former in the 1996 Champions League final and 1997 semi-finals. That was at the time when Van der Sar was still playing for the Amsterdam side. Ironically, the 6ft 6in. goalkeeper moved to Italy shortly thereafter to spend two years in Turin, but, he now says, those years weren't his happiest time as a footballer. After Ajax's triumph in Turin, Van der Sar expressed his deep satisfaction with the club's progress: 'It's great that all the puzzle pieces finally are coming together. Sometimes it doesn't work in one go. But this is what you've been working for, investing in and putting up with crap for, for years on end. Then it is very nice if you get this result. In terms of budget, we are at the bottom of the list at this stage of the Champions League. But Ajax is a big name in football. As football players in the Netherlands, we can all be proud and happy that we pulled it off.' And as a pleasing footnote: reaching the last four earned Ajax another €12 million.

Measured by investment in player acquisition and salaries, Ajax were the smallest semi-finalist in the Champions League since Villarreal in 2006. But that was a different time. The dominance by the superclubs was not yet a fact. In 2005 PSV was the last Dutch club in the last four, stumbling over AC Milan. In 2004 FC Porto won the final against AS Monaco, after knocking out Spanish side Deportivo La Coruña in the semi-finals. Such a mosaic of teams in the highest circles of European tournament football became impossible with the rise of the superclubs. In the last ten years Europe's elite clubs took an almost insurmountable lead. Thanks to countless millions poured into clubs by Arabian oil sheiks and Chinese business moguls, and the explosive growth of television and marketing money, these clubs have gained a financial edge that is difficult to compete with for clubs in smaller leagues.

In Spain, FC Barcelona and Real Madrid pushed each other to the edge – Barcelona nearly fell off – spurred on by sponsorship deals and duelling prima donnas Lionel Messi and Cristiano Ronaldo. Bayern Munich ran away in Germany. In Italy, Juventus pulled themselves out of the morass of scandal, with a relentless dominance in Serie A, winning the scudetto nine times during the previous decade. Of the four clubs in the semi-finals of the 2019 Champions League, Ajax had spent the least amount of money in the previous five years. FC Barcelona had spent €930 million; Liverpool, €770 million; Tottenham Hotspur, €445 million, and Ajax, €145 million. The fact that Ajax managed to squeeze itself between these footballing behemoths, completely against the current, was an unprecedented achievement. Ajax's advance to the Champions League semi-finals made the team the talk of European football.

• • •

Ajax supporters took the Tube to Seven Sisters and walked down Tottenham High Road. After half an hour of walking between neighbourhood shops and uninviting restaurants with lots of neon lights, something futuristic suddenly popped up. To the Dutch fans, Tottenham Hotspur's new home was something phenomenal. Everyone decided for themselves whether or not it was beautiful, but all Dutchmen agreed that there was nothing else like Spurs' stadium. Spurs supporters do not have a reputation of being fanatics, but the acoustics inside were so extraordinary that 'Oh When the Spurs Go Marching In' could not possibly have been any louder. But only Ajax did the marching on the pitch.

It should have been Tottenham's party: a first Champions League semi-final in their magnificent new stadium. But Donny van de Beek's 15th-minute goal, the only one of the match, put Erik ten Hag's exciting young team in the driver's seat going into the second leg in Amsterdam. Ajax neutralised the Tottenham effort and the English team was forced to lob one long ball forward after another to try to get something out of the game. Spurs struggled to overcome the absence of Harry Kane and Son Heung-min – injured and suspended respectively. Occasionally, Fernando Llorente would create something, but more often not. Ajax came close to adding a second goal when David Neres struck the inside of the post, with Spurs goalkeeper and captain Lloris beaten.

Matthijs de Ligt was the youngest player ever in a Europa League final at 17 years old. Two years later, he had already played 75 games in the Eredivisie. At Tottenham, the 19-year-old team captain

Ten Hag with his local team SV Bon Boys, in the Dutch village of Haaksbergen, where he was born (top row, third from the right).

Making his professional debut for FC Twente in 1989.

As a player for De Graafschap in the early nineties.

Ten Hag retires as a player for FC Twente in 2002,
but stays on at the club as head of training.

During his time as FC Twente's assistant
coach, talking to head coach Steve
McClaren on the bench.

Whilst Ten Hag was PSV Eindhoven's
assistant coach, at the City Ground for
Nottingham Forest against PSV Eindhoven.

Ten Hag, as head coach at Ajax, greeting Cristiano Ronaldo (top image) and celebrating with players (lower image) after they defeat Juventus.

Celebrating Ajax's 4–1 victory over Real Madrid at the Bernabéu Stadium with André Onana.

Ajax win the KNVB Cup Final on 5 May 2019, Dutch National Liberation Day.

With Matthijs de Ligt for De Graafschap against Ajax at the De Vijverberg, the Netherlands.

After Ajax against PSV Eindhoven, the Johan Cruyff Schaal (Dutch Super Cup), in Amsterdam.

With Edwin van der Sar before Ajax defeat FC Emmen in Amsterdam.

At an Ajax training session at Quinta do Lago in Portugal.

With player escorts at GelreDome in Arnhem for Vitesse against Ajax.

Celebrating Ajax's triumph over SC Heerenveen (top image: with Dušan Tadić, bottom image: jubilant Ajax players throw Ten Hag into the air).

Posing at Old Trafford after being appointed manager of Manchester United, 2022.

Manchester United's 4–0 victory over Liverpool at Rajamangala National Stadium, Bangkok.

With Marcus Rashford celebrating victory over Leeds United at Elland Road (top image).
Manchester United win the Carabao Cup at Wembley Stadium,
defeating Newcastle United 2–0 (bottom image).

showed leadership qualities beyond his years in defence, organising and directing more experienced teammates with confidence and expertise. With Frenkie de Jong, 21, and fellow midfielder Van de Beek, just a year older, this was an Ajax team with the class and youthful appearance that harked back to the club's origins. 'The Dutch did, the English hesitated,' *The Times* wrote. Erik ten Hag simply said, 'Winning 1–0 at Tottenham is an amazing result. We have to learn lessons from tonight, and next week we have to finish it. It's an excellent result. We're good in defence too. We can play football in different styles, defend really well. We won, we are satisfied – but we are only halfway through. If you want to get to the final, you have to improve – every day we want to get better.'

Ajax lost only once during the 17-match stretch of the 2018–19 Champions League campaign. The club won a match in the semi-finals of the Champions League for the first time since 17 April 1996, when Ajax beat Panathinaikos 3–0 in Greece, with goals from Jari Litmanen and Nordin Wooter. The 2019 goal scorer Donny van de Beek was born a year later. Ajax also recorded a clean sheet for the first time since 1996 in an away match in the knockout phase of the Champions League. It was the first time in 20 consecutive Champions League games for Tottenham Hotspur that the team did not score. That last happened on 2 November 2016, when Bayer Leverkusen won 1–0 at Wembley.

Regardless of all the plaudits, the Champions League tournament ended in tragedy for Ajax and Ten Hag. The way Tottenham Hotspur slammed the door to the final shut was particularly painful. When De Ligt and Ziyech ensured a 2–0 half-time score in the return, Ajax fans were already scanning their mobile phones for plane tickets to the final. In the second half, however, Lucas Moura became arch-enemy number one in Amsterdam. With a hat-trick, the Brazilian single-handedly eliminated Ajax and secured a place in the final for Tottenham. After this hammer blow Ten Hag said, 'The Champions League final is unique, the players understand that very well. You need time to process this. That won't happen in a day. But we have to start that process on time, otherwise we won't be ready for the game next Sunday.' The incredible episode will long be remembered by thousands of supporters, who were singing with pride in their club shirts on Bairro Alto in Lisbon, Plaza Mayor in Madrid and Piazza San Carlo in Turin.

Journalists from the largest newspapers across Europe wanted to know more about the seemingly imperturbable, unknown man managing Ajax. An Israeli TV camera crew made its way from Tel Aviv to Haaksbergen, visiting his amateur club Bon Boys to uncover the hidden springs of the genius football tactician. Meanwhile, Ten Hag was more interested in large-scale analysis. Even with the huge financial and resource disparities among European clubs, which make it 'impossible for a club from the Netherlands, Belgium or Portugal to insert itself', Ten Hag understood what Ajax had achieved: 'We were so close. I think we played a good game, but of course there were also bad moments. We played a fantastic series. We have grown incredibly as a team and as individuals, have done an amazing job. We have to process this, but eventually we have to get up.' FIFA shortlisted him for best coach in the world after the sensational performance. The modest football master responded, 'That doesn't mean much to me.'

Onno Aerden is a writer who gives 'unsolicited communication advice' to Dutch notorieties in a weekly blog. He wrote a paean to trainer Erik ten Hag:

A few minutes after the improbable loss of your club Ajax, in the semi-final of the Champions League, you said this in front of the cameras. You said it in a hoarse voice, but calmly, in full control of yourself. No tears, no big words, no curse. Every word lucid. Here stood a man who, on the most insane night of a crazy football season, radiated the calmness of a great leader. Crisp, businesslike, with a beautiful Twente accent: your conversations with representatives of the media are a relief to listen to among all the inflated bleatings of quite a few colleagues and commentators. That class is all the more remarkable because you have been ridiculed for months by 'football experts'. These gentlemen had no use for your extremely successful coaching career, which, among other things, three years ago, yielded the national trainer's prize – named after a coach whom they do consider great, Rinus Michels. On the eve of the KNVB Cup final won by your team, we were granted an insight into your deeper self through two aphorisms that could be put on a plaque: 'The person is worth more to me than the athlete,' and 'Ultimately, the leader is part of the process and must be able to subordinate himself to it.' My awe of you, already considerable during this season, has been greatly increased by the almost stoic way in which you react publicly – not only to wins and painful losses, but to the rats who completely wrongly keep gnawing at the legs of your chair. You are a communicator, a trainer, a world-class person.

Ajax won the KNVB Cup final on 5 May, Dutch National Liberation Day. When Ten Hag took over, Ajax hadn't won the cup in eight years. It had been four years since they had gone past the round of 16. While Frank de Boer dominated the Eredivisie for four years, he never managed to win the cup. It was a classic clash between a top club and a provincial challenger for whom the final could momentarily interrupt an otherwise anonymous existence. Ajax was a team of motivated players dressed in their black-and-beige away kit, the colours that Europe had become well-acquainted with. They were supervised from the touchline by Ten Hag, who takes all competitions equally seriously, whether cup, national title or Champions League. The game ended in a 4–0 drubbing of Tilburg's Willem II. The frustration had come to an end, the longest period the club had gone without winning a trophy in 53 years, and five years since their last prize. After the cup win, Erik ten Hag said on FOX Sports, 'The first prize has been won, but we are not satisfied yet. It's nice that we have something tangible. I am very happy to win this prize for the fans, because they have had to wait a long time for it.'

There had been concern after the Tottenham defeat that the season might collapse before its end. But Ajax overcame their Champions League disappointment and brought the national title back to Amsterdam for the first time since 2014. During the domestic 2018–19 season – in a blistering title battle with PSV – quite a few important hurdles were cleared. After the difficult start to the competition, Ajax recovered and strung together a series of big victories. FC Emmen and AZ were defeated 5–0, and the victories over Excelsior (7–1) and De Graafschap (8–0) were even more lopsided. After the winter break, Ajax dropped points against SC Heerenveen and lost away to Feyenoord, Heracles Almelo and AZ. The match against leaders PSV therefore was vital. The Eindhoven team was five points ahead and could decide the title fight in Amsterdam. But Ten Hag's team dictated the game and took the lead thanks to an own goal by PSV centre back Daniel Schwaab. After the break the game was turned on its head when Noussair Mazraoui received a red card, and the subsequent equaliser was scored by Luuk de Jong. The championship was within PSV's reach. But down to ten men, Ajax showed real character. Dušan Tadić scored a penalty, regaining the lead, and in the dying seconds David Neres decided the game.

Ten Hag insisted that his team would end the season 'with style and class' in Doetinchem. Defending champions PSV Eindhoven were the only side who could have mathematically caught Ajax, but their 3–1 win over Heracles was rendered irrelevant following their rival's 4–1 victory at De Graafschap. Ajax only needed a point from their final match of the season to secure the title, but ended up taking all three courtesy of goals from Schöne, Tagliafico and two from top goal scorer Tadić. Ajax ended the season with impressive stats: 86 points and 119 goals in 34 Eredivisie games. Ajax secured the Eredivisie title and sealed their first domestic double in 17 years.

During the 2019 Dutch Trainers' Congress, Erik ten Hag again received the Rinus Michels Award. He had won the national title, the KNVB Cup and guided Ajax to the semi-finals of the Champions League. He had gradually moulded his team into a smooth-running collective that played the football he wanted: placing early pressure on the opponent, responding immediately when gaining or losing possession, and playing in the opponent's half without getting caught off-guard in front of their own goal. In the Eredivisie, the style he advocated went painfully wrong a few times, including against PSV and Feyenoord. But in Europe it led to a truly impressive series – 18 matches in all – of compelling games that excited fans from the first to the final minutes. Ten Hag will forever be associated with the dazzling Ajax football of the 2018–19 season. In June 2019 his contract was extended until mid-2022.

11

FOOTBALL ARCHITECT

'An Architect is a person with Introverted, Intuitive, Thinking, and Judging personality traits. These thoughtful tacticians love perfecting the details of life, applying creativity and rationality to everything they do. Their inner world is often a private, complex one.'

MYERS-BRIGGS 16 PERSONALITY TYPES

Passengers landing at Schiphol Airport for the first time are struck by the Dutch landscape. Unlike almost any other in the world, it is perfectly two-dimensional: it is completely flat and looks like a huge grid of green squares – endless cow pastures and fields of sugar beets and corn, separated from each other by narrow drainage canals and rows of poplars. It may appear like an agricultural Manhattan (the once-upon-a-time New Amsterdam) with the grid of streets and avenues replaced by one of ditches and canals, or to football lovers, like a giant football training ground with an uncountable number of adjoining pitches. Some visitors find the structure and regimentation of the landscape oppressive; others find it fascinating. The Dutch take great pride in their civil engineering abilities and their capacity for creating land where once there was none. They have expanded the original landmass of the country significantly by transforming flooded marshlands, lakes and even parts of the sea into fertile new territory. They are fond of saying that 'God created the earth, but the Dutch created Holland.'

The geometry of the landscape is reflected in Dutch art. The great Dutch painters, like Rembrandt and Vermeer, were masters of perspective. Their contemporary Jan Steen was so famous for painting the messy interiors of seventeenth-century households that he earned himself a permanent place in the vernacular. 'A household of Jan Steen' is a derogation and means that someone cannot keep his home in order. But the apparent disorderliness of Steen's painting disguises a clear plan: each item has a strategic location and a specific purpose in the grand scheme of the design. Their lesser known contemporary Pieter Jansz. Saenredam almost exclusively painted the interiors of whitewashed churches. He is known to have taken extensive and exact measurements of the churches and produced several studies before getting down to the business of creating his highly stylised mathematical masterpieces in oil. Although they are light years apart in purpose, tradition and style, one of the best-known painters of the twentieth century, Piet Mondrian, had a similar obsession with linear design, which he ultimately reduced to its most basic form. Almost everyone in the world has seen a reproduction of his paintings on things ranging from Nike sneakers to Yves Saint Laurent dresses, with the distinctive black lines and white, black, red, blue and yellow rectangles.

Although the football field is the same size anywhere in the world, Dutch coaches and players learn to exploit the fixed space to the maximum. This is caused by an additional geographic peculiarity: the lack of space in the Netherlands. In terms of size, the country is ranked 131st in the world. In terms of people, it is the 16th most densely populated country, outranked mostly by compact city nations like Hong Kong, Singapore and Monaco. Space is at a premium and he or she who manages it well takes the honours. Hence, there is a certain compulsion in the Dutch attraction to 'the architect', not only the one who designs the buildings and the bridges, but also the one who draws the lines on the football pitch. Players like Johan Cruyff and Danny Blind have the ability to take a bird's-eye view of the entire football match in progress. Cruyff in particular was able to look at the pitch the Dutch way and is admired for his innate understanding of the geometric order of the field – a Euclid of football or 'Pythagoras in boots'. His masterly freeflowing style was only possible because he perfectly grasped the underlying order of the game, the potential lines of play.

In the movie *The Matrix Reloaded* (2003), Neo meets the Architect, a genius computer program that is the 'father' of the uncanny virtual world that humanity is trapped within. Other than the beard, Erik ten Hag bears little resemblance to this dystopian villain, and his purpose and motivation are not as sinister as those of the digital genius. But when it comes to designing, crafting, perfecting a network of component parts that matchlessly work together, he is just as competent. The strategies and tactics in operation on a football pitch have little in common with those working off the field. Teams playing a game follow a different set of rules and principles than people do on public transportation or in a restaurant. On the pitch, players are not allowed to use their hands, an odd feature absent from life in a corporate office. There is no offside rule in operation at a discotheque. The football world and the ordinary world are dramatically different. This is one of the reasons why some brilliant team players can be socially maladroit or even problematic outside the stadium. Football intelligence and regular intelligence have little in common with each other. Ten Hag possesses both, an essential requirement for a great football coach.

• • •

No understanding of Ajax is complete without reference to the godfather of Dutch football, Rinus Michels. The coaching legend – The Bull, The General, The Sphinx – was proclaimed by FIFA 'coach of the century' in 1999. Michels was one of the greatest coaches ever. He was also the inventor of 'total football', the influential tactical theory in which any player should be able to take over the role of any other player in the team. In total football, which Michels developed while head coach of Ajax, a player who moves out of his position is immediately replaced by a teammate. Thus the team retains its organisational structure. No player is fixed in his nominal role; anyone can be successfully a defender, midfielder and an attacker. Total football's tactical success depends largely on the adaptability of each player within the team, in particular his ability to quickly change positions depending on the situation. The theory requires players to be comfortable in multiple positions and to be able to exert the additional effort required to make such transitions. Hence it puts high technical and physical demands on them.

With its emphasis on attacking, total football became almost the religion of Dutch football fans. Yet it started out as something different. It was created by Michels not for aesthetic reasons but to win football matches. First at Ajax and later in the Dutch national team, his players were artists. But they were also extremely tough and assertive. Their tactics – pressing, position-switching, relentless attack – were designed purely for victory. Total football was the result of the search for a way to break open entrenched defences. This required actions during the build-up and attack that would surprise the opponent. Frequent changes in positions, within and between the three lines – defence, midfield and forward line – were required. All players were encouraged to participate in the build-up and attack as long as they were also responsible for their defensive duties. The creation of space was central to total football. The constant switching of positions only was possible because of spatial awareness. It was about making a space-filled architecture on the football pitch.

For those who espouse the total football philosophy, the biggest problems are team building and strategy. It is important for the system to bring the skills of the team to the highest level through the establishment of clear relations between strikers, midfielders and defenders. Once players understand the core of modern football, they are able to use their unique qualities and skills for the team. Total football does not distinguish between defenders and attacking players. Strikers should actively participate in the defence. In the past, a striker did not join the defence because he thought he had already done enough if he had scored a goal. It is a minus for the whole team if the offensive players only attack.

The main aim of this type of attacking, pressing football was to regain possession as soon as possible after the ball was lost in the other half during an attack. The trapping of the opponents in their own half is only possible when all the lines are pushed forward and the team plays close together. The coach plans to play mostly in the opponent's half of the pitch, meaning the players will therefore have to defend far away from their own goal. This automatically means that the pressing team gives away a lot of space in its own half and is vulnerable to counter-attacks. Consequently, the team cannot afford to lose possession of the ball during this build-up play.

Total football, and the attacking pressure that is part of it, creates a spectacular kind of game. It is a feast for the spectators, and the Dutch fans have come to almost expect it from their teams, especially at Ajax. However, it puts great demands on individual players and the team as a whole. It requires top fitness and physical stamina, and it demands personal excellence and group integration. The approach requires deliberate player selection and structural team building. The assumption is that the coach will carry the play forward as much as possible. This is quite challenging and only a few coaches are audacious enough to fully commit to such tactics.

Johan Cruyff, the system's most famous exponent after Michels, said about Michels, 'I always greatly admired his leadership. Both as a player and as a coach there is nobody who taught me as much as he did. He was a sportsman who put the Netherlands on the map in such a way that almost everybody still benefits from it. There is no one I learned more from than Rinus Michels. I often tried to imitate him, and that's the greatest compliment one could give.' In many ways, total football was made for the greatest Dutch player of all time. Although Cruyff was fielded as centre forward, he wandered all over the pitch, popping up wherever he could do most damage to the opposing team.

The 1972 European Cup final proved to be total football's defining moment. After Ajax's 2–0 victory over Inter Milan, newspapers around Europe reported the death of *catenaccio* and the triumph of total football. The Dutch newspaper *Algemeen Dagblad* declared, 'The Inter system undermined. Defensive football is destroyed.' In 1972 Ajax won the European Cup, the Dutch league, Dutch Cup, Intercontinental Cup and European Super Cup. So far, only Pep Guardiola's Barcelona, in 2009, and Hansi Flick's Bayern, in 2020, have been able to improve on that.

Ajax became a club steeped in the total football philosophy of Michels and fired up by the attack-minded Cruyff. The *meevoetballende* goalkeeper, 'football-playing' keeper, drew the last man further away from the goal than more conventional playing styles warranted. Ajax's approach required a goalkeeper who did not comfortably remain in the penalty box, but who intercepted balls that fell behind the defence. He shared responsibility for the build-up of the attack and the rapid counters. This created an attractive but risky game. Flexibility was needed. If the attack encountered too much resistance on the right, a shift to the other wing might be needed. The wingers had to be prepared to suddenly receive the ball on the touchline and carry it forward, thus keeping the play wide. Every player had to be keenly aware of his own position and that of his teammates. This required team discipline, and the entire team had to be able to shift over the field as a unit.

Critics suggest that the intense pressing and high offside trap that total football prescribes – in order to keep the field small when out of possession and as wide as possible when in possession to retain the ball – was unsustainable. Particularly in modern times, the number of games and the pace at which they're played have become prohibitive in that regard. British sports writer Jonathan Wilson suggests in his book *Inverting the Pyramid: The History of Football Tactics* that even the great Ajax of the 1970s couldn't really pull it off. According to his research, 'Their team doctor had them on a steady diet of amphetamines, painkillers and muscle-relaxants.' According to the sceptics, many of the modern players are primarily specialists, unprepared to play in every position the way the rapid swapping of positions of total football demands.

In addition, clubs go through players so quickly today that many don't have the time to master the system, whereas the Ajax teams of the 1970s to the 1990s had been staffed largely from within, growing up together and learning the system in the academy. These days, players know they're more valuable if they play one position well, rather than being passable in two or three. In total football, the individual becomes a part of the machinery for the greater good. Self-sacrifice is irreconcilable with the mindset of the modern footballer. Ironically, the blame for that lies partly with Johan Cruyff, a child of the 1960s and an individualist who became the first Dutch football star to cross over into pop culture.

On the wall of Ten Hag's modest office are three black-and-white photos of ex-Ajax managers Rinus Michels, Johan Cruyff and Louis van Gaal. They are as much enlightening examples as they are reminders of the expectation that comes with being coach of Ajax's first team. In a *Guardian* article of 2015, Jonathan Wilson argued,

> The predominant style was that which has sustained Barcelona since the arrival of the Ajax coach Rinus Michels in 1971. He brought with him total football, a belief in possession football, rooted in a high offside line, pressing, and the interchange of players on the field and, in 1973, the great Dutch forward Johan Cruyff. When Cruyff became Barcelona's manager in 1988, he reinforced this philosophy and, although he saw the version of the game practised by his successor as manager, Louis van Gaal, as overly mechanised, the starting point was the same. This was perhaps the greatest coaching seminar in history, and the philosophy it taught was that which had been flowing from Ajax to Barcelona, which believed the same things but had more money, for three decades: what we might perhaps term the Barçajax school.

That creative, attacking style has been endemic to the Johan Cruyff Arena ever since, and Erik ten Hag was a strong and proud proponent.

Ten Hag holds Johan Cruyff in high regard, and the famous number 14 has been a source of inspiration for him. That is why there are photos of both the player and the trainer Cruyff in Ten Hag's office. 'I am sure that Cruyff would be the best as a footballer and as a trainer again. You can say that of only very few people because in football many people are dated at some point. That would never happen to Cruyff. Cruyff is timeless.' Ten Hag finds it difficult to say which Cruyff has inspired him more, the football player or the trainer. 'The two are connected. You cannot see them separately. As a football player he already was a trainer. He was so good that he could translate his way of thinking into the game. He was the trainer on the field and directed the entire team. Cruyff stood for creative, attacking football. Winning is important, but it also has to be done in an attractive way. You play football for the people, that was his view. I also apply those Cruyff ideals in my current work. I think Cruyff still walks around here [at Ajax] every day. You can feel his DNA here. I think the word "gogme" applies particularly well to that.' *Gogme*, a word regularly used by Cruyff, is another heirloom of Ajax-Jewish origin. It is originally a Yiddish word, derived from the Hebrew *chochmah*, meaning wisdom. It refers to insight, cleverness and cunning – three things a good Ajax player should possess in order to contribute to the team performance and style.

The golden days of Spanish football were defined by tiki-taka, the Spanish style of play characterised by short passing and movement, one-touch football, working the ball through the channels and maintaining possession. Its development and influence goes back to Johan Cruyff's tenure as Barcelona manager in the early 1990s. Tiki-taka methods were fine-tuned by Barcelona after the turn of the millennium, especially during the era of Pep Guardiola. But the current Manchester City manager eventually distanced himself and the club from the style, saying, 'I loathe all that passing for the sake of it. You have to pass the ball with a clear intention, with the aim of making it into the opposition's goal.' The enduring influence of the style was seen during Louis van Gaal's rather unfortunate spell as manager of Manchester United from 2014 to 2016, albeit without the speed, the precision and, most importantly, the effectiveness. Van Gaal was asked why he let the team play sideways, instead of forward. The fans hated it and it produced no results apart from possession stats upward of 60 per cent. The manager, meanwhile, condescendingly observed that during a game 'we still played the long ball', and that, of course, went against the tenets of the faith.

Erik ten Hag is much more pragmatic. 'Of course, I discuss with my team to what extent we should build up. If you do that right, you can control and dominate. That is a means to get a hold of the match, and that is ultimately what you want to achieve. But I deliberately do not say that we prefer to build up, because the long ball can also be an excellent means of creating a scoring opportunity. We should always keep that option open. If we can force an opponent who wants to pin us down high to defend one-on-one in the back, then a long ball can be an excellent choice. If an opponent blocks us one-on-one, I prefer to see a focused long ball. That long ball preferably should be given quickly, before the opponent has had the chance to get organised. But sometimes it happens that the keeper first gives a signal before playing the long ball and ensures that the whole team is in compact formation before he kicks the ball. It is important to have people making runs, players who can be reached by one of the strikers to extend the pass. That can be another striker, but also a midfielder or even a wing defender. In the end, players have to make their own risk assessment in the match. What I mainly do as a trainer is to provide opportunities to escape the pressure of the opponent.'

In an interview with *Voetbal International* he explained how important moments of transition are: 'The turnover is key. This has increasingly become a crucial element in international football today. We have to deal with that. And not only from a defensive point of view, but above all: what do we do when we win the ball? I often thought that at Ajax we think: winning the ball is playing possession. But if you win the ball, and the opponent is open, you have to recognise the moment and must immediately play forward. With FC Utrecht we were at the top halfway through the season in the percentage of goals scored within four passes after regaining possession. Ajax was in the middle bracket although these are often the moments when you can score, especially at Ajax, which often plays against closed defences. Of course it is not always possible. If the opponent is in a good position and the remaining defence is in order, you have to play on possession. But if they don't line up, you have to immediately take advantage and hurt the opponent. I also experienced it at FC Utrecht, this Hollanditis. If we won the ball, we played around in the back for a while, from central defender to central defender. I don't think there is any country in the world where defenders play the ball to each other so often. We have the ball, and we are going to play for possession. But possession then becomes an end instead of a means. You have to change that on the training ground, get it into players' heads. There has to be a lot of movement, not only where the ball is, but also on the opposite side, so that you can immediately play on the counter.'

The Dutch tendency to mindlessly play possession annoyed Ten Hag. He eradicated the disease of possession for its own sake by the root, with almost 60 per cent of Ajax's successful combinations taking place in the opponent's half. During the 2020–1 Eredivisie season, Ryan Gravenberch was the only player who managed to give a team-mate a pass in the opponent's half more than a thousand times. Daley Blind was in second place. That is indicative of the way Ajax generally found its way forward: via the creative left side. To score goals, you generally have to get into the opponent's box. In 2020–1, 85 per cent of the Eredivisie goals were scored from within the penalty area. The attacking mindset is also reflected in other statistics. Ajax were at the top of the ranking in terms of creating opportunities. In total, the opponent's goal was fired on about 20 times per game, of which 7.7 attempts went between the posts. This made Ajax more dominant in numbers in the Eredivisie than any club in a European top competition. Bayern Munich came closest with 16.7 shots per game, of which 6.8 were on target.

Wherever Ten Hag goes, he innovates. At Go Ahead Eagles he developed a counter system with which he outwitted the entire Eerste Divisie and advanced to the Eredivisie. At FC Utrecht he introduced a diamond in the midfield that was difficult to play against. At Ajax he took a good look at the available material and developed the 'Tadić variant' for the Champions League. The Serb played as a roaming centre forward, flanked by Hakim Ziyech and David Neres in a 4-2-3-1 formation, with Donny van de Beek behind playing as the number 10. 'At every club where I work, I stimulate things. Sometimes it is very simple. At Go Ahead I made everything more professional: there was a weight room, beds for the players to rest, and we served lunch. That was new there. At Utrecht I changed the system and in that way took the team out of their comfort zone. Peter Bosz, my predecessor at Ajax, started with putting high pressure, and we continued with that. It's not new, but we make different combinations. I am always looking for ways to innovate and move things forward.'

Ten Hag recognised that when people have to deal with changes, there is resistance, but he liked to, in his words, 'broaden things' at each club he was appointed to. He said, 'Over the decades, Ajax has been the poster boy of Dutch football. But you have to conclude that Dutch football has certainly not been revolutionary for some time.

In the Netherlands we still very much have the idea that we are the innovators. But if you are realistic, you have to conclude that we aren't at the moment. You should be talking about Spain and Germany. England is coming up, with the influences of the foreign coaches there. They lead the way. We don't. If we do not adapt, do not become innovative ourselves, then we will get stuck at the current level. There still is the feeling: *the way we do it, that is the truth.* At the very least, I question that. We have to go to a higher level, higher demands, higher standards. The trick is to stay true to yourself, but also to bring in things from outside that can contribute to positive development.'

In that last regard he admitted, 'There are many German elements in the way I work. I was at Bayern Munich for two years, after all. Through my interactions with athletes, I understood that my generation was brought up harder than the current generation. The generation before had an even tougher upbringing. Humiliating comments were certainly made, but the idea was that it made us more resilient. In top sport you have to push boundaries. Many studies have been done, especially in education, that show that the softer and positive approach yields better results with the current generation. A very critical approach is no longer accepted. That is the paradox of the story. The world around us has become so much harder. Just look at the media and social media and what they can do to athletes. They are full of anonymous negative things. You have to be able to handle that. The outside world is getting more aggressive. But internally we are getting softer, at school and also in top sport. Is that making talented players resilient? I don't judge these developments, but I do ask myself a lot of questions. It has been proven that being positive has the right effect. But it may also result in some top talent not crossing the boundary that top sport requires.' He concludes, 'Being the best requires a degree of toughness.'

Former De Graafschap coach Simon Kistemaker once called Ten Hag a hybrid model between the obsolete cult coach and the modern laptop trainer. 'He's a blend. Less hard than I am. A man who sticks to the facts, but not a laptop trainer who bases everything on data and statistics. Rather, a practical man who can really put himself in the shoes of players.' As head of the youth academy at FC Twente, Ten Hag introduced the club to mental coaching. He says, 'That was groundbreaking at the time. We had personalities of the young players analysed. I still do that to this day. All athletes need incentives, but some people need a different approach than others. That is not new anymore, but it continues to be very important. I also think it is very important to remember that you coach on behaviour, never on the person. That's where the borderline is for me.'

In terms of formation, Ten Hag hasn't really been tied down to one particular shape. He is able to effectively adapt his tactics to the individuals within the team. In Utrecht, he mostly used a 4-4-2 diamond or 4-3-3, although he occasionally reverted to a 5-3-2/3-5-2. At Ajax, he has used both 4-2-3-1 and 4-3-3. However, his teams rarely stick to these rigid structures when in possession. Instead, there is a lot of positional fluidity as they look to move forward and create an overload, with the full-backs always looking to push high in order to support the attack and force the opposition back. Ten Hag thinks that too much talk about systems misses the point. 'The qualities of the players determine the system, not the other way around. And it's not even about systems. One system is no longer applicable in current football anyway, that time is far behind us. In modern top football, it's about what you do in possession, when you lose possession and in moments of transition. You have to be able to be flexible.'

It is to Ten Hag's credit that he managed to pivot Ajax away from the traditional 4-3-3 – something that previously would have been considered sacrilegious – to a more fluid 4-2-3-1. The formation could shift to three at the back, or could morph into a 4-2-4, with a front four or even six at times. The two central midfielders were expected to do a lot of work. He turned to rising stars Ryan Gravenberch and Edson Álvarez to do that for him. Their role was as much playmaking as it was going from box to box. He tried to create conditions in which his players were in one-on-one situations. The wingers were aggressive and the team was expected to win the ball back immediately after losing it. He liked to play with both full-backs high on the pitch. It was the same with his two central defenders, Lisandro Martínez and Jurriën Timber, who were good on the ball and had pace. In addition, Martínez was tough when necessary and Timber had excellent defensive timing. The game plan had been fine-tuned so that players could use their specific skills as often as possible.

The coach said, 'Attack is the best defence. It's difficult to score against us because we attack with 11 and defend with 11. All the players in our way of playing have a job, and have to do that job with 100 per cent discipline. Achieve that, and it's difficult to score against your team.' He repeated ad nauseam that Ajax had more than 11 base players. In 2020–1, the depth and versatility of Ajax's selection was expressed in the number of goal scorers. No fewer than 20 different players scored for the Eredivisie champions. The number was a record in the Eredivisie's more than 60-year history.

Perhaps the greatest strength of Ten Hag's formation lies in the energy that is put into pressing the opponent. No one did that as successfully near the opponent's goal as Ajax. Ten Hag is an intensely attack-minded, possession-based manager who likes to press high up the pitch whenever possible, forcing the opposition into making mistakes close to their own goal. His style has been referred to as 'vertical tiki-taka', that is, possession with a purpose, where players look to build up from the back with many passing options for the man on the ball. Loss of possession triggers an aggressive, coordinated counter-press, which, if unsuccessful, can lead to being exposed on the counter-attack. For Ten Hag, the starting point is to force the opponent to the side by locking them in everywhere. Opponents were chased into their own penalty area by a winger who appeared next to the striker. That joint hunting ensured that opponents had little chance to launch effective counter-attacks. They often didn't even come close to the goal, and goalkeeper André Onana had little to do. Ajax kept the most clean sheets in the Eredivisie.

On the issue of clean sheets Ten Hag said, 'André is a great keeper. But it actually is the credit of the whole team. We are very disciplined in performing our duties. Defending is not something for the last line and the keeper, but for our entire team. It is an interplay between all players, chasing the ball up front, understanding each other and knowing what is being asked where. The players do that very well. To be in a good position in the organisation at all times and to be able to press as well. In top football you have to recognise the moments; because the speed is high, it comes down to anticipation. To confuse the opponent, we like to change position when we are in possession. But then it is also important to get into position quickly when you lose the ball.'

Ten Hag's team specialised in sharp, one-touch football utilising 'maximum width' – luring defenders out of position and then exploiting the emerging space. He likes his teams to 'shock and awe' opponents with quick starts. What animates Ten Hag most is the movement of his players when they don't have the ball. His players get extensive coaching on their positioning and the runs they're expected to make to create space for others. In an Ajax club interview, Ten Hag sits in the middle of an empty Johan Cruyff Arena, is shown five of the best Ajax team goals and asked to comment on them. The giant screen flashes on and shows a superb move against Willem II that culminates in a brilliant finish by Klaas-Jan Huntelaar. Ten Hag doesn't focus much on Huntelaar though, but is inspired by Dušan Tadić, who isn't even in the frame, distracting opposition defenders by moving close to the far post. 'That run is stressing out opponents,' Ten Hag explains. 'The foundation is teamwork. In order to destroy opponents, you need off-the-ball runs. Creating space for each other is really important.'

What is the key? According to Ten Hag, the priority is finding the balance. 'Bring together the right people. Van de Beek in midfield; Tadić up front.' The second? Awareness. He says, 'I constantly worked on that with the players. What is the essence of a functioning team? The key to winning is that the team has to defend well in order to be able to play attacking-style football. That requires player discipline. That is not a request, it is a demand. Number three: the tactics. What should you do? How are you positioned on the pitch when you are in possession, and what should you expect when you lose the ball? There also are different phases in a game. That's what we are training for, and the video analysis helps a lot with that. When they see the images, they understand things much more easily. And then you have to repeat, repeat, repeat. Until they recognise the situation ahead of time and can properly anticipate it.'

It all sounds very logical, but Ten Hag cautions, 'You do have to create the awareness that this is how it should be done. The turn-over, turnover, turnover. That's what matters to us, every day. When we lose the ball, we are leaving our spaces. How are you positioned at that moment? What do we do when we lose the ball? They have to be fully dedicated to working on that, only then it will function. Every hinge has to be right. The intensity with which you have to work on that is enormous. Maybe I have to push them even harder, make another step. But that naturally happens when you are more successful, then your authority increases automatically. As you grow through the years, you pull people along with you more easily.' The evolution of a team in this way is pivotal. 'The team is very closely connected. Wanting to work for each other, don't give up, keep faith, show resilience. It is a culture that you develop. Always wanting to get better. As an individual and as a team. There is hunger in this team. That is also what we demand, not only as staff of the players, but also among players themselves. That is very important to be successful as a team. All players are able to put their qualities at the service of the team. That starts with its composition, with the mix of different characters: leaders, team players and individualists. As a player you can have great qualities, but it is so important to have that mix as a whole. In addition to the characters, you consider the technical qualities, so you are looking for specialists and multifunctional players. The latter help your team become even more tactically variable. You look for the best mix in the team, where players complement and reinforce each other in the dressing room and on the field.'

What does this mean for football teams today, where, as Ten Hag says, a 'regular starting 11 has become pub talk. Fun to talk about with each other at the bar, but not of this time anymore'? The reality is that if you want to 'compete on three fronts, you need a wide selection of players. That mean that you have to vary who plays. Also, you have to regularly give enough minutes to the boys who play less frequently, so that they make an impact when called on. That makes the team stronger. To create multiple options in your group, you have to make those decisions continuously. You need at least 16 players who are equivalent to some extent. With the demands of the current playing calendar, that simply is a must to be successful at the end of the season.' Ten Hag doesn't change players for the sake of rotation. He keeps the faith with a familiar-looking first 11 in the big matches. But both the nature of the Eredivisie and Ajax's strength relative to other teams in the league mean he had the luxury of being able to shift out key personnel in matches against smaller teams.

Ten Hag has always tried to take the best from other coaches, those he worked with or closely observed: the human dimension and pragmatism of Guus Hiddink, Kistemaker's no-nonsense work ethic and pure dedication, the personal attention and empathy of Fred Rutten – especially when working with difficult players – and Guardiola's tactical intelligence and perfectionism. He speaks of the 'whole person principle', although he finds it a little pretentious to adopt the term coined by Louis van Gaal. But he manages his team in a similar way. He evaluates the functioning of his players on the basis of talent and character. Leadership is based on situational demands. 'When I coached a young team, my approach was different from when I worked with a more experienced team. When you are in a successful period, you are coaching differently from when you are in an unsuccessful period. So as a manager, you always have to adapt to the circumstances. You learn a lot and get more experience and you learn better how to deal with situations. I have improved as a manager.'

He claims, 'I focus on the things I can influence, I let go of the rest quite easily. Football is a complex sport. It is not only about tactics and technique, but also about physiological and social-emotional processes. A huge package. Fortunately, I can delegate things to people I trust. I ask them for feedback: am I doing it right? I don't gather a group of yes-men around me. You have to manage all the input. You don't learn that just at Go Ahead Eagles or FC Utrecht, where everything is much smaller. At Ajax, there is a constant flow of information, triggers and incentives. You have to channel all of that. Time management is very important. What do you prioritise? Ultimately, it's about making your team perform better. The rest is secondary. I will stay true to myself and will not change my view on coaching. The material always determines how you play, but I determine the requirements and the standards. I decide who fulfils which task. Whoever does not meet the requirements, will be told, regardless of who he is. I make no concessions in that regard.'

At the beginning of Ten Hag's journey with Ajax, there was, he admits, a lot of resistance. 'We had to initiate a transformation. There was a very negative mood within and around the club. The chagrin was palpable. It was a turbulent initial period, when the sentiment was very negative. I saw and heard everything, but chose my own path. That was a wise decision, focusing on my squad and developing the team. I didn't focus on fringe issues. Of course I had to manage a number of things, such as certain media, certain player situations and their interactions with the media. I had to convince the dressing room that we had to maintain our unity and do it together. Otherwise, we would end up pitted against each other, and that would not have yielded good returns for anyone. Over time, the dressing room has become tighter and more unified, and things have become calmer as a result. It was turned around and changed into a positive atmosphere. The club had to come a long way.'

12

AJAX HAT-TRICK

'Ten Hag has brought Ajax into modern times. There is more variation, less dogma, more end product.'

PIETER ZWART, *VOETBAL INTERNATIONAL*

The clouds hang low between the mountains and give the area a mysterious, even surreal appearance. The village of Bramberg am Wildkogel is sandwiched between the Zillertal and Kitzbüheler Alpen ski resorts. It is a popular destination for ski lovers in winter. In summer, the small town full of large chalets is quieter, the right setting for an intensive football camp. In July 2019, Ajax settle down for a week of training and two practice matches. The training is officially closed to the public. There is a sign: *ACHTUNG – Während der training von Ajax Amsterdam ist die Sportanlage gesperrt!* (ATTENTION – DURING THE TRAINING OF AJAX AMSTERDAM THE SPORTS FACILITIES ARE OFF LIMITS!) That does not discourage the locals from taking a peek, and the Ajax staff don't seem to mind.

There are the usual running drills, players moving the ball around the pitch, and a friendly game against Istanbul Başakşehir in the evening. Ajax fields almost two completely different teams in each half, and the match ends in a 2–1 win, albeit with the help of a Turkish own goal. Erik ten Hag can be heard instructing his players from some distance, the trainer's voice clearly audible in the crisp alpine air. He is the last to leave the field and is met by a group of fans at the gate. He patiently responds to every request for a selfie, gets on his mountain bike and follows his team to the luxurious players' hotel.

Ten Hag liked Austria: 'This environment gives off so much energy. We have many options for a good programme without attracting attention. In the Netherlands, everything and everyone is drawn to Ajax, but here we can work in peace. The players feel comfortable.' In terms of training for a new season, Ten Hag has a game plan already: 'Ajax has been successful, both in the Eredivisie and in the Champions League. Opponents are now adapting to our game, they are trying to disrupt it. So we must bring surprises, in the way we build up, in the way we get into attacking positions, and in the way we put pressure on our opponent. Modern top football requires being variable. The group is in good shape, but we still have to improve, in all areas. Moments of transition are always a crucial pillar of our game, just as pressure football should be a given. We also want to attack this season while keeping the back door locked. If you would single out an area for improvement, then I am thinking of dealing with the opportunistic play of an opponent, responding to a team who play the long ball.'

Success has its price at Dutch football clubs. At Ajax, in particular, team building is a revolving door. The great performances of the previous season got large European clubs interested, and Ajax lost its star players. Frenkie de Jong moved to FC Barcelona and Matthijs de Ligt to Juventus. That posed a challenge for Ten Hag. 'Of course we had a great season, but that is in the past. You can't simply compare the current performance with last season. Not just because we no longer have two key players, but also because all players together are a team. The nine who stayed can't play the same way with two different players around them. The team will have to take shape anew. People can expect us to go for the national title, and we are going to do that with an attractive team. But not that we are going to make it to the semi-finals of the Champions League again. Don't forget that until last season it was practically impossible for a Dutch club to qualify. We have to survive two rounds, the draw also plays a role, and there are no easy opponents in Europe. Don't get me wrong: Our ambitions are high, but we are just starting again empty-handed.'

That season, Ajax won almost all its matches in the Eredivisie and also seemed on the way to more Champions League glory in 2020, after 3–0 wins over both Valencia and Lille. But the game against Chelsea in Amsterdam was lost 1–0, and the return match at Stamford Bridge on 11 May 2019 produced bizarre statistics and controversial moments. After 55 minutes, Ajax was leading 4–1, but the match ended in a 4–4 draw. The goals scored at 1–0 and 3–1 were Chelsea own goals, courtesy of Tammy Abraham and goalkeeper Kepa Arrizabalaga. Thus Ajax became the first team to be gifted two own goals since Barcelona on 4 April 2018 against AS Roma. The 3–1 half-time score went on record as the first time in history that Chelsea had conceded three goals in the first half of a Champions League match. For Ajax it was the first time in history that they had scored three goals in the first half of a Champions League match. Daley Blind and Joël Veltman both received red cards within two minutes of each other. This made Ajax the first Dutch club to receive two red cards in a Champions League match since Feyenoord on 17 October 2001 against Sparta Prague. There was a lot to do with the red cards. Blind was shown a second yellow after an apparently minor foul, and Veltman was penalised for handball, although there was little he could have done to avoid it. Ajax was 4–2 ahead of the Londoners, but conceded two goals, playing with nine against 11.

With the injuries of Hakim Ziyech and newly arrived Quincy Promes, the team's performance became less powerful and at decisive moments disappointing. A narrow defeat against Valencia meant Ajax finished third in the group stage and were eliminated from the Champions League. Domestically things weren't much better, and a wandering Ajax was eliminated by FC Utrecht in the semi-final of the league cup. AZ was closing in on Ajax in the Eredivisie. It was up to Ten Hag and his team to restore the gap with Alkmaar in 2020 and to ensure rehabilitation in the Europa League.

On 1 December 2019, Noa Lang became the first Ajax player in 60 years to score a hat-trick on his first Eredivisie start, as Ajax came back from two goals down to beat Twente 5–2. Seven days before Christmas, Ajax played in front of 5,000 fans at second-tier SC Telstar in the KNVB Cup second round. Lang scored the opening goal in the 4–3 away win. If Lang, 20 at the time, felt he was entitled to be shown some leniency from his manager, he was in for a surprise. 'Noa, you have to run deep,' Ten Hag barked. Lang, 29 years Ten Hag's junior, had the gall to complain. 'You have to shut up,' the manager retorted. 'You have to listen. You just need to do it. It's our game, not just yours.' The camera cut back to Lang, completely humbled. Noussair Mazraoui, Ryan Gravenberch, Sergiño Dest, Jurriën Timber and Brian Brobbey all made their debut under Ten Hag and would develop into key Ajax players. Ten Hag also managed to transform the careers of older players like Dušan Tadić. The Serbian midfielder flourished after an underwhelming spell at English Premier League club Southampton. In his four years at Ajax he was to score more than triple the number of goals he scored during his four years in England.

When Ajax announced on 25 October that there would be a training camp in Qatar during the winter break, some Dutchmen and Dutchwomen were upset that the club would be using facilities in the oil state. With almost half of the population hailing from India, Pakistan, Iran and African nations, Qatar is highly dependent on immigrant labour for building its roads, bridges and stadiums. According to an Amnesty International report, exploitation and abuse are rampant, with workers exposed to forced labour, unpaid wages and excessive working hours. The team went anyway, Edwin van der Sar defending the decision by stating that football should be seen as separate from politics.

But taking such a stance in 2020 was problematic. On 3 January, the United States assassinated Iranian bête noire General Qassem Soleimani in a rocket attack. From 1998 until his assassination in 2020, he was the commander of the Quds Force, an Islamic Revolutionary Guard Corps division primarily responsible for extraterritorial and clandestine military operations. Relations with the Middle East were tense. Ajax full-back and US national team member Sergiño Dest felt unsafe and left the training camp early. Fortunately, politics did not monopolise attention. Erik ten Hag had brought promising young talents Sontje Hansen, Juan Familia-Castillo, Naci Ünüvar, Kenneth Taylor, Danilo Pereira da Silva and the Timber brothers. The debutants impressed in a friendly match against Belgian club KAS Eupen.

• • •

In 2020, the world was hit by COVID-19. Football clubs struggled with infections among players, empty stadiums and the financial impact of the pandemic. Ajax sent dozens of employees home and the club took advantage of government aid for office workers. From July to the end of December 2020, Ajax recorded a €31 million decrease in turnover. 'As a result of the corona crisis, the prospects are very gloomy,' a club press release announced. Paradoxically, Erik ten Hag and technical director Marc Overmars had conjured up the largest purchase in Eredivisie history during the 2020–1 winter transfer window. Ivory Coast striker Sébastien Haller cost Ajax €22.5 million in a move from West Ham United. What appeared to be an excessive expenditure in times of crisis was explained as a means of sustaining future earnings. Prizes in European football generate millions of euros with which the club could acquire expensive players to perpetuate its success. The vision was borne out by the result. The striker was involved in a goal or assist every 97 minutes, and produced the winners against Fortuna, Heerenveen and RKC Waalwijk.

The Eredivisie was the first major European league to come to a standstill due to the pandemic. On 10 March 2020, games in the southern province of Brabant were cancelled due to the expanding crisis. Two days later, all clubs had to close immediately, which meant training sessions were stopped. On 21 April, Prime Minister Mark Rutte announced that all professional football matches would be banned until 1 September. The KNVB then communicated its intention to UEFA not to resume the 2019–20 competition. On 24 April, the organisation declared positions in the league table final. Promotion and relegation were scrapped. Ajax were top of the Eredivisie table, ahead of AZ Alkmaar on goal difference with nine rounds left to play. Neither would be national champions, but Ajax advanced directly to the play-offs of the Champions League, with AZ playing in the second qualifying round.

In the summer of 2020, Ajax saw the departure of three of their strongest players to the English Premier League. Hakim Ziyech went to Chelsea, Donny van de Beek to Manchester United, and Joël Veltman to Brighton. Ten Hag had introduced young talent to his Ajax side with Jurriën Timber and Devyne Rensch at the right time. Younger players were also attracted, such as Ghanaian midfielder Mohammed Kudus and Brazilian winger Antony, while home-grown talent Ryan Gravenberch got a chance to expand his influence. COVID or not, in August 2020, Ajax took on FC Utrecht in the Johan Cruyff Arena. The second friendly match of the pre-season resulted in a 5–1 win for Ajax, with all Ajax goals coming in the first half. Judging by the game and the number of goals over three weeks of preparation, Ajax was on the right track: 6–0 against RKC, 5–1 against FC Utrecht, 4–1 against Red Bull Salzburg. Ten Hag said that 'Salzburg got away with one. We were sloppy in the finish due to fatigue. We could have scored more.' Ten Hag had no fewer than 11 players at his disposal for four attacking positions. 'Let them fight over it. The internal competition is great, it keeps everyone on their toes. Players have a better chance to get playing time, since five substitutions per game are allowed in the new season. That offers even more possibilities for tactical variation.'

The club was domestically dominant, defeat was again a rarity. Only FC Groningen and FC Twente beat Ajax during the season. Ajax's 35th national title was a fact after the 4–0 victory over FC Emmen, with a margin of 12 points. Goals from Jurriën Timber, Sébastien Haller, Devyne Rensch and Davy Klaassen sealed the deal. Because Ajax's competition for the title dropped points in matches against smaller teams, Ajax won the championship on match day 31, with a considerable goal difference. The 13–0 rout of VVV-Venlo in in their home stadium, De Koel, helped. Along with the 1971–2 and 1997–8 seasons, this was the third time in club history that Ajax had been certain of the Eredivisie title with at least three rounds to go. The team also scored the most goals, conceded the fewest and won the most points both at home and away. Ajax again took the double. In April 2021 his contract was extended until mid-2023. It was clear why Ajax believed in him.

Ten Hag was doing very well on the pitch, but at the turn of the year, he had to deal with some nasty surprises in the dressing room. Ajax had wanted to build upon the successes of the great 2018–19 season and brought striker Quincy Promes to the club. The sizeable sum of €15.7 million was transferred to Sevilla and the Dutch international got off to a flying start in Amsterdam. Ten Hag had previously worked with him in the youth teams at FC Twente and Go Ahead Eagles. After a strong first six months, Promes's performance levels dropped. In the subsequent season, the formerly lightning-fast attacker spent a lot of time on the bench.

Promes had a history of legal trouble. In June 2018 he was arrested in Ibiza when he got involved in a fight. He was released on bail, while the investigation continued. No charges were ultimately brought. In December 2020 Promes was detained in connection with an incident that had happened in the summer. He allegedly stabbed a cousin in the knee at a family party. Initially, he was prosecuted for aggravated assault, a charge that was later changed to attempted murder by the Public Prosecution Service. Erik ten Hag said, 'It is a deplorable affair. It touches me deeply, and I am deeply saddened. It is very regrettable that he has ended up in such a situation.' At the end of the season, Promes returned to Spartak Moscow, where he had played prior to joining Sevilla. Promes formally denies the charges.

Goalkeeper André Onana had made his debut at Jong Ajax (Young Ajax, the reserve team) as an 18-year-old. During his senior career he had shown some great performances over a span of five years. Because he had been instrumental in helping his club reach the Europa League final and the Champions League semi-finals, he was a crowd favourite. In February 2021 he tested positive for furosemide, a banned substance. Onana was banned from playing for 12 months by UEFA. He said he took his wife's medicine by mistake and the decision was appealed. Eventually, the ban was reduced to nine months by the Court of Arbitration for Sport. He was dropped to the bench as the second-choice goalkeeper at Ajax, but due to problems in that position – Remko Pasveer, Maarten Stekelenburg and Jay Gorter were all struggling with injuries – Ten Hag was forced to call on him. He seemed to have lost his touch and piled blunder upon blunder. The criticism increased. The keeper had set his sights on a transfer to Inter Milan and signed a multi-year contract. The fans were disenchanted with the Cameroonian, but he was indifferent. 'I don't care. I've done so much for this club. They can sing, they can cry, I don't care. I'll be here for a few more weeks and people will be critical of that. That's part of it.'

Ten Hag dealt with the issues as a 'sober and rational person'. He understood that 'These things happen to people. Usually I can forgive someone, but I never forget. I protect people outwardly. Internally, it can be different, if someone has crossed the line. Ultimately, this is top sport. You have to be able to trust each other, otherwise you cannot achieve results. If my protective attitude goes at the expense of myself, then so be it. I am the manager, the leader, I do that in the best interest of Ajax and the result. My own situation is secondary to that. When the judiciary draws conclusions, someone must bear the consequences. I have come to his [Promes's] defence. I am disappointed, but that does not mean I completely write him off or that he can no longer come to me.'

The situations of his players were, in his words, 'beyond my control'. The fact is 'you are dealing with humans, not robots. People make mistakes and have imperfections. You try to be ahead of things as a coach, but that doesn't always work. I have known Quincy for some time, he has matured in front of my eyes. His responsibilities increased, he has a wife and children. Of course I talk to him about all kinds of aspects of life, but in the end he makes his own decisions. His prosecution doesn't do the image of the team any good, leaving aside the question of guilt. And I have to protect the team. The same goes for Onana, although his situation is of a different order. I hope both players have learned from their mistakes and take those lessons to heart during the rest of their careers and lives. I have learned how important transparency is. André and Quincy have to accept the consequences, but I would have liked to have seen both make greater contributions to Ajax. Sometimes I am like a father to the team. Some players are very young, and they make choices that have big consequences. I can only set the standard and monitor it.'

In conclusion, he said, 'my profession is training, coaching, making analyses, but above all it is guiding people. This task has become much more intensive in the last 20 years. In the previous century, the world was still relatively comprehensible. The Internet has changed things a lot. People's problems are becoming more and more complex as society becomes more and more complex. You can also see that in football players. If you want to get the most out of people, you have to take an interest in them. Ajax is a very mixed club, a true reflection of society, with many cultures together. You have to seriously consider that.'

In 2021 Ajax won the double – the national title and the KNVB Cup – a second time, and Erik ten Hag won the Rinus Michels Award for the third time. The award had not been given in the 2019–20 season, which was interrupted by the COVID-19 pandemic. After receiving the 2021 trophy, Ten Hag gave a short speech, which he concluded with a self-deprecating wisecrack. 'You are only as good as your last game, so at the moment we are not very good,' hinting at the 4–0 loss in the battle for the Johan Cruyff Shield.

In the summer, Ajax managed to keep its star players for the first time in some years, while Ten Hag was able to add Steven Berghuis and Remko Pasveer. A special role was reserved for Berghuis, who, after starting as a winger, was given a chance in the number 10 position. Ajax ended up in a Champions League group with Borussia Dortmund, Sporting CP and Besiktas. Ajax secured a memorable 4–0 win over Borussia Dortmund in an electric performance in a sold-out Johan Cruyff Arena. The home side took the lead through an own goal by Dortmund captain Marco Reus, who deflected Dušan Tadić's free-kick into the net. After Daley Blind doubled the score, Ajax continued to dominate and kept creating chances. Brazilian winger Antony made it 3–0 after 57 minutes and Sébastien Haller headed in his sixth goal in three Champions League matches in the 72nd minute. Ajax could have scored even more, but the 4–0 victory saw the Amsterdam side record their biggest European win against a German side since 1973 when they beat Bayern Munich by the same scoreline, while Dortmund suffered its biggest ever Champions League defeat. Ajax secured the top spot in Group C and a place in the knockout phase of the Champions League after four group matches. The club won their away match against Borussia Dortmund by a final score of 3–1, overcoming a one-goal deficit late in the match against a home team that played with ten men for over an hour. The aggregate score was 7–1. 'Very nice: Four games. Twelve points,' said captain Dušan Tadić. Ajax could relax during its two remaining group matches against Besiktas and Sporting CP but didn't. They qualified from the group stage with a perfect record of six wins from six games, the first time any team from the Netherlands had done so. Only ten other sides in the competition's history have achieved this. In the process, they conceded just five goals, while scoring 20, a tally only bettered by Bayern Munich with 22.

It had been a long time since Ajax started a two-legged game in the round of 16 of the Champions League as the favourite. It showed how far Ajax had come since Ten Hag made his entry into the club. Sébastien Haller did not stop scoring in the Champions League. In the 2–2 tie against Benfica, he scored his eleventh goal in seven matches, making him the only player to have achieved such a feat in the competition. Up to that point, Erik ten Hag had only lost one of 21 Champions League away fixtures, the 1–0 defeat at Anfield in December 2020. However, having drawn the away leg 2–2 against Benfica, they ultimately lost the home tie 1–0 and were knocked out in the round of 16. Ajax dominated the game. They had 69 per cent possession, 16 shots to four, with Benfica's threat exclusively coming from set pieces. Benfica showed that Ajax could still fall into the trap of – in Johan Cruyffs terms – 'sly opponents'.

. . .

The concept of toxic masculinity has been around since the 1980s in academic discussions of traditional stereotypes of men as misogynistic and violent. More recently, the #MeToo movement began to draw public attention to the widespread culture of sexual abuse, sexual harassment and date rape. The scale of these excesses came into full public awareness when Hollywood film producer Harvey Weinstein and New York financier Jeffrey Epstein were convicted of numerous sex offences. The entertainment industry, it appeared, was rife with sexual exploitation and predation. Meanwhile, USA Gymnastics (USAG) was compromised by numerous sex abuse cases. Hundreds of people, mostly women, alleged that they were sexually assaulted by gym owners, coaches and staff working for gymnastics programmes over a period of two decades. It is more or less common knowledge by now that sex abuse in sports has been a well-established practice for a long time. No sport or location appears to be beyond its reach. An alleged sexual abuse scandal left Iceland's football association rudderless amid calls for change of an unacceptable culture at the highest level. And this was in a country with the reputation of being the 'best place to be a woman' because of its 12-year run atop the World Economic Forum's Gender Gap Index.

Football in the Netherlands is not immune to this social disease. Players and coaches of both the Baby Boomer generation and Generation X did not really question the status quo, and sexual harassment and derogatory language were par for the course. Off-the-pitch topics of conversation were mostly money and cars, women and sex. Humour in bad taste about women was a common ingredient of this volatile mix. As long as players scored on the pitch, they were alright. Football was a macho world, and there were only some of greater moral awareness and social sensibility who did not engage in these practices. At home with the wife it may have been a different story. But beyond the front door, sexist humour was a daily reality. Women who worked in the club environment had little choice but to endure the abuse. Sports commentators such as libertarian Johan Derksen have justified the practice by claiming that it simply was part of the zeitgeist. Dutch football greats such as Koeman, Van Basten and Rijkaard became more moderate in the choice of their words at a later stage in life.

For decades, Marc Overmars had been immersed in this rather one-dimensional football culture. In January 2022, when the ink on his new four-year deal had barely dried, a bomb exploded in Amsterdam. It was revealed that, over an extended period of time, the director of football affairs had sent intimidating sexual messages and 'dickpics' to several female colleagues. He had little choice but to respond to the issue directly: 'Last week I was confronted with reports about my behaviour and the impact it has had on others. Unfortunately, I didn't realise that I had crossed boundaries, but that has now become clear to me. I suddenly felt enormous pressure. I apologise. Certainly for someone in my position, this behaviour is unacceptable. I see that too now, but it's too late. I see no other option than to leave Ajax. This also has a major impact on my private circumstances. That is why I ask everyone to leave me and my family in peace.' The club announced in early February 2022 that Overmars was leaving with immediate effect.

The management commissioned an independent investigation into Ajax's corporate culture. The results confirmed earlier media speculation surrounding the case. 'The investigation has made it clear that a number of women within Ajax have been confronted with undesirable behaviour. This ranges from bad jokes and derogatory or hurtful comments, to an unwanted arm around the shoulder and other intrusive behaviour.' The organisation assured the public that steps towards the realisation of a safer sports and work climate at the club would be taken. The national champion engaged an outside specialised agency to help the club get there.

The collaboration between Overmars and Erik ten Hag had been very productive in more than one way. Territorial disputes were non-existent, and for the first time in years peace appeared to reign in the Ajax boardroom. Jointly they had brought in players from the Premier League. Overmars had pursued a financially daring players' policy and increased salaries significantly. The club had weathered the COVID storm well, and, unlike most other Dutch football clubs, the Ajax brand maintained and increased its value. Ten Hag's capacity for team building and player development was highly profitable. In the summer of 2019, having won the domestic double and reached the semi-finals of the Champions League,

Ajax lost Matthijs de Ligt, Frenkie de Jong, Lasse Schöne and Kasper Dolberg. The following summer Hakim Ziyech, Donny van de Beek and Joël Veltman departed, with David Neres joining Ajax in January 2022. Only Daley Blind, Dušan Tadić, Noussair Mazraoui, Nicolás Tagliafico and André Onana remained. In four years, Ten Hag had spent approximately €215 million, but recouped about €415 million, resulting in a profit of approximately €200 million. Then Ryan Gravenberch went to Bayern Munich for about €23 million, including add-ons. Ten Hag was able to retake Daley Blind, Dušan Tadić and Sébastien Haller from the Premier League and, by using academy graduates and smart scouting, he created another exciting, dominating side. Edson Álvarez, Lisandro Martínez and Antony were signed for a combined sum of about €40 million.

Ten Hag got to know Overmars at Go Ahead Eagles. During Ten Hag's time as head coach in Deventer, Overmars was head of football affairs. Ten Hag became Ajax manager through Overmars's mediation. The two not only worked closely together professionally. For public and personal reasons, Ten Hag understandably was the first to formulate a response to the Overmars affair. 'You have to be careful with the word "friend". But in Marc's case, I can say that. That's why this is particularly hard to take. But my first thoughts now turn to the women. I don't know all the facts either. That also has to do with privacy. Steps have been taken. These have been incredibly bad days. I was totally stunned. It was disastrous. Especially for the victims, especially for the women, the suffering that has been inflicted on them. I have a very hard time with that. It touches all of us to the very depths of our souls. Everyone processes this his own way. In such situations, I often withdraw. I am a bit quieter and have less energy at the moment. But in the first hours and first days it was particularly difficult. I think this is a social problem. It also plays into politics.

This week we saw another MP resign for the same reason. Football is a mirror of society. I think this happens in many organisations. Yes, we worked in tandem, but it's too early to make any statements about my future now. It's not about me right now. I have to let this settle first. After some time, I will think about the consequences.'

Ajax suddenly had to continue without a technical director. Together, Gerry Hamstra and Klaas-Jan Huntelaar took care of business in the interim. Following Overmars's departure, Ten Hag said, 'As a person I miss him every day, but also in terms of the club's functioning. We'll have to deal with that. We still text and call. And that is more than business. You cannot cut such a bond. He was involved. He was the director of this team. We have known for a long time which direction we wanted to take with all players. We decided that together. The things that were started will be followed up. My job is to keep things together. That includes sticking up for people. I do that from my heart too. We humans are in this world to help each other and not to shoot each other.'

It was difficult to gauge to what extent the Overmars imbroglio impacted the atmosphere in the dressing room. The performance on the pitch seemed to have suffered, with the media criticising the play and suggesting that it was predictable: opponents by now had caught on to the Ajax style of play and were able to respond to it more effectively. Ajax was not quite as overwhelming as before but still managed to get the points. Towards the end of the season, the team often struck in the final phase. Ajax scored against Willem II in the 81st minute, against RKC in injury time, against SC Cambuur in injury time, against Feyenoord in the 86th minute and against NEC in the 88th minute. Ajax did not drop many points in competition, as a result of which PSV's march on the top spot in the Eredivisie was held off. Ten Hag still managed to get his team to the top of the

Eredivisie with an incredible goal difference of 79, while they also reached the Champions League round of 16.

In a disappointing KNVB Cup final, Ajax lost 2–1 to rivals PSV, meaning a triple double would elude Ten Hag. Dressed in a suit jacket and sweater on a hot afternoon in Rotterdam, he stood quietly on the sideline. An occasional wave of the arm was about as animated as he got. Even when Ryan Gravenberch opened up the scoring, his reaction was an understated fist pump. The fourth official did get an icy glare when a penalty-box trip went unchecked by VAR. The goals that won PSV the final came from individual lapses rather than any tactical malfunctioning. They came within three minutes of each other, shortly after half-time. Ajax had appeared with a different line-up. Sébastien Haller, the principal striker with 33 goals in 37 games that season, was dropped to the bench and replaced with 20-year-old Brian Brobbey. Ten Hag brought on Haller with 18 minutes remaining. Troubled goalkeeper André Onana was left out of the squad altogether. Ajax's dominance with nearly 60 per cent possession didn't produce the needed equaliser. Ajax had cause to feel aggrieved as well. They scored two goals that were disallowed by the most fractional of VAR offside calls. Ten Hag concluded his post-match press conference by saying, 'I think this is the time to end the press conference. I will need 24 hours to recover from this.'

Erik ten Hag may not yet have had the name recognition enjoyed by Jürgen Klopp, Pep Guardiola, Carlo Ancelotti or Zinedine Zidane, but his game ideas and the way Ajax executed them drew attention across Europe. He had signed a new contract, but the pull from big-name clubs abroad increased with successive championship seasons. On the heels of Ajax's spectacular achievements in the Champions League, interest came from Bayern Munich. The Germans were not happy with coach Niko Kovač's work and would rather see Ten Hag in the dugout at the Allianz Arena. That call came too early, and Ajax was happy to keep their manager in Amsterdam.

After the successful 2018–19 season, opportunities had been presented to both Ten Hag and Overmars, but both decided to remain loyal to Ajax. Overmars had been a key factor for Ten Hag to continue at Ajax, so the departure of the technical director strengthened Ten Hag's conviction that it was time to take the next step. In the context of a changed environment at the Johan Cruyff Arena, football pundit Marcel van der Kraan had expected a Ten Hag move. 'The departure of Marc Overmars as technical director, Ten Hag's big friend on and off the pitch, has made it very obvious that Ten Hag is not looking for another season at Ajax. He has been there for four years, almost five. He's won five trophies, he's guided Ajax as far as he possibly can. He's built up brilliant teams, even after the sale of loads of top players and young talent. I can't see him doing another season there.'

Late in April, Ten Hag made an important announcement at Ajax's training grounds. After the morning training session, several members of the staff, including general manager Edwin van der Sar, team managers Herman Pinkster and Jan Siemerink, communications manager Miel Brinkhuis, and club doctor Niels Wijne, joined the players at the centre circle. Ten Hag told the group that he would be leaving Ajax to join Manchester United in the summer. After weeks of speculation, it did not come as a shock to anyone, and the team and staff warmly applauded and congratulated him. In fact, there was some comfort in knowing with certainty what the future would bring. Ten Hag, too, was happy that the word finally was out officially, but he assured those gathered that he would keep his priorities straight. 'I'm really looking forward to it, it's a great club. But everything is now focused on Ajax, the rest will come after this season.'

The 2021–2 season's title was Ajax's 36th and Ten Hag's third, not counting the interrupted season during the pandemic. He was the fourth trainer to win three national titles in sequence with Ajax. Frank de Boer won the championship four times in a row. Louis van Gaal and Rinus Michels won three consecutive national titles. Ajax had been the leader in the Eredivisie almost uninterrupted for four years. Ten Hag also won the KNVB Cup twice with Ajax and the Johan Cruyff Shield once. This makes him the best performing Eredivisie coach over at least a hundred games at a single club. Ten Hag had been in charge of 138 Ajax Eredivisie matches. His team won 109 matches and lost only 16. The games ended in a draw 13 times. The Amsterdam team scored 409 times and conceded 109 goals. No manager ever earned more points in his first 100 games in charge.

The club had made all the preparations for the award ceremony; supporters were already celebrating on the Leidseplein in Amsterdam, and the trophy had been brought to the Johan Cruyff Arena by KNVB director Marianne van Leeuwen. Erik ten Hag's team had an easy evening and secured the title against Heerenveen 5–0, with goals from Nicolás Tagliafico, Steven Berghuis, Sébastien Haller, Brian Brobbey and Edson Álvarez. Ajax was in control of the game from beginning to end, and the crowd in the packed home ground was treated to a game with numerous scintillating attacks. The performance was reminiscent of the self-confident style they had played with before the winter break. The win allowed Ten Hag's side to claim the Eredivisie with one game left to play.

The Amsterdam municipality was the wet blanket of the victory party. The official announcement from the Government of Amsterdam said:

The Amsterdam triangle – municipality, Public Prosecution Service, police – and Ajax would have preferred to organise the ceremony again on the Museumplein [the traditional venue for Ajax championship festivities]. However, a celebration in public space is not possible due to the severe shortage of security personnel. Experience shows that a tribute to Ajax in public space attracts 80,000 to 100,000 visitors, which amounts to at least 320 security guards. The municipality has approached 12 different companies, but the desired number of security officers has not been obtained. The city of Amsterdam now opts for a tribute to the team in the Johan Cruyff Arena, where this can be done safely and festively.

Half an hour after the final whistle, club icon Jari Litmanen handed the championship trophy to captain Dušan Tadić. Lisandro Martínez was named Player of the Year, while Jurriën Timber was recognised as Talent of the Year. The Johan Cruyff Arena had been transformed into a large party tent. The beat rumbled through the stadium, and the festivities began. The bars on Arena Boulevard came alive. FEBO Boulevard, near the main entrance, not only served the standard Heineken, but in honour of the Twente coach, kept the Grolsch flowing. Johan Cruyff, albeit in bronze form, kept watch just around the corner. Ajax's supporters clubhouse, burned down, presumably by rival fans, in 2015, and now situated in the bowels of the stadium, did brisk business. After the setbacks the club had to overcome this season, feelings of joy and relief were dominant. With fierce competition from a revived PSV, and to a lesser extent from Feyenoord, Ajax had been put to the test. They initially faltered, but stood their ground, winning the national title for the third time in a row. Even if the football wasn't always what Ten Hag, the team and the fans had envisioned, the points were accumulated, and an inexhaustible drive to win prevailed.

Special recognition was given to the champion trainer. During the ceremony, Ajax director Edwin van der Sar grabbed the microphone to address the departing Ten Hag. 'I am standing next to a man who came to Ajax four and a half years ago. Every now and then I thought: *what a weird guy you are, Erik*. I still remember our first conversation. What were you going to do with Ajax? You have exceeded all expectations. You let Ajax play dominant football, attractive football. You have won trophies, reached the semi-finals of the Champions League. You are going to make the step to one of the biggest clubs in the world, in a fantastic competition, a club that I also support. I wish you a lot of success. You go out through the front door of the Johan Cruyff Arena and I hope to see you again soon.' A prolonged standing ovation from the fans for the manager followed, after which he was tossed into the air by his players and caught again. Every player received a big hug from the coach, accompanied by some affirmative words. It was the culmination of a special period in Amsterdam.

About his departure, Ten Hag said, 'Of course it's a shame that we can't celebrate this with the supporters under normal circumstances. Two years ago the party on the Museumplein made such an impression on everyone. You want to experience something like this again, but because of the pandemic that is not possible now. I am happy with the pure joy in the dressing room, of the players, of all the people involved. This title definitely is also for the supporters. We missed them in this season, but hopefully we were able to give them some beautiful moments.'

Ten Hag acknowledged that his time at Ajax had been meaningful to him: 'This Tukker has become a bit of an Ajax player. You never deny your roots, but I feel at home here. I enjoyed this great journey, it was a beautiful era. I look back with great satisfaction. I've come to love the club, and I really enjoyed working here. When I started here four and a half years ago, I had to prepare Ajax for Europe again. That succeeded beyond expectation. I enjoyed our home game against Borussia Dortmund in the Champions League the most this season. It was of such a high level, even comparable to those matches in Turin and Madrid. We've also had a lot of setbacks this season. In the last few weeks I had to use more players than I actually wanted. But I've said before that we have more than 11 starters, and we have seen that young players are breaking through again. The foundation of Ajax good.' He noted that the atmosphere surrounding Ajax had changed dramatically. 'We have also created a culture of winning. If you look at the facts, we've created a pattern of huge expectations. We can hardly meet those anymore. The disappointment was great when we were eliminated by Benfica, the whole of the Netherlands was disappointed.'

Ten Hag emphatically wanted to involve Marc Overmars in the championship celebration. At Ajax, staff and management carefully skirted the controversies surrounding the former director of football affairs. Questions about Overmars were not answered and his contributions seemed no longer relevant. He was persona non grata, eliminated from conversation as if he had never existed. Ten Hag did not ignore the moral challenges that the Overmars affair posed, but he nonetheless paid tribute to a fallen football leader for the value he had contributed. He showed a degree of loyalty you do not often encounter in the world of professional football, with its ever fluctuating alliances. He did not drop his discredited friend. To him, the former left winger continued to be a prominent colleague with whom he had built the new Ajax. That is why he had to be named in the title celebration. 'We've done it together for several years. This title of Ajax also belongs to Marc Overmars.'

After the championship celebration, the manager also gave credit to others who had contributed to the success of Team Ten Hag. 'When I think of structure, I first of all think of our way of playing football. But the professionalisation of the organisation in the field of sport has also undergone a good development. I'm talking about the cooperation between the different parts of the club: medical, performance, technical. The integration of Jong Ajax within the club and its management is a good example of how it can yield returns. We have brought it closer to Ajax 1, resulting in close cooperation. Players in the U23 team must learn to win a competition, but ultimately the progression of players to the first team is central. I therefore attach great value to the U23 team. This has been achieved at Ajax, partly due to the excellent youth academy of the club. I would like to mention Saïd Ouaali, the head of youth education. Someone who always thinks in the service of the club, who thinks along with the first team, who has so much knowledge and expertise, and with whom you can work well together. This also applied to the interaction with scouting, with Henk Veldmate and his crew. It fit, it was right. The cooperation between the different departments was very good.'

In conclusion he said, 'We've had great years. I think that Ajax has played Ajax-style under my leadership, always with the intention to play good and attractive football, an adventuresome and beautiful game. That led to a lot of goals. A more winning mentality, a winning culture, has settled at the club. Perhaps that is where my greatest influence has been. In the Netherlands there is often insufficient attention for that. Trainers are preoccupied with tactics, but mentality is an equally important factor.'

Erik ten Hag averaged 2.44 points per Eredivisie match, a higher point average than all of his predecessors besides Romanian Ştefan Kovács, Ajax coach in the early 1970s, with 2.69 points per game. When he left, a year before his contract expired, a sentiment of foreboding could be felt in Amsterdam. There was some apprehension that Ajax would collapse without Ten Hag, the team thinker who balanced attacking and defending, who linked attractive play to realism, who gave opportunities to creative players. The departure of the atypical Ajax coach left many with a feeling of abandonment.

13

MANCHESTER MAGNETISM

*'We cannot solve our problems with the
same thinking we used when we created them.'*
ALBERT EINSTEIN

The Tour de France was not part of Manchester United's pre-season training, but it did nicely coincide. Erik ten Hag would play a decisive role in formulating the master plan that led to the win of the most prestigious bicycle road race by Dutch team Jumbo-Visma. The team produced Tour winner Jonas Vingegaard and also took home the green jersey and the polka dot jersey. Facing some unexpected hurdles in the run-up to the Tour de France, Jumbo-Visma technical director Merijn Zeeman decided to get in touch with the new Manchester United coach. 'Ten Hag has helped me a lot,' Zeeman revealed. 'He is someone who works in a completely different sport, but I wanted to learn from him: how do you come up with your tactics? What is the essence of your sport for you? What is behind making a game plan? I got to talk with him about that a few times.' It turned out to be part of the winning strategy for the 109th Tour. Zeeman learned what he had to do: stay away from the beaten track, approach the sport in a different way. He kept in mind the adage, 'If you do what you always did, you will get what you always got.'

It was to data analysts that Zeeman turned, to ask the 'central questions such as: what can we do better? What are we not doing well? What are our competitors doing? We had already done quite a lot of reconnaissance. We knew the course better and better.' At the top of the agenda was always that one question: where are the weaknesses of key opponent Tadej Pogačar? 'We were still looking for that. We knew what Pogačar was especially good at. But what are his pitfalls, where is his weakness, what kind of team does he have, where can we hit them? And how do you translate that into our qualities in the course?' The conclusion was: if Pogačar wastes a lot of energy before a long hard climb, then he can be caught. The solution is the tough mountain stages.

The eye fell on stages 11 and 12 of the Tour. The rides to Col du Granon and Alpe d'Huez. With Jumbo-Visma rider Primož Roglič still high in the standings at the time, Pogačar couldn't afford to let him pull away. Roglič's teammate Jonas Vingegaard was even closer and was certainly not allowed to get any space from the two-time Tour winner. With that knowledge Vingegaard and Roglič started attacking Pogačar alternately. Not two or three times, but six times, seven times. The plan went off like clockwork. Pogačar was slowly taken apart. He finally surrendered to Vingegaard's attack, just under three miles from the finish. He crossed the finish line 2 minutes and 51 seconds after Vingegaard, who pulled the yellow jersey off his Slovenian competitor in the eleventh stage and did not relinquish it again. The Tour was decided.

• • •

Professional football, more so than the manufacturing and service industries, is a heavily internationalised enterprise. This is the result of the nature of the game. Whereas other commercial enterprises only take on their competitors indirectly in the free market, direct engagement of foreign competitors at international tournaments is a regular part of the football business. In addition, most higher-level clubs are heavily populated with experts and adepts of foreign origin. This exposes both players and coaches to intensive interaction with foreign 'products' – football cultures, strategies and personalities. Hence, importing new styles and ways comes relatively more easily to football organisations than other businesses. A good example is the 'Dutch school' of football – total football – which really is no longer 'Dutch' but has become the collective property of footballing humanity. Within the football world, as elsewhere, tendencies towards convention and self-preservation persist only among the mediocre, and at their own peril.

The principle of using outside talent to add a missing dimension to an existing organisation is constantly and effectively applied in the world of football. For years, British teams, because of their reliance on high speed, limited build-up strategies, and therefore average positional play, had a tough time competing against teams from the European mainland. This was the reason that British teams had to change strategy and adapt their style of play and training methods. To achieve this, coaches were hired from abroad who were well-educated and experienced in the team tactical aspects of the game. Sven-Göran Eriksson's transformation of English national football comes to mind. As an outsider, the cool Swede was unaffected by the then accepted customs of British muscular-but-brainless football and hence free to make the needed changes. Eriksson improved England's position in the FIFA World Rankings from seventeenth place in January 2001 to fifth in July 2006, reaching fourth during the 2006 World Cup. Portuguese manager José Mourinho at Chelsea and the more recent managerial stars at Manchester City and Liverpool,

Spain's Pep Guardiola and Germany's Jürgen Klopp, each significantly impacted the Premier League. In fact, none of the so-called big six of the Premier League had an English coach for some time until Graham Potter suddenly replaced Thomas Tuchel at Chelsea after a mediocre start to the 2022 league season. The honeymoon lasted for six months, and Potter is now gone. Foreign managers are greatly valued and the salaries drawing them to England are high. As a result, coaches in England are among the best paid in the world.

On Christmas Eve 2021, Erik ten Hag announced, 'There will come a time when Ajax and I will part. That may take a while, but it can also happen quickly, because you are only as good as your last game. That's why I live from match to match. In Germany they say: *himmelhoch jauchzend, zum Tode betrübt* ['rejoicing to high heavens, plunged to the depth of despair' – a line taken from Johann Wolfgang von Goethe's play *Egmont*]. If I move, I want to work for an organisation with a clear philosophy, attainable ambitions and honest people. If I don't have the right impression, I won't start on it. The last thing I want is to look over my shoulder to make sure they don't shoot me in the back.'

What would lure Ten Hag to managing in a bigger league one day? 'The challenge: can I do it there, too? See if my bar can be set even higher. Why did I go from FC Utrecht to Ajax? To see whether I could also be successful at the top club in the Netherlands. To challenge is human. I think that applies to everyone in life, no matter in which sector you work. But for me it is never at all costs. I am not obsessed with a top competition. It's always about perspective for me. What is the plan and philosophy of a club? Do they match my ideas? Are the goals realistic and achievable? Can I find a way to get them there? That counts for me before I consider a transition. There may be a club where all the questions I just asked are answered positively. If there is a good working climate, fertile soil for development, people I can trust and with whom I have a good feeling, I would consider it. I've always said, I've never been hunting for anything in my life. For my wife, yes, but nothing else.'

The history of Manchester United over the last few decades is somewhat of an anomaly in the world of professional football. Unlike employees at other types of companies, those working in football are accustomed to very short periods of employment. Both players and managers move from club to club at irregular intervals, often after two or three years, sometimes even less. In the UK, contracts tend to be somewhat longer than on the continent. Sir Alex Ferguson's two and a half decades at United were extraordinary not only because of the sheer length of his tenure but because of the outstanding results they yielded. His managerial journey produced two UEFA Champions League titles, the European Cup Winners' Cup, UEFA Super Cup, 13 Premier League crowns, five FA Cups and four League Cups. It would be a hard act to follow for anyone.

The announcement that Alex Ferguson was retiring was worldwide news. Sir Alex's decision, after 26 years in charge, meant he relinquished his title as Europe's longest-serving coach after the final game of the Premier League campaign, his 1,500th in charge of United. The honour thus passed to Portadown FC coach Ronnie McFall, who was appointed six weeks after Ferguson took charge at Old Trafford and lasted a full three decades at the Northern Irish League outfit.

The scenario of a larger-than-life figure overshadowing those who come after him proved problematic. Ferguson appointed his own successor in 2013. He had moulded the club and didn't want to squander his carefully constructed legacy. At his home, over a cup of tea, he decided who would become the manager of the richest club in the world. Sir Alex had earned that right by building Manchester

United, brick by brick, into the institution it had become by the first decade of the new millennium. The choice fell on his country-man David Moyes. Ferguson had faith in him because he saw in his compatriot a younger version of himself. In 11 years, without too much fuss and with few resources, Moyes had built Everton into a stable mid-league performer, sufficient reason for United to immedi-ately offer him a six-year contract. When Ferguson gave an emotional farewell address to Old Trafford there was a mix of celebration and apprehension in the air – *what's next?* Twelve league defeats later, the answer was painfully clear. The spirit that had built up over a quarter of a century was obliterated within a season. It is unfair to lay all the blame for the dramatic undoing of Manchester United at the feet of Moyes. Cracks had been emerging at the organisation for some time. Ferguson had been the glue that held an ailing side together, and without the supervision of the tough taskmaster it came apart at the seams. United quickly admitted that the Moyes experiment had been the wretched failure of a good man and a decent coach floundering out of his depth.

Dutch fitness coach Raymond Verheijen was a steady critic of United's decision to install Moyes. Verheijen worked alongside the late Gary Speed for Wales and knows British football well. In 2013 he challenged Moyes's training methods after an injury suffered by Robin van Persie during pre-season training. He claimed Moyes was a 'dinosaur' and that Van Persie had been 'overtrained'. Verheijen thought United's hierarchy were rather naive to bring in Moyes from Everton. 'I don't think it is so much the problem and responsibility of David Moyes. But if the people at United had done their homework they would never have appointed Moyes, they would have selected someone else. When you are managing Manchester United you need different tactical qualities as when you are an underdog like Everton.

It has to do with tactical flexibility.' After Alex Ferguson's departure, the club went from David Moyes's long balls to possession under Louis van Gaal, followed by counter-attacking with José Mourinho, nostalgic club feeling with Ole Gunnar Solskjær and pressing with Ralf Rangnick. There was no clear vision, no consistent strategy, no organisational and managerial expertise.

Erik ten Hag is facing a similar task today that Sir Alex Ferguson was faced with in 1986 when he came from Aberdeen and had to start from scratch to make Manchester United a challenger to England's best teams at the time. Ferguson was concerned that many of the players were drinking more than their due and was 'depressed' by their level of fitness. He increased discipline and his team finished the season in 11th place, up from 21st (second from bottom) when he took over. Alcohol abuse is not something Ten Hag will have to fight with. Rather, lack of fitness, technique, morale, discipline, focus and organisation are what he'll need to combat.

What makes his job even more challenging is the changed football landscape. The Premier League of 2022 is not the First Division of 1986. Ferguson's job was to dethrone Liverpool. Ten Hag has to deal with Arsenal, Chelsea, Manchester City, Liverpool, Tottenham and, possibly, Newcastle United. A newcomer to the Premier League's top table, Newcastle now has the ambition and the money to grow, just like Manchester City, into a brand with a permanent place at the apex of English football. Ten Hag is embarking on a challenge that will demand everything he can muster as a person and trainer. José Mourinho had to get the club a prize. Ten Hag has to give the club an identity. He will have to determine the direction and prove that his tactical ingenuity, training system and people management can transform the club from an underperforming straggler into a winning team.

The Manchester United leadership was inspired by Ten Hag. He had a better overall record than the other potential new manager Mauricio Pochettino and, apparently, a better story as well. Ajax still had five Eredivisie games to play. Ten Hag was committed to retaining the title. He would only speak to United officials on his one free afternoon a week. During talks in March with director of football John Murtough, technical director Darren Fletcher and CEO Richard Arnold in Amsterdam, he captivated the guests from England with his vision for the long term. This energy and enthusiasm for the challenge ahead was among the decisive factors in eventually hiring Ten Hag. Conclusions were not reached overnight on either side. A dossier was drafted on the state of affairs at United and the potential way forward was outlined before a contract was signed. Immediately after Ajax's final game on 15 May, Ten Hag flew to England. More meetings were held with senior executives at the club's Mayfair offices in London, together with Ten Hag's intended assistants Mitchell van der Gaag and Steve McClaren.

Ten Hag also spoke with the Glazers, the less-than-popular American owners of the club, and laid down a number of clear requirements in terms of transfers. No player would enter the squad without his deliberate engagement and approval. Ten Hag had no desire to end up in the same situation as Solskjær, who had been confronted with players that did not correspond to the needs of the team. The return of Cristiano Ronaldo was cause for celebration at Old Trafford. But putting together a squad involves more than bringing in good players. Ten Hag's countryman and predecessor Louis van Gaal succinctly summarised the coach's challenge: 'I do not need the eleven best; I need the best eleven.' Ten Hag needed fresh recruits that matched his philosophy and corresponded with the reality on the pitch.

When Van Gaal became Manchester United's manager in the summer of 2014, director Ed Woodward called him not only intelligent and thoughtful, but a 'larger than life character'. The former Ajax coach made a grand entrance into the Premier League. Street vendors sold shirts reading 'King Louis' at United's first league game. His performance did not meet expectations. Under Van Gaal's leadership, United played dull, predictable and defensive football and scored the fewest goals in his final season since 1989–90. In his second season, United did win the FA Cup, but landed in fifth place in the Premier League table, meaning the club would not play in the Champions League the following season. As a result, Manchester United missed out on more than €50 million and had to play in the much less profitable and not-so prestigious Europa League. Meanwhile, an agreement had already been reached with José Mourinho behind Van Gaal's back. Commentators in the Netherlands thought that the way Van Gaal was shown the door in Manchester did not deserve the beauty prize. His wife, Truus, revealed in the 2022 film *Louis* that he cried after his dismissal.

Van Gaal later described Ed Woodward as 'somebody with zero understanding of football who was previously an investment banker. The balance between the football department and commercial department is not right and even is slanted towards the commercial. It cannot be a good thing when a club is run solely from a commercially driven perspective.' There is little doubt that the club's interest was not advanced by Woodward's holding sway over football technical policy for ten years. Van Gaal thought Ten Hag would be ill-advised to make a move to Manchester. 'Erik ten Hag is a great coach, and that is always good for a club. But Manchester United are a commercial club, so it's a difficult choice for a coach. The structure is not so bad but the chief executive's right-hand man has to be a technical director with a football view, not somebody with a banker's role. Unfortunately, we are talking about a commercial club, not a football club. I spoke to Ferguson about this and in his last years, he also had problems with it. I'm not going to advise Ten Hag. But he must choose a football club and not a commercial club.'

In this context, José Mourinho's time at Manchester United is instructive. He would have loved to succeed Alex Ferguson in 2013. Back then, the leadership thought his views on football didn't fit with the United way. But that appeared to have changed three years later. Woodward had gained more power as director within the organisation. He was inspired by the methods of Florentino Pérez at Real Madrid: making the club commercially interesting by bringing in big stars, after which, it was assumed, the results would follow automatically. Paul Pogba came from Juventus for more than €100 million (£94.5 million). With this new strategy, United acquired a cache of highly rated, expensive players whose presence alone seemed to overshadow the club and its interests. The era of the superstars had arrived. The American owners were happy that with Mourinho on the sidelines, the marketing department was humming. In 2017 United still topped the Deloitte Football Money League as the club with the largest turn-over. The football was less spectacular than the economic figures. Meanwhile, Mourinho did what he does everywhere. He set up a team that played ultra-defensive football when necessary. It did have some effect. United won the Community Shield, the League Cup and the Europa League. But Mourinho's pragmatism has a limited shelf life. After starting the 2018–19 season with just seven wins in the first 17 Premier League games, he was sacked by the club in December 2018.

Ruud Gullit joined the chorus of Dutch pundits warning Ten Hag about working at Manchester United. 'Is it the right choice?

Time will tell. They also want to play the football he plays, but it's going to be a really terrible job. The TV studios are full of former players: Gary Neville, Rio Ferdinand, Paul Scholes … There is constant pressure on the team, which is not easy. Know what to expect, it's a huge job. He also has to be given the time, but I don't know if you get the time at Manchester United. The former football players are constantly carping, you are constantly getting things on your plate. You have to be able to handle that.'

Others had more faith. Former Ajax president Michael van Praag was impressed with Ten Hag, saying that he had done 'a tremendous job' with Ajax. 'When he started in Amsterdam, everyone had to get used to his media appearances. Then people made the mistake of quickly basing their opinion about his entire functioning on that. He completely dispelled that wrongfooted notion. I don't know Ten Hag well, but I spoke with him on the sidelines of a Dutch national team match. I immediately thought he was a very sensible and engaging person, who works in a well-considered and convincing way. That is why I think he will succeed at Manchester United. With the much greater pressure in England, his imperturbability will be an important asset.'

Manchester United won hearts and minds through recognisable, stylish, attacking and winning football. It is an incomparable football empire that is admired and closely followed by nearly one in ten people on the planet. A 2012 study found that the happiness of 325 million Asians, 90 million Europeans, 173 million people in the Middle East and 71 million inhabitants of the Americas is closely connected to the club in northwestern England. The numbers may have changed somewhat over a decade, but Manchester United is still a global brand. Through clever exploitation of the fanbase, the club generated a revenue of approx. £480 million in the 2020–1 season, compared to about £90 million in the late 1990s. Its stars made such an impression that they have featured in advertisements the world over – from Malaysian computer chips to Nigerian beer and Indonesian noodles. Manchester United blurred boundaries. If United were a religion, as a supporters' slogan claims, by sheer numbers it would have more devotees than Buddhism.

Yet many think that there is something rotten in the red side of Manchester. 'A club without identity', 'a graveyard for reputations', 'profile of a club in decline', 'sinking to the point of competitive irrelevance', 'lacking the fundamentals of football', 'a club spitting coaches like bubble gum for the past decade', 'a squad teetering on the verge of collective personality breakdown', 'a club lacking method, structure, coherent culture', 'a team on the pitch that has no connection', 'near-decade of mediocrity', 'a hollowed-out robot replicant of a club', 'a club in absolute chaos', 'Total Non-Football': these were just some of the insults and accusations hurled at Manchester United, its management and players. Erik ten Hag was forewarned: 'Without full say in transfer policy, the coach will sink into a quagmire.' There would be a lengthy to-do list: 'tackling a toxic dressing room', 'overcoming the slump at Old Trafford', 'reshaping the club from the ground up', 'breaking the cycle of mediocrity', 'bringing warmth and coherence to an ailing celebrity club', 'putting a firewall between the coach and the layers of middle management inserted by the ownership' and 'anticipating a very long road to recovery'. The idea was that Ten Hag had better think twice before wading into such a morass. It might spell the end of his credibility, his reputation, his managerial career. 'Welcome to Manchester United, Erik,' was the caustic conclusion.

To fans of Manchester United, all of this must have sounded painfully familiar. But Erik ten Hag is always looking for new challenges. The ascent of his coaching career – Go Ahead Eagles, FC

Utrecht, Ajax, Manchester United; the county, the province, the nation, the world – is astoundingly steep. But there is distinct danger looming ahead for the man hailing from the quietude of the eastern Dutch borderland. Only three managers have ever won the league at Manchester United. This is a club with 42 major trophies, 33 of them won by two tough Scotsmen in two distinct spells. The pattern is one of stagnation, decline, crisis, revolution. Sir Matt Busby saved a club that had been bombed into the dust by the Luftwaffe; Sir Alex Ferguson steered to safety and success a rudderless ship without a league title in 20 years.

Fellow Dutchman Jaap Stam played at Old Trafford between 1998 and 2001. He recognises that it will be difficult for Ten Hag to be as dominant in Manchester as he was at Ajax. 'The quality of the other teams is much higher in England. To do the same in the Premier League, the club must spend money on players that fit his philosophy and way of playing. He did that in the Netherlands and he will probably do that there too. By adding your own players to the roster, you can implement your playing style to get results during the season. If you belong to the biggest clubs in the world, you are obliged to compete for the prizes every season. You may not have time to build or follow a bad season with a good season. Every year they must at least compete for the FA Cup and the Premier League, as well as go far in the Champions League.'

Dutch football analyst Sam Planting thought Ten Hag might be getting himself into a predicament. 'The most important legacy he leaves in Amsterdam is that tactics matter. Frank de Boer built up credit by winning titles, but tactically it wasn't much. Ten Hag has created a tactical framework in which old leaders such as Tadić and Blind, young talent such as Gravenberch and Timber, and new acquisitions such as Antony and Álvarez succeeded. The playing style under Ten Hag was clear and the bar was set high. What he accomplished with Ajax is great. Thanks to his tactical skills Ajax has again become a relevant team in Europe. All in all, he is leaving a great legacy that you hope won't be ruined. Ten Hag's departure was inevitable. Because of the performances in the Champions League, it was also likely that he would work with a big club, although I am surprised that the choice fell on Manchester United. Maybe I had hoped he'd hold on to his cards a little longer and pick a more stable club. Manchester United imagine they are world class, but in terms of play it really isn't good. Manchester City and Liverpool have expanded enormously in recent years, but in the meantime expectations at United remain high. They do not see that the club needs to be rebuilt. I am curious whether Ten Hag will get that space.'

In addition to the technical challenges of the football club, Ten Hag will have to deal with the cultural differences in a new country. Being a manager in England is different from being a head coach in the Netherlands. The English manager is the club's banner. He has to deal with sports journalists who have to fill several pages every day. The Dutch proverbial wisdom that the Netherlands has newspapers and England has the press particularly applies in the field of sports. René Meulensteen worked at Manchester United from 2001 to 2013 in various positions. During his last five years he was assistant to Alex Ferguson. He had some words of caution for Ten Hag. 'The challenge for him will mainly lie in dealing with the greatness of Manchester United. Erik expresses himself in his own way, there is nothing wrong with that at Ajax, everyone in the Netherlands got used to it. I do know that communication at a club like Manchester United is crucial: that you can convey your vision, your faith and that you get everyone on board, your players, the media, the supporters. When Klopp is in front of the camera, I see an enormous personality, someone who speaks excellently and has a great charisma. Liverpool fans see that too: look at that manager of ours, always has his chest out. United need a man like that. Someone of whom everyone knows: he has a clear plan, we must continue to support him. I am not saying that Ten Hag cannot live up to that, but I just indicate that you should not underestimate that aspect.'

Ten Hag, for all his extraordinary qualities as a coach, has never been a media star. He does not have the winning charm of Leo Beenhakker or the natural communication skills of Guus Hiddink. Although he is not given to lecturing representatives of the media like his colleague Louis van Gaal, he had difficulties with journalists at Ajax, particularly in the early stages of his work there. When he started bringing in results, the media became more accommodating because everyone loves a winner. At Manchester United another ingredient was added to the volatile communication mix: the mysterious thing called the English language, with its intractable grammatical logic and pronunciation hurdles. If he had returned to Bayern Munich, as he almost did at one point, he would have been fine. He grew up next to the German border and like many in the area has German as his second language. English, however, is not within his comfort zone. A manager who takes charge of one of the biggest clubs in the world, with the media and publicity circus surrounding it, should have a decent command of the English language.

On 19 July 2022 Samuel Luckhurst wrote in the *Manchester Evening News*,

By appointing Ten Hag, United have restored authority to the manager's role after a four-year absence. Ten Hag has been laconic in the three rounds of briefings we have had with him. In his press conferences, the questions have run longer than some of the answers. Ten Hag talks concisely and authoritatively.

Ten Hag clearly knows what he is talking about when it comes to football. Still, people in the Netherlands were a little bemused by comments in the English media that he communicates quite well in the local language. Maybe his hosts were just being polite? Dutchmen who have mastered the language on a passable level are not impressed with what they consider Ten Hag's *steenkolen-engels*, 'coal English' – the Dutch derogation of pidgin English. His habit to literally translate Dutch idioms into English – linguists refer to the impulse as 'interference' – must cause some consternation to his British audience.

There are some problems with evaluating the professional competence of a non-native speaker primarily by judging his or her language fluency. The speaker invariably appears less competent or even less intelligent in a second language than he or she really is. How this is interpreted depends to a considerable degree on the sex of the speaker. Men often find women who speak with an accent exotic, intriguing and attractive. That may have something to do with the male stereotype of the 'fair sex' having to be more emotionally appealing than intellectually convincing. To many men, women should be playful and a little vulnerable. Women may understandably chafe at such sexism, but many men find the utterances of Monica Bellucci or Penelope Cruz compelling. But when it comes to evaluating men, who traditionally are expected to convey strength and command respect, it is a different story. Expressing oneself in less-than-fluent English is considered a liability, particularly when one occupies a position of influence. Business leaders, politicians and generals need to convince people by the soundness of their arguments and the plausibility of their plans. In short, they need to make sense.

A football manager is expected to be the boss, the leader, the gaffer, the man who has things under control. Obviously, he needs to know what he is talking about. Like troops heading into battle or pilgrims on a quest for the Holy Grail – the league trophy – his audience hangs on his every word and needs to be able to both understand and believe in what he says. Erik ten Hag, with his 'weird Dutch' at Ajax, and his less-than-polished English at Manchester United, does not fit that bill very well – say the critics. At Ajax, his image was not congruent with the picture of the gutsy and streetwise Amsterdam coach who outmanoeuvres everyone in the room with his camera-ready answers and convincing sound bites. English audiences got used to listening to Claudio Ranieri and Antonio Conte, so perhaps they will cut Ten Hag some slack?

When Erik ten Hag was appointed as the new manager of Manchester United, the Dutch media gleefully used the opportunity to try and pull the rug from under his feet. *Today Inside* analysts René van der Gijp and Valentijn Driessen suggested that, with his poor English, he was the spitting image of Carlo Boszhard. Boszhard, a TV host/funny man in the Netherlands, impersonated Ten Hag on several occasions on the RTL 4 programme *TV Kantine*, to public acclaim. Presenter Wilfred Genee introduced a segment of Ten Hag answering questions from the English press prior to the famous cup final against PSV. Ten Hag explained with some difficulty that he was still busy with Ajax and not with United. Well-known commentator Johan Derksen predicted that Ten Hag would be tripping over his words and have problems getting his message across to his players in England. 'He is going to the nuns in Vught [a convent renowned for its second-language education programmes] for a week, but I would make it three.'

Pieter de Jongh is the national coach of Somalia. In 2021 he went viral with a video in which he responded to questions of the

Zimbabwean press after a match his team had won in a language that, Dutch commentators decided, 'only showed some remote resemblance to English'. In a gesture of collegial largesse, the football coach from the small town of Asperen, who calls himself 'The Champ', offered to help Erik ten Hag learn proper English. 'Only I think that it important is that you a good teacher have for English. And the champ is available you to teach English. Erik, only a call and I'm coming from Africa to Holland you to teach English [sic].' The Manchester fans indeed may have to get used to English laced with the heavy, sharp consonants the Dutch do not easily shed. Ten Hag seems to have weathered his first English press conferences rather well. He does sometimes puzzle his audience, but people are willing – for now – to forgive him for his slightly laboured syntax, his staccato style, his Dutchisms and his curious pronunciation.

In the opposite direction, Manchester United staff and supporters, and media covering the club, may have some difficulty with pronouncing, and writing, Erik ten Hag's name correctly. The first name is straightforward: just a 'k' instead of a 'c' at the end. The problem is the surname. 'Ten' has nothing to do with maths, but is a simple preposition that means 'at,' 'of' or 'from', pointing to the geographical location the first name-bearer came from. The 't' is always in the lowercase when you are including the first name – Erik ten Hag – and capitalised when you are just using the surname, Ten Hag. The vowel sound is neither as in 'hag' – the shrew transporting herself via broom – nor as in 'hog.' It is something in-between, like the 'a' in 'art'. The 'g' at the end is problematic and sounds a little like someone with a cold clearing their throat. The Dutch have been amused by brave attempts on English TV to get it right. Fortunately, the lovely MUTV presenter Pien Meulensteen came to the rescue, instructing United fans in her equally flawless English and Dutch.

Regardless of well-meant caution, on one side, and ill-willed disparagement, on the other, Erik ten Hag did sign a contract with Manchester United until 2025. A video was released to introduce the new manager, *Announcing Erik ten Hag*. In it, the United camp explain how 'in our conversations with Erik leading up to this appointment, we were deeply impressed with his long-term vision for returning Manchester United to the level we want to be competing at, and his drive and determination to achieve that.' He will earn £9 million per season, which makes him the fifth highest-paid manager in England and the highest-paid Dutch coach in the history of the Premier League. In Manchester, Ten Hag makes in one month almost as much as he earned in a year in Amsterdam.

Interviewed by Pien Meulensteen, he displayed his typical confidence. 'I know the history of Man United, I know the big times and the audience, the vibe that can be around Old Trafford. I watched them in their big times, when Sir Alex Ferguson was manager, during the really successful times when they won titles and were dominating Europe. But also before Sir Alex, Man United was a really big club and I know names like Busby and Charlton that gave Man United a presence to the outside world with winning, and winning in a spectacular way, winning so they entertain people. What stays with me is that there was always a fighting culture. They fight together and they get success. I'm not a dreamer. I live day by day and give my best. I make my decisions based on clearness and logic. We need a good concept and we need the right people around it. Then, if we give everything, every day, we will get success. Live by the day, focus on titles. Don't dream about other things, what may happen in the future.'

Under Alex Ferguson, René Meulensteen won the Champions League and the Club World Cup with United once, two League Cups and the Premier League four times. He has said, 'It will be a very big

job for Erik: the size of the club, the pressure that comes with it …
At United you have to do one: win, and two: play attractive football.
That's the hardest thing there is for a trainer. In principle that was
also the case at Ajax, but the big difference is that you can win many
matches there by playing at 60 per cent. That is never the case in
the Premier League. There you have to work hard every three days,
out and at home. That's completely different. Manchester United are
used to taking home trophies; that hasn't happened for five years
now and then you get a slap. You can also see that in the very slow
way of hitting the transfer market. Liverpool already have Darwin
Núñez and Manchester City Erling Haaland, but at United it squeaks
and creaks. At those clubs you also know exactly where you stand.
Liverpool is intensity, energy, direct and dynamic football. City is
more for short passes, tiki-taka. But United have completely lost their
identity in recent years. I have no idea what the club stands for now.
It is Erik's job to bring that back so that big players want to go back
to Old Trafford. It is also hoped for the entire Dutch trainers' guild
that it will go well.'

Jaap Stam said, 'Most difficult will be implementing his playing
style. He will undoubtedly have been obtained because of his way
of playing football at Ajax. He will also have to take care of that at
United. Then he will have to train and improve the current players,
because you can't get 11 new players. They will have to think differently about football and filling their position. There are many places
that need to be filled in differently, or where players simply have to
perform better. For example, there is very little attacking power
from the rear. The backs are unstable, not dynamic enough and do
not bring enough quality. The rearguard turned out to be a major
flaw in the build-up, but also purely defensively. They conceded far
too many goals.'

Asked by the BBC whether he was wise to put his growing reputation on the line with 'a club that a lot of people are thinking is not doing very well', Ten Hag responded without batting an eyelid, 'I don't see it as a risk. This club has a great history. So now, let's make a future. I am really excited to do that with the people who are at the club. We will bring some people into the staff, and we will analyse the squad. We will go from day to day: work hard, and I am sure we'll get success.' About Klopp and Guardiola: do they need to leave before others can have a shot at the crown? 'In this moment, I admire them. I admire them both very much. At the moment, they play really fantastic football, Liverpool and Man City. But you will always see that an era can come to an end. I am looking forward to doing battle with them. And I am sure that, in the Premier League, all the other clubs will want to do the same. The reason I am here is that there is great potential for the future. That is why I am here.'

Menno Pot, Ajax podcast host and a bit of a Ten Hag connoisseur, says, 'Erik comes across as a very, very focused man, very serious and with an enormous work ethic. He is always talking about football and thinks it should be better. It took some time for people to get used to him [at Ajax] because he didn't turn things around immediately. By the time he started his first proper season he had lost much of his credit and it was a thin line. And it was hard for him at first. But slowly, people started to understand what he was doing, results started coming, the team started improving and that's when the magic happened. I think we have come to love him as a person as well. With his integrity and his seriousness, he is a bit of a professor and people can smile about that now. When I think of Erik, I am totally convinced that he will read about Manchester United, that he knows the club, knows how they have played in the past and what the philosophy of the club is. He will take that into account and implement his own vision along with it so it will become something better. He is very, very aware of the traditions of the club and what people will want to see at Old Trafford.'

In an interview with *Voetbal International* Ten Hag said, 'It feels like a difficult but great challenge. That is also the most beautiful thing there is. There is also something to build at United and something to gain. Manchester United is such a big name in football history. It feels like a challenge to put the club back on the track of winning. Old Trafford is nicknamed the Theatre of Dreams for a reason. It is a club with name, fame and allure in international football. Everyone knows the history of the beautiful teams. From Sir Alex Ferguson of course, but also further back in time. The great team of the late fifties, which suddenly disappeared with the plane crash. The history is impressive, but I also started to delve into the present and the future, and the options that are available. They are there, also financially. If you also get a good feeling from the people who are there, then the picture is right and then the factors are present to take this step.'

Andy Mitten, editor-in-chief of *United We Stand*, the largest United supporters' fanzine, thinks Ten Hag will get some time, but only so much. 'It is the most difficult job in football. And everyone seems to think he's a superhero. People crave success to such an extent that he can fill in everything according to his own insight. And there is money enough to attract stars. Ajax is big, Manchester United gigantic. Ten Hag starts with the wind in his sails. Once the ball rolls, it can turn quickly. But we all hope he's "the one".'

14

THEATRE OF NEW DREAMS

'Atmosphere great, welcome fantastic,
organisation really, really good. But result not.'
JÜRGEN KLOPP, AFTER LIVERPOOL'S 4–0 LOSS TO
MANCHESTER UNITED IN BANGKOK, 12 JULY 2022

At top-level games there are instances when one moment of mental weakness from one player decides the course of a match and, hence, the championship or tournament. The situation on the pitch is such that an opponent will immediately profit from a moment of inattention. It is down to the coach to get his players in the right frame of mind to avoid this. The purpose of training is to acquire not only tactical skills but the mental framework that underlies the game. A coach who can convince his players of this is invaluable. The best players know that football is played more without the ball than with the ball. The more they play with their head, the easier it will be on their legs, and the more energy they will conserve.

Such football intelligence is created from a number of match-related mental qualities. The emphasis varies from player to player, but to a greater or lesser degree they are essential for every top-level player: conviction to be a winner; courage, self-confidence and a controlled fear of losing; controlled aggressiveness and stamina; the ability to accept and deal with a defeat, to take and demand responsibility, to maintain team discipline and team spirit; and engender a sense of responsibility for the team. Naturally, a ball virtuoso will not become a fighter in duels with an opponent. A true goal scorer will not get thrown off balance by blasting a shot into row Z, but another player might be too scared to shoot or make a long pass. The solidarity players feel with each other has a positive influence on their mentality. The willingness to take personal responsibility for achieving a good collective performance is the most important tool available to the coach to influence the mentality of individual players.

The environment a manager creates at a club is vital in achieving this. This is not an easy assignment, and there is no ready recipe for preserving a positive atmosphere: maintaining the set-up demands the constant attention of the coach. When holding a training camp that lasts for a few weeks he has to deal with all kinds of problems. The quality of the facilities must be exceptionally good. It is not always easy to find the ideal hotel. Another important aspect is to find a good balance between tension and relaxation. There are a number of 'empty' hours that need to be filled by a group that is exclusively made up of males, many, if not all of them, millionaires.

The most successful teams have a dominant character at the top. Erik ten Hag knows this, and he immediately put his stamp on Carrington culture by instituting his own regimen. He took the initiative to foster a sense of togetherness after a season in which the dressing room became fractured and dominated by cliques. All the players eat dinner and breakfast together. In the past, players were permitted to eat breakfast later on their own, but Ten Hag wants all of his squad to eat at the same time. Fines or punishments will now be meted out to any player or staff member who is late for a team meeting, meal or training. Ten Hag was pleased with how the team responded to his demands, including the arrival time at the

Carrington complex of 9am, which was previously only applicable to youth players.

Another rule is that players will not be allowed to drink alcohol during game weeks to ensure that they will be at their maximum conditioning level. Each player will have a custom-made diet plan and a monthly BMI check-up. Players will no longer employ their own catering staff; the same chefs will prepare meals for everyone. The food menu at Carrington was changed, with fish and vegetables featuring more prominently. The manager has also asked his players to come see him, rather than their agents, if they have any issues. This will prevent dressing room leaks and unnecessary tension. Ten Hag is down-to-earth and communicates in a very direct way. Although his training sessions are intense, they are easy to understand. Meetings with players beyond training-specific instructions are kept to a minimum. He is enthusiastic on the pitch, which has considerably improved the mood around Carrington. Unlike his immediate prede-cessors, Ten Hag leads every element of training – even to the extent of rearranging cones. Van der Gaag and McClaren are also hands-on, helped by Darren Fletcher and Eric Ramsay.

Erik ten Hag is not intimidated by the Manchester United chal-lenge. But he does not think he has to take on rebuilding the team single-handedly. He is not an office man – if he was he would have joined his dad in the real estate business. He will not go down the route of traditional English management and constantly be on the phone to agents. He wants a sporting director or an assistant to do that. He spends an incredible amount of time on the training pitch. He wants to be in a tracksuit whenever he can. Whereas many coaches focus only on the first team, Ten Hag doesn't just pay atten-tion to the star players. He also goes beyond the first 11 to the 19th or 20th most important player. If they show promise and work hard, he will give all of them his time. Even with those who have a difficult background, if he thinks the talent is there, he will make sure they fit in. He wins the trust and respect of his players because they see the effort he puts into improving them individually.

Mitchell van der Gaag was a young centre back at PSV Eindhoven until he suffered a serious injury that sidelined him for more than two years. He played abroad at Motherwell in Scotland but was most successful in Portugal with Madeiran club Marítimo. He concluded his playing career in Saudi Arabia. He moved to Ajax in 2019 as the head coach of Jong Ajax and earned a reputation for developing young players. In 2021 Van der Gaag was appointed as first-team assistant coach to Ten Hag. At Ajax, he often watched games up in the stand to get a better view, effectively serving as a second pair of eyes for Ten Hag. He is known as a coach who excels in organising defences. He has outstanding man-management skills and is an effective communicator, which is underlined by his fluency in five languages – Dutch, English, Spanish, Portuguese and French.

Van der Gaag explained his methods in an interview in Holland: 'I used to have discussions with the whole team, but as field coach I am moving away from that more and more. Players increasingly prefer individual conversations. That takes a lot more time and energy, but I have the feeling that I can reach my players better that way. I sit down with players every week and we look at how they have performed, together with the footage. As a result, I can demand much more and you also get more sense of responsibility from the player. They can hide in a group. These are not just fair weather conversations either. If I'm not satisfied, I'll say so. Then everyone will know where he stands. I talk to everyone. If I don't, and suddenly we have to call on a substitute, I don't want to be paying attention to that player for the first time. You don't want a player to think, *ah, he suddenly has time for me, now I am suddenly important.* I am naturally quite calm, but I do not run away from a conflict.'

Ten Hag felt that Van der Gaag was a great fit as assistant at United. 'My vision evolves, but in many areas the essence remains the same. The bigger the club, the more you have to deal with many stakeholders who influence the process. And you have to guide that yourself. Much more is asked of you as a manager. If you don't have competent people around you, you can't delegate either, and then you end up doing it all yourself anyway. If you do have competent people, you can do it well. And that also depends on your leadership style. Above all, you have to inspire people with your vision and then you can assign tasks. An example is the training process: I know that this is in good hands with Mitchell van der Gaag. In return, I benefit from that on the field. Because he is at the training sessions, I often get to take the bird's-eye view. And then, as a manager, you get a much better view than when you are involved with the exercise yourself.'

United returned to training on 27 June and flew out to Thailand 12 days later. Ten Hag clearly outlined his expectations of the pre-season journey: 'I have to learn, to know my squad, the personnel, the individuals, the players. That is, I think, one of the biggest advantages of the tour. We have two weeks to work really closely together and we will learn about each other. I want to learn about them, and they want to learn about me, my coaches and assistants. We'll spend a lot of time together and do it with a lot of team football. But there will also be time in locations not directly in connection with football, to learn about each other in a personal way as well.' Pre-season is not only a chance to gather knowledge about the team, but an important opportunity 'to get the players physically and also mentally fit and to get a team. Of course, it will improve during the season, but you are setting high standards and demands, establishing values and making rules, so you get organised to go into the season. What I want to see is that they learn but also they show themselves because they have to deserve a position in top football. You have to earn your position. That means you have to deliver every day. That demands a certain style, a certain way of life that they have to adapt to, that they probably don't know yet. I hope they can prove themselves and they will come into the squad.'

United flew to Bangkok on a Boeing 747 furnished entirely with business class seats by specialist carrier Atlas. With Ukraine airspace closed to civilian flights since February, the United plane was directed south of the war zone when they ordinarily would have flown through Ukraine and Russia, the detour prolonging the flight by more than two hours. On the flight Ten Hag walked through the plane asking employees about their role at the club and their background, demonstrating that his warmth extends to everyone at United. He understands what a grind a long tour can be and so constantly expressed his appreciation for staff. The five-star Athenee Hotel in the Sukhumvit Ploenchit area of Bangkok has eight restaurants and bars, a spa and roof-top pool. United had two floors sectioned off for their 120-strong tour party. The hotel was mobbed with supporters as soon as Ten Hag and his players arrived. An area was cordoned off in the lobby for fans to pose for pictures with their heroes and get autographs. There was another area sectioned off outside – away from United's two giant red tour buses –for those who had not been able to get inside.

The heat in Thailand in summer is made oppressive by the 80 to 90 per cent humidity. Manchester United and Liverpool are the two most popular Premier League clubs in the Far East. Taken together, this created a boiling and noisy mixture inside Bangkok's Rajamangala

Stadium. In the second half Manchester and Liverpool fans donned disposable raincoats to protect themselves against another instalment of the monsoon rains that Thai people take for granted in summer. United started the game on the front foot. There were six players inside the Liverpool third for the first press; the full-backs doubled as wingers. The starting United side set up in a 4-2-3-1 formation and the second team was in a 4-3-3. At times, United overcommitted but their goal led a charmed life when the post, and not the back of the net, was struck twice within a minute. As in April, the score-line ended 4–0, only this time it was reversed. Some Liverpool fans sported '9–0' shirts, celebrating their aggregate drubbing of United the previous season. Manchester United last defeated Liverpool 4–0 in April 2003.

Beating Liverpool is always a good start for a United manager, whatever the context. In Bangkok, Erik ten Hag received his first silverware. After the match, he observed, 'I have seen some really good things. I think we have a lot of creativity and speed up front, so we have potential. The experience from the team, the heart we played with. We were very brave, proactive. I was very happy to see that we transferred what we trained on during the last two weeks. So, well done. We have made our first step, and now we have to build on that. We have a lot of work to do.'

United then moved on to Australia for the next part of their pre-season tour. The 100,000 spectators in the Melbourne Cricket Ground were in festive mood. The stadium, the largest in Australia by some distance, holds almost twice the number of spectators as the Rajamangala, a circular, southern-hemisphere Camp Nou. Melbourne Victory midfielder Chris Ikonomidis scored within five minutes to give the Australian outfit a 1–0 lead. Aussie fans were chanting 'you're getting sacked in the morning!' at Ten Hag before his competitive tenure at United had even started. Manchester United had to battle a Melbourne side that did plenty of parking the bus. But the team dealt effectively with the Australian defensive barrier, producing a comfortable 4–1 win.

Perth was ravaged by torrential rain during the Manchester United–Aston Villa game. The pitch in the Optus Stadium was soaked and uneven, and cut up terribly in the second half. It clearly affected both teams' attempts to play passing football in the closing stages, but Ten Hag offered no excuses. 'These are the circumstances we have to deal with on a football field. It's equal and you have to turn it into an advantage. The first half was a decent performance, 2–0 up. But in the second half, we had control of the game, and we gave it away. That's not good, so that is a lesson for the players, for the team. I think we make a lot of progress, a lot of positive aspects. A season is not always going up, you also have setbacks and have to deal with that. A loss of focus is unacceptable. But I'm glad it's happening now. Because now I can tell them it shouldn't happen.'

Back in Europe, Manchester United had to play two matches in a little over 24 hours, so Ten Hag divided his squad: the strongest team lost 1–0 to Atlético Madrid in Oslo on a Saturday before the second string side drew 1–1 with Rayo Vallecano at Old Trafford on Sunday. It meant that United ended pre-season with three wins, two draws and one defeat, with 14 goals scored and six conceded.

There is a very close relationship between how much a club spends and what success can be expected. It is obvious that the results attained by Real Madrid, Paris Saint-Germain, Bayern Munich and Manchester City are to a large extent the product of their spending power. In *Soccernomics*, the economist Stefan Szymanski and the journalist Simon Kuper argue that money determines somewhere between 80 and 90 per cent of the performance of professional football clubs.

That leaves 10 or 20 per cent for other factors, one of which is the manager. Their influence could be compared to that of prime ministers on the economy: probably no other single individual has more influence, but it's still limited. Judging by the words of Richard Arnold, football cannot be reduced to mere mathematics. The Manchester United chief executive, who succeeded Ed Woodward in early 2022, was open about the club's recruitment problems when speaking to supporters. 'We spent a billion pounds on players. We have spent more than anyone in Europe. I'm not thrilled with where we are. It doesn't sit easy with me and I worry how we get this sorted out for the future. We have blown through an enormous amount of money.'

Manchester United is one of the greatest clubs in the world, an institution with an awe-inspiring past and a global presence. But the organisation has forgotten, in part due to its American ownership, that football should be the primary consideration of a football company. The transfer period is a good indicator for top clubs. Pep Guardiola and Jürgen Klopp chose Erling Haaland and Darwin Núñez. Like many other top clubs, Manchester United expressed interest in Robert Lewandowski. But the best players in the world are not really interested in the Europa League and do not want to be 20 or 30 points behind in fourth, fifth or sixth place in the table. United's detractors speak of 'the club no player in the world wants to move to'. That is exaggerated, but Ten Hag had some difficulty convincing players to join him in Manchester. He has to pull the club from an extremely difficult position while expectations and demands remain high.

In every organisation it's important to have good cooperation. Ten Hag's pas de deux with Overmars at Ajax was fine-tuned to great effect. Until Overmars's sudden departure, the club had an effective machine that allowed Ten Hag to focus on training the team, leaving the politics and transfer negotiations to Overmars and Van der Sar.

At United, it is different. After years of turbulence, this is seen as a fresh start, but the club is playing catch-up in the transfermarket. At Ajax, there is an almost annual upheaval as the club loses its best players. Ten Hag won't have that problem at United. Matt Judge, the man who previously handled transfer negotiations, departed along with chief scout Jim Lawlor and head of global scouting Marcel Bout. With the exit of the much-maligned Ed Woodward, it marked the exodus of senior staff. The solution was to entrust the rebuild to the football experts, with less boardroom interference, giving space to Erik ten Hag and director of football John Murtough. Judging by the targets identified, Murtough decided to give Ten Hag what he wants.

The head coach's extensive influence on recruitment strategy is still a little unusual at an English top club. But Ten Hag understands the reality of football very well and can find the right combination of player acquisition and moulding a team into a winning force on the training ground. Wherever he goes he has been directly and intensely involved in determining the transfer policy of his club. He said, 'I set requirements in advance about how I want to work. If they aren't granted, I won't do it. I am ultimately responsible and I am judged on the results. I don't want to be the sole ruler, I stand for cooperation, but having a say in transfers is a condition for me.' Once the personnel question is settled – the 'player material', as Ten Hag likes to call it – he is prepared to do anything to coax that extra 10 or 20 per cent (whatever it really is) out of his players.

Interim manager Ralf Rangnick reached an alarming conclusion when he was asked how United could close the gap with Manchester City and Liverpool: 'six to ten players must come'. For his predecessor Ole Gunnar Solskjær, designing a team and leading one did not seem to go together well. Under his watch, Manchester United brought in Cristiano Ronaldo, Harry Maguire and Aaron

Wan-Bissaka. But taken together, all the beautiful names did not form a coherent whole. There was a pervasive lack of vision and clarity. For one reason or another, Solskjær did not get the players that could have improved team performance. Transfer policy became so muddled in recent years that Manchester United put together a roster for five different game systems.

By contrast, Ten Hag selects transfer targets that fit his philosophy. His assessment of the squad was that it was grossly imbalanced, short on tactically gifted thinkers, lacking in speed and the conditioning was well below what was needed to implement his high-tempo style. He recognised that certain players had not been used according to their strengths. He planned to cure the ills through intense training, a change in psychology and focused transfers. Following the departures of Jesse Lingard, Paul Pogba, Juan Mata, Nemanja Matić, Edinson Cavani and Andreas Pereira, he outlined what reinforcements he needed. He wanted the bulk of the transfer business completed before the team flew out for their pre-season tour on 8 July, which proved to be an elusive goal. He assured nervous fans that there would be no desperation-buying. 'We need the right player,' he asserted. 'We have a list of players who have the attributes to play that role. We will strike the moment the player is available. We need new players, we need quality players and we will do everything to convince them to come.'

New coaches strengthen their teams by contracting the most suitable players – often with a contingent from their home countries. With Ten Hag, an influx of players from the Netherlands was to be expected at United. At Go Ahead Eagles (Quincy Promes and Deniz Türüç), FC Utrecht (Andreas Ludwig and Rico Strieder) and Ajax (Zakaria Labyad, Sean Klaiber and Sébastien Haller), Ten Hag surrounded himself with old acquaintances. This was in keeping with his character as a coach, prioritising loyalty and trust, and essential to the way he likes to play – a physically and tactically demanding style that requires intensive preparation. The coach is keenly interested in introducing his system as quickly as possible, which is essential at a club like Manchester United where performance is rated from one game to the next. He is inclined to employ players who are already familiar with his game principles. If 20 or 30 per cent of the team have already mastered the system, the collective learning curve is not as steep.

Ten Hag wants to direct matches and control them in the opponent's half. In this way his team plays with a lot of space in the back, meaning you need players who are quick and not afraid to cover. Tyrell Malacia and Lisandro Martínez have those qualities. Manchester United bought Malacia from Feyenoord in July 2022. The left back traded Rotterdam's De Kuip for Old Trafford for a transfer fee of €15 million, excluding €2 million in bonuses. He signed a contract until the summer of 2026 with an option for another season. The pundits predicted that at Manchester United he would have to compete with England international Luke Shaw in the left-back position – a battle he appears to be largely winning. He was very happy with his move, saying, 'It's an incredible feeling to be at Manchester United. This is a new chapter for me, a new league with new teammates and a great manager. From playing against his team in the Eredivisie, I know what qualities he has and what he demands of his players.'

Christian Eriksen has a long connection with Ajax. Danny Blind travelled to Denmark to sign the 16-year-old from Odense in 2008. United was among those to show an interest in the teenage prodigy – the youngest player to appear at the 2010 World Cup in South Africa – but he opted for Ajax instead. Six and a half years at Spurs followed, before he moved to Italy to play under Antonio Conte at Inter. He suffered a cardiac arrest while playing for Denmark at his country's opening game of Euro 2020; following this he was fitted with an implantable cardioverter defibrillator (ICD). He was no longer permitted to play in Italy and exited Inter Milan. Back at Ajax once more in an unsigned capacity, he began his road to recovery, training with the reserves while Ten Hag was at the helm of the first team. 'I am very happy to be here,' the Dane said at the time in fluent Dutch. 'At Ajax I know the people; it feels like coming home because I was here for so long.' Slowly, he pieced his life back together. In January, when he had been cleared to play, newly promoted Premier League club Brentford offered him a short-term deal.

The 30-year-old is starting a new chapter now after signing a three-year deal with Manchester United. On the move, Eriksen said, 'I have seen Erik's work at Ajax and know the level of detail and preparation that he and his staff put into every day. It is clear that he is a fantastic coach. Having spoken with him and learning more about his vision and the way he wants the team to play, I am even more excited for the future.' Some questions were asked when the Dane was taken on a free transfer. But Ten Hag knew exactly how important Eriksen's creativity and his ability to open up defences would become for his team. Eriksen is a stable and consistent influence. He has the awareness and ability to make passes that few others can. At United, where attacking talent has foundered partly through the lack of chances created, that is a priceless asset. Eriksen is capable of creating scoring opportunities, as he once did for Harry Kane at Tottenham and more recently Romelu Lukaku at Inter Milan. He is the calm brain in the centre of the pitch who can complement the instinctive talent of attacking players like Bruno Fernandes.

With his limited height, Lisandro Martínez raised a few eyebrows in England. At 5ft 9in. he does not seem to be made for Premier

League football, where defenders have to be ready to guard against numerous long balls and win a lot of aerial duels. But at his previous clubs Martínez won more duels on average than defenders of considerably greater stature, such as Matthijs de Ligt. Despite being almost eight inches shorter than Harry Maguire – and playing six league games fewer because of injury – Martínez still managed to win 80 aerial duels to Maguire's 75. During the 2021–2 season at Ajax, Martínez ranked higher than United's defenders per 90 minutes for passes, forward passes, aerial duels won, interceptions and possession won. He also won more tackles and completed more dribbles than United's centre backs. The 24-year-old won two Dutch titles in three years under Ten Hag and was Ajax's player of the year. That quality came with a hefty price tag: Ajax received €57 million for Martínez, with the caveat that the fee could rise an additional €10 million with bonuses.

Strikers win matches but defenders win titles, is the adage. Ten Hag likes his players to find solutions on the pitch, and he acquired a centre back who will do just that. Martínez epitomises the sort of front-foot defending that Erik ten Hag wants to see. He is a ball-playing defender with the aggression the Manchester defence has been deficient in. Martínez said, 'I am called the Carnicero – the Butcher – of Amsterdam. We Argentines do everything with passion, and when I go out on the pitch I fight for every ball. If I have to step over dead bodies, I do it. I want to win every 50-50 situation because I know that I am fighting for food for every member of my family and for my friends. That is the feeling I have – and that every Argentinian has. It is the kind of motivation I cannot explain.' He is not overly fond of 'The Butcher' moniker that was given to him in Amsterdam. In Argentina, he is known as 'The Pitbull'. He fits the trend of most major clubs – in the Premier League and beyond

– to have a left-footed defender playing a key role in the team. A lot will be said about Martínez's height for a little while. He is a full head shorter than the giants he will encounter. But Ten Hag is unfazed because he knows how easily Martínez held his own against Erling Haaland in the 4–0 home win against Borussia Dortmund. His versatility is a weapon.

With Tyrell Malacia, Christian Eriksen and Lisandro Martínez, the manager indicated the desired profile shift: technically skilled and tactically intelligent players that can help United become a team dominant in possession. Ten Hag said, 'Eriksen is an experienced player, he's played in Holland, Italy and especially England with Spurs, so a long career and also a lot of caps for the Danish national squad. I think the whole Premier League knows what he can do, what he can contribute to the team, and I would call that creativity. Martínez is a different type. He's a warrior, he brings aggressiveness, but he can also play football and has a good left foot. That is also what you need in the balance of the team, players who can create and also players who can defend. In the defending part we want to be proactive and to be of the highest intensity.'

Roy Keane risked sounding like a broken record on Sky Sports, bewailing the lack of firm command at his former club. Clearly, there is no one of his calibre at United when it comes to leadership, but then there are few like him in today's football at all. Still, establishing an order of players to depend on is an absolute necessity. That was part of Ten Hag's thinking when he signed Real Madrid midfielder Casemiro. He lauded the 30-year-old, explaining the ways in which the five-time Champions League winner would drive the team forward. 'He has won so many trophies in his career. He knows the road: how you win games and how you win trophies. We now have more players who have won already many trophies in their careers.

That has to be a guidance for the rest of the team, so they know and they understand how to win games.'

When Casemiro left Real Madrid, Luka Modric called him a 'true leader' and 'the best bodyguard in the world.' Toni Kroos said, 'With you, even the Turkish bath was a gym and you only allowed people to lie down when it was time to do sit-ups.'

His move brought an end to United's search for a much-needed defensive midfielder. He was introduced to fans at the first league match against Liverpool. 'I think it was quite good for him to see the Premier League, it's a different style,' Ten Hag said. 'Now we have to integrate him in the team in the way of play and the way of working with his teammates.' Ten Hag came another step closer towards completing his complex jigsaw.

Developing a new, functional team cannot just be up to new transfers. Those that are already in the squad must buy into the new manager's philosophy and methods. Ten Hag explained, 'I think that, as a trainer, you should always work first with the players you already have available. The position of right-wing defender in our selection is a good example of this. In the beginning I also had my doubts about whether we should look for reinforcements there, but then you start working with your team and you come to new insights. A player like Diogo Dalot did very well in that place during preparation, and I saw the potential of that boy.'

After a dreadful 2021–2 season, there were challenges for many. The ball needed to be moved with greater speed and precision, the first touch had to be better, some of the positioning needed correcting and not only was the movement of players too sluggish, but there was not enough communication. High-quality intensity takes time to develop. Ten Hag wants his teams to be able to keep the ball in tight spots and manipulate space effectively. He tested the players' first touch, reaction times, quick thinking, movement and fitness. 'Every new season is a new start. We don't have to look back at the past, we have to look to the future. These players have great potential. When we construct a team, and they take responsibility for their fitness, I am sure they will perform, and we will get the right results. It's always a matter of developing. That's true with experienced players and with younger players. I am a coach, I am not afraid. If players are good enough, I will use them. We set a high standard, and the team responds to it. We are happy with that.'

Jadon Sancho and Marcus Rashford were two of the players who did not reach their potential under the previous regime, struggling after Euro disappointment and in a lacklustre club campaign. Ten Hag built them back up. Sancho fits well into the Ten Hag system. He has the close control and intelligence to combine in small triangles and find space in tight areas. Rashford looked in excellent shape when he returned from a working holiday in the United States. He did a lot of warm-weather training at Nike's HQ, was in superb physical condition and had a point to prove after the worst season of his career. He said, 'The manager just wants us to be positive. He wants us to do everything in a positive manner, so for us it means a lot of forward runs, a lot of interchanging positions, trying to link with each other on the ball. It's fun to play in, we're enjoying it, so hopefully we can kick on and offer these type of performances come the season.'

Bruno Fernandes has the individual brilliance that Ajax relied upon with Dušan Tadić. Used as one of the more advanced midfielders, he can thrive under Ten Hag. He will need to be more patient in possession, with his coach preferring to wait for the best moment rather than pounce on the earliest one. He loses the ball, but then, all creative players do because they are the ones taking risks to make things happen. Like Tadić, Fernandes is a leader on the pitch and arguably will be one of United's most important players.

By adventurous nature and out of economic necessity, reliance on young talent is a Dutch speciality. This is particularly emphasised at Ajax where the annually recurring migration of top players heading west and south in Europe depletes the first team. Ten Hag has a strong record of bringing on academy graduates both in his time at Bayern Munich and Ajax. His most recent Ajax team had ten regular outfield players of whom six were 24 or younger and three were over 30 years old. He was happy to see a promising crop of young players at Old Trafford. Youngster Zidane Iqbal put in some impressive performances during pre-season, while Charlie Savage also held his own. Alejandro Garnacho is on the shortlist to make a first-team appearance. There are more.

In an interview with *Voetbal International*, Ten Hag explained his perspective on youth. 'Just as at Ajax, at Manchester United the second team was isolated when I came in. It wasn't really part of the academy anymore, but it wasn't part of the first team either. I immediately changed that, just like I did when I started in Amsterdam. The second team became the responsibility of the head coach. This allows me to exert influence on player transition. Of course I give the coaches freedom, but I can also give directions, for instance by saying, "I want that particular player to get minutes in that position". The final responsibility lies with me – how that team performs and the movement from the second to the first team. That is completely new for Manchester United, but I had already discussed it during the introductory meetings with the club management. The continuous influx of talent – I explained that. The basis for the first team is the youth academy.'

Before the first game of the 2022–3 against Brighton, protests by United fans forced the club shop to close as a crowd gathered in front of the megastore. Co-owner Avram Glazer, making a rare visit and later watching the match from the directors' box, must have noticed. The result was a 2–1 loss. The match was a plea for a striker, someone to fill the role Robin van Persie or Wayne Rooney once occupied. Anthony Martial, who started very well in the warm-up, was injured. United started with Christian Eriksen as a false number 9. Ten Hag said, 'If I had a real striker at my disposal, I would have fielded him. With Martial out, we did not have a good replacement and then we struggled. You need that depth when you have injuries and games every three days, and players who are not recovered to play the next game.' Süleyman Öztürk, a senior pundit at *Voetbal International*, declared, 'Manchester United are doomed (and so is Erik ten Hag).'

However, Ten Hag insisted that individual errors cost them against Brighton. He said, with utter certainty, 'I get it done – and I'm convinced I'll get it done here as well.' He operates a '24-hour rule – you celebrate, or moan, after that you move on'. He continued, 'Of course it starts with the result, but also the performance, in many aspects we were not good. But it is quite normal though in the start of the season when you have to get together and when you want to get a way of playing. You miss two players against a good team. We were confident in pre-season, good pressing and decisions, but that was clearly not the case in the first half against Brighton, when we obviously made mistakes and they punished us. You have to be mentally strong at the start of the season as you will make mistakes.'

Manchester United followed up their humbling at Brighton with an embarrassing 4–0 defeat against Brentford. All of the goals came in the first half and the result left United bottom of the table after two games. Ten Hag admitted, 'Brentford were more hungry. We conceded goals from individual mistakes. You can't have a tactical plan but then put it in the bin. I asked them to play with belief and take responsibility for their performance, and that's what they didn't do. I definitely was not happy. You can talk about football, you can talk about the plan and philosophy, but it starts with the basic stuff, the right attitude, a fighting attitude, and I didn't see that from minute one. Bring it on the pitch in every game. It starts with yourself, act as a team, follow the rules and principles and work hard, as hard as you can. If you do that you can build confidence. It's not difficult to motivate this team because my experience is that they work really well on the training pitch. It's a normal week as a manager: you see a game, you have a plan, a way of playing and then you check how the game went. Then you clearly analyse and see what's wrong and what's good.'

Manchester United was originally founded under the name Newton Heath Lancashire and Yorkshire Railway Football Club in 1878, and eventually changed to its current name in 1902, moving to Old Trafford eight years later. Newton Heath played in a bold yellow-and-green strip throughout their 24-year existence, with the squad populated by railway workers full of passion for the game, building a strong foundation for the values that still are cherished today. United's fanbase now wear yellow-and-green scarves as a reminder to the powers that be of those values. The supporters' call for the departure of the hated American owners that took place hours before the Manchester United–Liverpool kick-off made Ten Hag decide to cancel a team meeting at Manchester's Lowry Hotel. A police cordon kept watch in front of the stadium as a protest marched against the Glazer family. Inside the stadium, the muggy air was thick with cordite from the green and yellow flares. The night was one of the most raucous in Old Trafford's recent history, fuelled by demoralising defeats, simmering antipathy towards absentee owners and the loathed opposition.

An awesome Manchester United resurrection took place under these grim circumstances. Ten Hag forcefully intervened after the previous humiliations and found the way to let his team rise above itself. With aggression, energy and urgency, United displayed mental resilience. The speed of Anthony Elanga got Liverpool into continuous trouble. His assist was the start of an unreal evening. Jadon Sancho showed superb control and composure to deservedly put United in front after 16 minutes, before Marcus Rashford raced clear to beat Alisson from substitute Anthony Martial's pass eight minutes after the interval. Mo Salah scrambled in a header with nine minutes left, but the evening could not go wrong for Ten Hag. After the match Rashford said, 'For me it is about my mentality, when I am happy and feel happy I will play well, score goals and help the team.' He wasn't the only one who was happy.

Erik ten Hag said, 'We can talk about tactics but it is all about attitude. There was communication and a fighting spirit. I wanted a different approach and a different attitude and that is what they brought on the pitch. It is only a start. We can play with much more composure and much more danger. Be a team and have a good spirit – and that is what we saw today. It is not always about what I said. We have to act and not talk a lot and make sure you are a team and battle and be brave and give each other options. It makes me happy that Rashford and Sancho got the goals. Fernandes took responsibility and the captaincy encouraged him. He showed leadership with Varane. They made a huge difference. It is not just them; we need more leaders. When you want to win you need leaders and the spirit we showed today. I am happy with the performance but we have to bring it every game. Don't just bring it against Liverpool. Every Premier League game is difficult, we need to bring it to every game. It starts, once again, with the spirit.'

The counterplay style was not new to fans at Old Trafford. 'When you talk about Manchester United, you talk about speed,' Liverpool assistant Pepijn Lijnders summarised in his analysis of the Manchester rivals in his book *Intensity*. United's best finishes since Alex Ferguson's departure came when José Mourinho and Ole Gunnar Solskjær played purely on the counter-attack – playing with black, Ten Hag calls it. Unfortunately, Ten Hag still had to do a lot of work with a team that was accustomed to that type of football. As club icon Wayne Rooney put it, 'He needs time. He inherited a lot of players from the previous managers.' United have never looked comfortable playing out from the back, nor have they pressed with any sense of cohesion or purpose. Both are critical elements to Ten Hag's style of play. Against Liverpool the coach showed that he understood the problem and proved that he can compromise and play to the current strengths of his team. To negate the high press from Liverpool, he opted for long balls from his goalkeeper. The manager demonstrated his versatility and pragmatism, adapting to present realities while continuing to work on getting his team to where he really wants them to be.

Ten Hag's prayers for a striker were answered when Brazilian forward Antony was signed shortly before the closing of the transfer window. Manchester United's primary attacking target was finally secured in a deal worth an initial €95 million (£82 million) plus €5 million (£4.3 million) in bonuses. In 2020, Antony had made his debut for Ajax in an away match against Sparta Rotterdam. He scored the only goal of the match. He smartly received a pass on his foot, followed by a dribble inside and a shot into the far corner.

Ten Hag immediately felt he was someone special. 'A very sharp guy, who picks things up quickly. Antony is a true footballer, a wonderful player who has the ball on a string. At Ajax, we made it clear to him at the beginning what we wanted from him. We worked with profiles per position: what is expected in possession when choosing position in the build-up and offensively, how we want to put pressure. But without an excessive number of tasks and assignments. To a large degree, this kind of player has to figure things out and feel freedom on the pitch. From the first moment, he really impressed in terms of his football qualities and as a person. He's a fighter and someone who has a real willingness to win games, I like that. He showed that from the first moment in Amsterdam, from the first game with the winning goal. That is what he always contributes to the team – a fighting spirit who creates actions, and I expect the same from him in Manchester. I think the fans will be excited by him and the way he plays his game.'

Antony Matheus dos Santos was on from the kick-off in the match against Arsenal, which says a lot about his status. His manager did not think it necessary to let him acclimatise in England a little. The game is 35 minutes old when Bruno Fernandes passes across the axis of the pitch, right through the heart of the Arsenal defence. The ball gets to Marcus Rashford, who smartly extends to Antony, and the Brazilian slides the ball into the far corner for his debut goal: 1–0. Old Trafford explodes with joy and the player is buried in the corner of the pitch by his teammates. Antony ferociously hits the Manchester United logo on his chest in front of the Arsenal supporters. He impersonates a tiger, making claw gestures towards the camera, and tucks a ball under his shirt, sucking his thumb like a baby. Old Trafford immediately gets the whole package, complete with the exuberance, aggression and theatre. Erik ten Hag said afterwards, 'I know what he can bring with his threat, with his actions and his speed. That's why I put him on right away.'

The £225 million outlay on Antony, Casemiro, Lisandro Martínez, Tyrell Malacia and Christian Eriksen is unprecedented in the club's history. United's previous biggest summer spending was £153 million under Ole Gunnar Solskjaer in 2019. Ten Hag explained the spending was unavoidable. 'If you want to compete at the top, you don't have a choice. If you want to fight for the top four positions you have to do it, and we have the ambition, especially over the long term, to play for trophies. We were on one page from the first talks I had with the club. They also saw the positions which we definitely had to strengthen. I'm happy that we analysed those positions, we analysed the squad and [are] succeeding in filling those positions with quality players. There are more options in several positions. We are really happy with the players we brought in. They have quality football-wise, but also as people, they suit Manchester United. We want to compete with the best clubs and we want to win every game, so you need a good squad. During the season you have injuries, suspensions and loss of form, so then you need substitutes to fill in the role. You need quality and I think now we have a squad which has the quality.'

Ten Hag concluded, 'You want to win and you want to win in a certain way, so be proactive, brave, adventurous. I think that belongs to the culture of Manchester United, and we want to bring it in. But if you cannot win in a good way, in an entertaining way, you still have to win. That is the mentality, attitude that we bring in.' He highlighted the importance of the supporters to the new project, saying, 'I hope for good cooperation from the fans. But we have to give the example on the pitch. If we have the right attitude – and by that I mean doing hard work and also being brave – then the fans will like it and it will bring the fight back. There will be setbacks and disappointments and we will have to deal with it. I know that because that's life – a sporting life. Every club, every team and every supporter has to deal with it. That is the attitude we all need. When you show it and you have a good plan, in the end you will achieve success. I am 100 per cent confident of that.'

15

THE MAN IN CHARGE

'This above all: to thine own self be true,
And it must follow, as the night the day,
Thou canst not then be false to any man.'
WILLIAM SHAKESPEARE

'Something had to happen in Amsterdam. There was a vibe of "we know it all" there. They did linger too long in their historic successes. Football has developed. There was too much resistance and that culture needed shaking up. Which is why Alfred Schreuder [Ten Hag's on-again off-again assistant] and I were brought in. We were coaching from outside of the club and that always brings resistance. My mission wasn't merely "make Ajax champions". My mission also was also to make Ajax Europe-proof, and to introduce modern elements of the game. In Amsterdam, there also is the superiority, the "We are Ajax!" mantra. I see the benefits of this, don't get me wrong, but I also see the danger. We introduced a modern approach and it worked. All energy and focus goes to the team and the process. I do enjoy successes, but briefly. It's not who I am. I want to stay sharp. Some people start to believe in the stories about themselves and I try to remain realistic. In the media, some people painted me as a loser last season. This season, I saw some in the media use the word "legend". I have to laugh about both. It's ridiculous. I do monitor the messages in the media for the impact they can have on the team. Good or bad, it will reach me and the dressing room and then I need to manage it. Simple.'

• • •

Ten Hag greets the media at Old Trafford less than 24 hours after he watched from the stands as his new side brought an end to their worst season in the Premier League era with a fitting 1–0 defeat at Crystal Palace. He enters the Old Trafford press suite and does not immediately sit down. He approaches the journalists, and those in the front row receive a warm handshake. A round of introductions follows and pleasant surprise can be read on the faces of the English journalists. 'Today I like to meet you all,' Ten Hag says with a smile. He engenders enthusiasm, even before he says a single word. After a wave and a wink at the Dutch media present, he seats himself behind the table and the questions are fired at him. On his first impressions of England and United, his expectations of Cristiano Ronaldo, the label Louis van Gaal put on the club, the changes in the player roster and his feeling at the club. Ten Hag responds to the questions in his characteristic way. His answers are short and offer scant detail. He does not reveal too much but does try to reply to all questions with a fitting response. After 19 minutes, the United press secretary says that enough is enough.

Long-serving Manchester United employees believe there has not been such a clear path, as well as emotional investment, since Sir Alex Ferguson's retirement. Ten Hag's opening weeks in charge demonstrated a willpower and commitment to help redeem the club well beyond the pitch. Manchester United staff were introduced almost casually to the Erik ten Hag managerial style. One employee said, 'It was great to see Erik introduce himself to the office staff. He had a warming presence and seemed extremely personable. He immediately made you feel welcome and valued.' Another staff member commented, 'For a man who surely needed little introduction as the new manager of Manchester United, Erik ten Hag's willingness to speak with new colleagues at Old Trafford was as refreshing as it was engaging. Ten Hag has spoken about his quest to unify all areas of the club and his presence at our home stadium was an impressive launchpad to fulfil just that.'

Ten Hag introduced himself to everyone, including staff in the canteen, and spoke to them all personally, which 'absolutely reinforced the theme of cooperation that he'd alluded to in his press conference only a short time before'. An employee by the name of Maddy said, 'Erik made sure he introduced himself to every single member of staff that he came across at Old Trafford, and showed real class. He genuinely wanted to make sure that everyone felt part of the team, reminding us that "we will all work together".' Nick, who had spent the day with Erik, said, 'While his energy and enthusiasm was infectious, I was personally moved by the respect he paid when walking through the Munich Tunnel. Although his schedule was busy, he spent a considerable amount of time reading each tribute, learning more about the history of this special club. It was a powerful and moving moment that I felt privileged to have seen first-hand.'

Ten Hag looked shellshocked during the 45-minute humiliation at the Brentford Community Stadium. He made his feelings known to the players at half-time and then again at full-time, before informing them that tomorrow's scheduled day off was cancelled. The squad, who arrived back home from London around 11pm, were ordered to report to the club's Carrington training base at 9am on Sunday, where Ten Hag's retribution continued. To compound the humiliation, statistics showed that United's players had run a total distance of 95.6km compared to Brentford's 109.4km. Ten Hag set up a session that required every player, even those who did not start on Saturday, to run the 13.8km difference between the two teams' combined distances. He wanted to make the emphatic point that he would not tolerate his players being outworked by modest opponents like Brentford, who had finished 13th the previous season in their first year ever as a Premier League club. United's players were far from happy when they found out they had been hauled in to run one-third of a marathon in blistering heat.

They were stunned, however, to learn the manager was running it with them. Ten Hag did penance with his players. He shared the punishment that he meted out to his under-performing stars. It was his way of telling the players that he shared responsibility and was equally culpable for how he had set them up and the instructions he had given to them. Some of the talking heads on TV and in the news-papers questioned the 'old school' management and '1980s' approach. But the Manchester United players did not. The move gained respect and won over members of the squad who had yet to be convinced by Ten Hag. He requires discipline from everyone at United, beginning with himself. He laid down the gauntlet to his players and everyone associated with the club.

Ten Hag elaborated on the notorious episode later, 'I cancelled the day off. They understood that, but the fact that I then confronted them with their performance set things in motion. I said, "Unacceptable. We are going to run the 13.8km we fell short of yesterday." If I'm being honest, I wanted to do something even more extreme, but I decided against that, because in the end it's about the objective – what you unleash with the players. I also did the run myself, because I'm part of the team. Those 13.8km were purely a metaphor, because it's not really about how many metres you run.

It's more about the intensive metres, but in that area too Brentford outdid us by far. I had to show my teeth at that moment, otherwise I would deviate from my own vision and approach. All the teams I have coached had a winning mentality, whether it was Go Ahead Eagles, FC Utrecht or Ajax. That is because the manager sets the standard and then intervenes and adjusts things at the right times.'

Ten Hag was no longer 25, he was 52. He struggled to get through the run. 'Don't get me wrong, managers are responsible as well. It's a big responsibility and I take that. I will work on that. That's our job. First, I look at myself and make a clear analysis. I take some notice of some criticism: some of it is really good, good advice. But some is not that good, so I lay it to the side. They also have to get it by themselves because they know they are good players. Now we have to be a team and take responsibility. We work from game to game, and Liverpool are next: obviously we know what's going on when we play Liverpool – you have to be ready – to fight yourself into the season.' Ten Hag taught his pupils that character counts, leadership matters. He taught not in words, but through action.

The lesson was learned and worked its wonders. On the pitch Manchester United showed more passion and intent against Liverpool in the first ten minutes than they had in two whole league matches against the same opponent the previous season. They ran 18.2km more than they had against Brentford. The biggest winner was Ten Hag, whose stature rose after he made big calls and produced a tactical game plan that worked to perfection. He dropped captain Harry Maguire and the superstar Cristiano Ronaldo to the bench and witnessed United produce a performance of intensity, defensive solidity and bravery. He got it all right, and United tore into Liverpool from the kick-off. It proved that Ten Hag, regardless of the opposition, is prepared to make bold decisions for the good of the team, even if it risks upsetting some of the high-profile players in the squad. He operates differently by focusing on the team and its collective responsibility, instead of sustaining the self-image of star players who think they ought to be guaranteed a weekly starting berth. He wants his players to fight for their positions and justify their inclusion.

Erik ten Hag feels sympathy with and respect for frustrated and disappointed Manchester United fans. But he took the high road by publicly supporting the club's ownership. He defended the Glazers by stating that Manchester United's owners 'want to win' before more protests against the American family's ownership took place. The manager was asked about this. 'I can only say the owners want to win and the fans – we want them behind the club. I can understand the sentiment sometimes, but I am not that long in the club, to see all the backgrounds. We have to fight together and be unified.' It is not a charm offensive or a lack of courage to meet necessary challenges. It is part of the essential Ten Hag: you show unity, you work together, you are a team – on the pitch, and off. Manchester Undivided.

After Manchester United firmly halted Arsenal's five-game opening winning streak on Sunday, 4 September 2022, the *Daily Mail* wrote breathlessly:

> Erik ten Hag's resurgent Red Devils make it four wins in a row … Suddenly, everything Ten Hag touches is turning to gold … Marcus Rashford, a man reborn, struck twice in the space of 10 minutes to take the game away from Arsenal … Take your pick of the best performers: Christian Eriksen, Bruno Fernandes, Lisandro Martinez, Rashford. There's fight

in this United team too, something that was sorely missing before. It's a dubious accolade but no Premier League team can match their 20 yellow cards this season ... The celebrations around Old Trafford were unbridled. The hope tangible. 'I understand the fans are dreaming,' said Ten Hag, and who can blame them? ...

Cultural differences show up in the use of language. Whereas in England the man in charge is the 'manager' or 'gaffer', in the Netherlands he is the 'coach' or 'trainer'. The British press invested considerable stock in portraying Erik ten Hag as someone who brooks no dissent and cracks the whip at the slightest challenge to his regime. Further nurturing this stereotype, video clips of Ten Hag bellowing orders at his charges are an online staple. These manifestations of authority meet with approval from United fans, who are comforted at the thought that, at last, there is someone in the dugout who shows everyone who's boss. In light of recent United experiences, such endorsements are understandable. Under men such as Solskjær, the team seemed at times to veer close to mutiny. Everyone in and around Old Trafford was longing for someone who would clearly stamp his authority on the team and the club.

Tottenham had considered Erik ten Hag two years earlier when they searched for a replacement for José Mourinho, but they passed on the Ajax coach for reasons that do not look too clever in retrospect. A lack of charisma was cited as one factor in the London club's decision to look elsewhere. United saw something in Ten Hag that Spurs did not and rightly appreciated his directness. The Dutchman's communication skills are among his greatest strengths: there is no ambiguity in what he says. By now, the impact Ten Hag has had at Manchester United is well documented. After a decade of managerial ineptitude, there is relief and joy that there is a someone at the helm with the stature and skill to steer United out of the doldrums.

Inevitably, this has led to comparisons with Alex Ferguson. Manchester United watchers believe they recognise 'the hand of Sir Alex' in player management or see 'vintage Ferguson' in tactical interventions. Yet the two men are different in significant ways. Grouchy, dictatorial and blunt, Ferguson was able to inspire his teams to top performances. He may not have been an innovator when it came to football strategy, but he was brilliant at adapting to the game's changing trends. He made superstars out of players like Ryan Giggs, David Beckham and Paul Scholes. He tolerated no voice but his own, as players quickly learned, and referees, opposing coaches and reporters were well aware of the force of his personality and his ability to intimidate. Ferguson combined his natural authority with a love of football, self-belief, insatiable desire for victory and great staying power.

Erik ten Hag is not an imposing figure but is personable and has a peculiar sense of humour. His authority comes from his tactical acumen, self-confidence, honesty and unpretentiousness, his people skills, the uncompromising striving towards perfection, relentless work ethic and the ability to almost always get results. Discipline matters, but Ten Hag does not think that fines are a very effective form of punishment for millionaires. He believes that if a player's behaviour affects the team, the penalty should give a sporting sting. When Marcus Rashford was late for a team meeting because he overslept, he was dropped, despite United being short on strikers. Asked about his decision to sideline Rashford, who came off the bench to score the winning goal against Wolves, Ten Hag replied, 'If it's the right person, the right human being and the right character, they will react like this. Related to Marcus, I was quite convinced about it because I have known him for seven or eight months and could expect that reaction.'

Ferguson and Ten Hag are nearly 30 years apart in age. Ferguson is a proud member of the wartime or 'silent' generation, whereas Ten Hag is part of the Generation X – notepads vs. iPads, broadsheets vs. Twitter. Ferguson's resolve originates back in the dockyard unions of Glasgow. 'In the trade union I was a shop steward. I learned how to make decisions and had the strength of character to take me into management.' Ten Hag developed the art of persuasion in the relative comfort of the Dutch countryside as the son of a successful businessman. The differences were on display on the training ground, at media briefings and in the style of their outfits: suits, ties and dress shoes gave way to cardigans, khakis and sneakers. Former United midfielder Ander Herrera adequately assessed the difference in scope of the challenge facing the two men. 'When people compare United managers to Sir Alex Ferguson, I always tell them to realise there were fewer title contenders in that period. Sir Alex has done incredibly well, but he really only had to compete with Arsenal and Liverpool. Ten Hag now also has to compete with Chelsea, City, Tottenham and even Newcastle United. That's not easy. It's not easy being United's manager.' Over time with Ten Hag, United would become more comfortable within themselves, with fans and pundits relenting and accepting that their team could be successful even when they were not 'playing like a Sir Alex Ferguson side'.

• • •

The star player adds extra value for the team, and often has the sympathy of the fans and the media. This is a tough problem for the manager to deal with. The star may not be aware that a team tactical problem exists. But players have to put their qualities to work for the team without making themselves subservient. The manager tries to create a natural balance between individual initiative and team cooperation. He accepts technical and tactical mistakes but does not tolerate mental trespasses, because they threaten the team effort. One or several star players do not make a team. The coach has no room for stars who do not want to do some of the hard work. A coach also cannot take players' pasts into account. He has to build the team, refine the way of playing, manage the dressing room and field the best football players. One person cannot and should not dominate a team.

Football is a team sport, not an individual sport like tennis or golf. All the personal plaudits and awards are won because the star has other players around him who make it possible for him to excel. Former England manager Kevin Keegan said, 'There has to be selflessness. All the top players in teams will tell you that you can't win European Footballer of the Year on your own. You need five, six or maybe seven good players around you.' The special talent must understand that the team is more important than he is, and that he needs the team. For him to flourish, the team needs to flourish too. The mutual dependence of individual brilliance and a high-performing team becomes a winning formula if these priorities are kept straight. Great talent that is simultaneously unselfish is not easy to find. Some are particularly ego-driven and insufficiently team-oriented to put their skills in service of the team. The most serious challenges the manager faces are the threats to balance. He has to make sure that individual player skills and abilities are blended together and used purely for the benefit of the team and the result.

On 27 August 2021, Manchester United announced they had reached an agreement with Juventus to re-sign Cristiano Ronaldo. He was given the number 7 shirt after Edinson Cavani agreed to switch to 21. The first 24 hours of Ronaldo shirt sales broke the all-time record following a transfer. Expectations were high, but he experienced a difficult relationship with his teammates and interim manager Ralf Rangnick. Ronaldo equalled his worst scoring run since 2010 at Real Madrid: two months without a goal. He still finished the troubled season with 24 goals in all competitions, 18 of them in the Premier League. His goals helped United escape some hazardous situations, but a number of those predicaments were of his own making. Everything had to go through him; he was the game plan. While he scored his goals, it ensured that no one else was scoring. United as a whole netted 16 fewer goals than the previous season and finished in sixth place. For the first time since 2010, Ronaldo failed to win a trophy.

The Glazers had hoped Ronaldo's second coming would give Manchester United the silverware-winning impact that Tom Brady brought to their NFL team, the Tampa Bay Buccaneers. The board were seduced by the marketing and business potential of the 'Ronaldo effect', as well as the entertainment allure of his megastar status. They were bringing in one of the game's greatest players of all time, a hero whose social media following and brand outrank everyone else in football, and in sport as a whole. Indeed, the off-pitch impact was as impressive as ever: in 2022 Ronaldo brought New York's Times Square to a halt during the presentation of his wax figure at Madame Tussauds. But bringing him back on £26.8 million a year turned into a strategic mistake from the owners, who aimed for a quick fix. He had an inhibiting effect on the group process and earned far too much money compared to his sporting input.

Nevertheless, Erik ten Hag began his first summer wanting to work with Ronaldo, endorsing the player in glowing terms. 'From the start we said we planned with Ronaldo. Cristiano is an example to every player. How he heads the ball – that timing and jump, just like his shot and free kicks – involve thousands of hours of training.

Being so extremely talented and still having the commitment to get the most out of yourself; that's what distinguishes top from sub-top. The way of playing, the set of demands … you can see in training he has the ability. He fits in because – and it doesn't need further explanation – he is a great player with great capabilities. He fits in every system and every style. We are on the same page, and he knows what the demands are. We are happy with him. He's happy to be here, and we want to make the season a success together.' In an interview with the club in early June 2022, Ronaldo spoke almost as positively about Erik ten Hag, 'I know he did a fantastic job for Ajax and that he's an experienced coach, but we need to give him time. Things need to change the way he wants. We are happy and excited – not just the players, but the supporters as well. I wish him the best. Let's believe that next year we're going to win trophies.'

But trouble started brewing early. Ronaldo missed pre-season because of family circumstances and played his first minutes against Rayo Vallecano. The Madrid club came to Manchester for United's last pre-season game, in what was Ten Hag's debut match at Old Trafford, 'The Theatre of Dreams'. Ronaldo announced in his inimitable way that he would be on the pitch from the start. 'Sunday, the king plays,' he posted on Instagram before the friendly. Just prior to the game, Ten Hag made it clear that Ronaldo was a long way behind. 'He is not yet at the level of the rest of the squad because he has not been here for many weeks. He needs matches and lots of training.' The striker lasted for 45 minutes.

The early substitution did not go down well with Ronaldo. He left Old Trafford before the final whistle. He was not the only one to leave early, but players were not indulged by their new manager as they had been before. They were publicly rebuked by Ten Hag for leaving without permission. 'I certainly don't condone this. This is unacceptable for everyone. We are a team, and you have to stay until the end. You are always judged by what you are now, what you are presenting now, how you are performing now. The team, and Cristiano himself, have to prove it.' By the time the transfer window closed, Ten Hag might have been happier to let Ronaldo leave. The problem was that the only offer came from Saudi Arabia, despite Ronaldo's agent Jorge Mendes' extensive exploratory pitching. No top club was prepared to take on the salary of about £500,000 a week for the 37-year-old.

Tottenham turned up at Old Trafford with the same record as Manchester City in the season – seven wins, two draws, one defeat. The game plan was obvious before the ball was kicked. 'We will have to be good and creative to find gaps against Conte's way of playing,' said Ten Hag, 'because he is good at protecting his goal while attacking the other way.' He raised his arms in jubilation when Bruno Fernandes bent a brilliant finish past Hugo Lloris in the 69th minute. United dominated from first whistle to last. Ten Hag wants his team to attack first and exert complete control, as evidenced by the final figure of 28 shots to Tottenham's pitiful nine. United's total of 19 shots in the first half was more than any team in a Premier League up to that point of the season. Spurs had captain Hugo Lloris to thank for keeping the score respectable. Antony struck the foot of the far post, while Lloris was forced into smart saves to deny Marcus Rashford, Bruno Fernandes, Fred and Luke Shaw. The players put in tremendous effort as they collectively covered 114.4km – nearly 20km more than they managed in the 4–0 humiliation by Brentford.

Ten Hag opted for a different tactical plan and made one change to the team that was held at home to Newcastle, bringing in Marcus Rashford for Cristiano Ronaldo. He saw that his principles are more closely aligned with Rashford as the focal point of the attack. Jadon

Sancho, Marcus Rashford and Antony formed the agile vanguard. Ten Hag cited the intensity of Rashford's pressing as justification for choosing the England international over the veteran attacker. 'It was magnificent from all 11 players. It was also a performance from the substitutes who came on. It was a squad performance. I think what we have seen is 11 players who defend and 11 who attack. I was pleased. Against this Tottenham team you need good pressing, good counter-pressing; from there you can create chances. So, you need good pressing players. Offensive-wise you need that dynamic. That is what Marcus brings.'

There was no footballing reason to incorporate Ronaldo into a progressive side that favoured a fluid, dynamic attack. Despite United having only made three of their five permitted substitutions in the 2–0 home win, Ronaldo decided to leave the bench early and disappeared down the Old Trafford tunnel. He left in the 89th minute, after remaining an unused replacement. It came three days after he showed his displeasure at being substituted against Newcastle. Fans witnessed the finest display of their team in recent memory and saw Ronaldo stomp off because Scott McTominay, Christian Eriksen and Anthony Elanga were preferred. Later it became evident that he had been asked to come on in the final minutes of the game, but had refused. Ten Hag said, 'I will deal with that tomorrow, not today. We are now celebrating this victory.'

In the previous season Ronaldo had been United's top scorer, but the stats backed up Ten Hag's use of him. Under Ten Hag, United played their best football and achieved their best results without Ronaldo. Up to the Tottenham match, he started only two of Manchester United's first 12 Premier League matches. The only full game he played was the 4–0 defeat at Brentford. Manchester United won 75 per cent of their Premier League matches without Ronaldo in the starting 11. That rate was slashed to just 25 per cent in the four games he did start. United's points return also soared 120 per cent, from 1.0 to 2.2 per game without him, while their return in front of goal nearly quadrupled – letting in fewer at the other end, too. Without Ronaldo, United recorded top-level returns for fast breaks, goals, expected goals, shots on target and pressing in the final third, and the team ran, on average, 4km more per game.

Respect for Ronaldo was eroding – not for the talent, dedication, serial silverware, personal honours and 817 career goals – but for someone who appeared to be the antithesis of the all-for-one ethos Ten Hag knew was essential to achieving success. Jamie Jackson wrote in the *Guardian*, 'In exiting on Wednesday Ronaldo bolstered Ten Hag's assessment that he is peripheral to United – there to be deployed when and if required but in no way a shoo-in for the 11 on the grounds of former glories and a glittering CV … Ronaldo striding off is apt: it points to the sense of him as a cipher, a garlanded perfectionist who, despite being one of the greats, remains unknowable, whose profile beyond the pitch is via image-conscious, choreographed social media posts, with the true persona fiercely guarded.'

Being a great doesn't end at scoring goals. Jaap Stam thought Ronaldo's leaving a game early was unacceptable and said Sir Alex Ferguson would not have tolerated it within his side. 'Ronaldo would have gotten the "hairdryer treatment" under Sir Alex.' Ex-United goalkeeper Peter Schmeichel said, 'It's the first time I can say that I am disappointed with him. Normally I back him, I understand his situation. We are in transition. Manchester United are now five managers down the road since Alex Ferguson. We have got Erik ten Hag now, who has very clear ideas about the way he wants to play football. We need understanding and time from everyone. We don't need distractions like that, and that's a disappointment, I would say.'

Ronaldo was unrepentant. He released a statement which said, 'As I've always done throughout my career, I try to live and play respectfully towards my colleagues, my adversaries and my coaches. That hasn't changed. I haven't changed. I've always tried to set an example for the youngsters in all the teams that I've represented. Unfortunately, that's not always possible and sometimes the heat of the moment gets the best of us. Right now, I just feel like I have to keep working hard in Carrington, support my teammates and be ready for everything in any given game. Giving in to the pressure is not an option. It never was. This is Manchester United and united we must stand. Soon we'll be together again.'

Ten Hag had faced player mutiny before. In March 2018, winger Amin Younes refused to come on for Ajax in the final phase of a 4–1 home win over SC Heerenveen. Ten Hag exiled the recalcitrant German to the under-21 team for two weeks. After a conversation between the two, Ten Hag recalled, 'He said he didn't like his reaction. But it's not just about saying it, he has to show it and do it. Gündoğan comes on for Manchester City [against Stoke City] in the 91st minute. Do you want to be part of the team or not? And Younes showed that he didn't want to. I thought it was strange that he didn't want to come on – you could see that from my reaction. One hundred per cent commitment: that's what it's all about in my eyes. He says he wants to give everything for Ajax, but then you have to show that too.' Younes didn't play again for Ajax after the incident, and was transferred to Napoli at the end of the season. There is a considerable difference in how the transgressions of Younes and Ronaldo were handled. The first incident didn't cause a ripple outside of Holland; in Ronaldo's case, it made headlines across the world.

Ten Hag managed a fraught situation well. He decided to discipline the player, receiving the backing of football director John

Murtough and chief executive Richard Arnold. The club released a statement about Ronaldo: 'Cristiano will not be part of the Manchester United squad for this Saturday's game against Chelsea. The rest of the squad is fully focused on preparing for that fixture.' Ten Hag elaborated, 'I am the manager, I'm responsible for the top sport culture here and I have to set standards and values. We are in a team. After Rayo Vallecano, I said this was unacceptable, but he wasn't the only one. This is for everyone. When it's the second time there will be consequences. That is what we did. We'll miss him tomorrow. It's a miss for the squad, but I think it's important for the attitude, the mentality of the group. I think it will be a moment of reflection for him and also for everyone else. I gave him a warning at the start of the season, and the next time there must be consequences. You are living together, playing together. Football is a team sport and you have to fulfil certain standards – and I have to control them.'

The noise around Ronaldo was an unwelcome distraction. Ten Hag said, 'It's about Chelsea. We have a big game to play, all my focus is on that game, all the focus of the staff and the players is on that game. We have to win that game and do everything we can, so we need full concentration to prepare for it and play our best. When you play in top football sometimes there are rumours and noise, but you have to focus on the job, and that is to perform tomorrow. To get top sport culture and to set the highest standards, we have to live them. That is what we do at the moment. It is not something you can construct in a couple of weeks. It takes time. Cristiano achieved a lot in his career. It is brilliant. But he has to be aware you get judged by how you are acting today – it is not about age or reputation.'

Samuel Luckhurst wrote in the *Manchester Evening News*, 'Ronaldo misread the room against Tottenham. United produced their best performance in five and a half years. With authority restored to the

United manager's role with Ten Hag, the player-power era is well and truly over. You cannot imagine Ten Hag, a renowned disciplinarian in the Netherlands, pandering as subserviently to Paul Pogba as Ole Gunnar Solskjær did. Ronaldo is marooned in Manchester and in danger of becoming an irrelevance at the club whose stadium has a suite that doubles as a shrine to Ronaldo. Ten Hag has almost obsequiously supported Ronaldo, refusing to single him out for his early departure against Vallecano and the exaggerated applause as Ronaldo trudged off with 20 minutes to play and the game deadlocked against Newcastle. On Wednesday night, the allowances expired. United fully back Ten Hag's decision to drop Ronaldo from the squad against Chelsea on Saturday and his insistence on discipline.'

Social media was awash with vociferous Ronaldo fan comments calling for Ten Hag's head. But the manager's decision to reprimand the striker had nothing to do with him pulling rank. It was an affirmation that no one is justified to break the rules – a principled stand. Consistency is essential in an environment where everyone has his own strong opinion and there is a plethora of changes every day. Dissent of an influential player impacts a manager's ability to coach. Team members might not respond as instinctively to instructions from the dugout if there is a hint of rebellion. Ten Hag had no regrets over excluding Ronaldo. 'It is more important to have the right culture and standards and values. For the longer term, that is always more important.' Most observers agreed that Ten Hag came through the standoff with his status enhanced and Ronaldo with his diminished. His insistence on fairness and discipline went down well in the dressing room.

Ronaldo's bombshell interview with TalkTV, published by the *Sun* on 13 November, saw the striker criticise the club and the manager. In a 90-minute interview with *Piers Morgan Uncensored*,

Ronaldo claimed Ten Hag and others wanted him out of Old Trafford. When Morgan asked Ronaldo about Erik ten Hag, Ronaldo replied, 'I don't have respect for him because he doesn't show respect for me. If you don't have respect for me, I'm never gonna have respect for you. I think it was a strategy from the club for me to react that way. I was very, very, very, very disappointed with the communication of Manchester United. To be honest, I've never had a problem with any club, with any coach. And they suspend me for three days, which I felt was a lot. It was a shame.'

Many Manchester United supporters reacted to Ronaldo's attack with indignation, particularly his comments about Ten Hag. Wayne Rooney gave voice to widespread sentiment when he said, 'I just think the things [Ronaldo] has done from the start of the season are not acceptable for Manchester United. I've seen Roy Keane defending him. Roy wouldn't accept that. Roy wouldn't accept that at all. It is a distraction which Manchester United don't need at the minute, when they are trying to rebuild. For Cristiano, get your head down, work and be ready when the manager needs you. If he does, he will be an asset. If he doesn't, it will become an unwanted distraction. I think Ten Hag has done really well. He's come in and stamped his authority on the team, and for the first time in about two or three years I'm starting to see an identity with Manchester United. He's shown his strength and his character with how he dealt with Cristiano at times, and with the stuff he's been up to. He's the right man for the job. I think it will take time but it's a real step in the right direction to finish in that top four and get Champions League football again. I'm very close with Darren Fletcher so I know what he's doing and how he's going about his work. I know the players and staff are a lot happier than they have been over the last couple of years.'

Ronaldo reached extraordinary levels with unshakable belief in his own ability. There was a time when his goalscoring record was so stunning that a club could tolerate the ego and the selfishness, but three goals in a season are hardly worthy of the special treatment the striker demanded. United terminated Ronaldo's contract by 'mutual consent' two days before Portugal's World Cup campaign began. A terse message bade the player farewell. 'Cristiano Ronaldo is to leave Manchester United by mutual agreement, with immediate effect. The club thanks him for his immense contribution across two spells at Old Trafford, scoring 145 goals in 346 appearances, and wishes him and his family well for the future.'

Once it was clear that the breakup was unavoidable, Ten Hag wisely prepared for Ronaldo's exit. Under close media scrutiny, the pressure to recreate a functioning squad was immense, but Ten Hag made it look easy. Ten Hag kept his composure; Ronaldo didn't. Sam Wallace surmised in the *Telegraph*, 'One suspects that Ronaldo's exit is exactly what Ten Hag wanted all along.' However, this manager is not conniving or Machiavellian. As a tactician, Ten Hag is cunning and unpredictable; as a person he is honest and straightforward. When he said he wanted to work with Ronaldo, he meant it. The Portuguese superstar made that impossible.

Speaking to journalists for the first time about Ronaldo's exit during United's mid-season trip to Spain, Ten Hag said that once he saw the notorious interview there was no way back. 'I have seen most of it. I had to do it. It is part of my job. As a club, I think, you can't accept the interview. To make that step he knew the consequences. It was quite clear that he wanted to leave. And when a player definitely doesn't want to be in this club, then he has to go. But he never told me before. Until that moment he never told me, "I want to leave". In the summer we had one talk. He came in and said, "I will tell you in seven days if I want to stay". He came back and said he did. Until the interview I never heard anything else. I like to work with world-class players. I know they can make a difference and help you to achieve your objectives. That is why you want to have such players in your dressing room. I wanted him to stay from the first moment until now. I did everything to bring him into the team because I value his quality. We wanted him to be part of our project and for him to contribute to Manchester United because he is a great player and has such a great history.'

Ten Hag never exposed Ronaldo. During his absence in the pre-season tour, Ten Hag reminded his audience the decision was for personal reasons. When the forward did return to Carrington for training, the manager chose to highlight how hard he was working. Even when admonishing his behaviour, Ten Hag emphasised, 'We miss him. For the squad it's a miss.' Ten Hag was never against the idea of a new contract. 'Last year he scored 24 goals. What does this team need? We need goals. We want a new future for Manchester United and he didn't want to be part of it. What happened, happened. I have to make choices around players who are not performing and pick the best team. All my accountability is in favour of the club and the team. There are decisions I have to make, and it doesn't matter which person it is. It is about how we perform now. I believe our performances will confirm that we are going in the right direction.'

'Pain, uncertainty and constant work' were the words of Hollywood psychotherapist Phil Stutz that were quoted in a message from Cristiano Ronaldo on his Instagram account, two days after Portugal's elimination from the Qatar World Cup. The 1–0 quarter-final made Morocco the first African or Arab team to reach the semi-finals of a World Cup. The superstar played as supporting cast for his country, fielded in the 51st minute. Lionel Messi willed

Argentina to World Cup victory by scoring seven goals and assisting on three others, and Kylian Mbappé brought runners-up France eight goals and joy. In Portugal's game against Ghana, Ronaldo opened the scoring from the penalty spot, his only goal in Qatar. He walked off the international stage, alone with his tears, after bowing out in a game in which he had 10 touches, gave away possession five times and completed just three of an attempted six passes in 40 minutes.

Gary Neville said on ITV, 'When it happened at Manchester United, the suggestion was that Erik ten Hag was trying to make a move on Ronaldo, but Fernando Santos is a manager who has had an unbelievable relationship with Ronaldo for eight years. There are a lot of Ronaldo fans who aren't willing to tell him the truth. I think he does need to listen to the truth. It's becoming a bit of a scruffy end. The petulance, the sulking, it's got to stop because it doesn't reflect well on him at all. His long-term legacy is set as one of the great all-time players, but in the short term he's got to do a lot better. Is the Juventus manager wrong? Is the Manchester United manager wrong? And now the Portugal manager is wrong? Three of them have now done the same thing with him.' Ronaldo would continue his club career on the Arabian Peninsula, in a competition ranked in 67th place by teamform.com, just above the English League One and the Italian Serie C.

Ten Hag handled a very difficult situation impressively. He engaged in an all-out effort to rebuild Manchester United. Ronaldo could have made a contribution to that process. But for a man who has spent 20 years as the star of the show and the centre of attention, that was never going to be enough. Ten Hag constantly emphasised the value of team spirit and unity, whereas Ronaldo placed himself outside the group. The problem for Ten Hag was attempting to build a new team with the presence of one of football's biggest superstars on his back. The progress Ten Hag made at Carrington and at Old Trafford came in spite of Ronaldo. Until his departure, the Portuguese dominated every press conference. For good or (mostly) bad his shadow loomed large over everything the manager tried to do. Too much of Ten Hag's time involved dealing with Ronaldo. The manager was relieved when he no longer had to talk about the elephant in the room.

Ronaldo's exit meant Ten Hag had more power than any other Manchester United manager since the retirement of Sir Alex Ferguson. United managers have been hamstrung by their own employers in the past when a difficult decision on a player was required, but Ten Hag is now clearly the one calling the shots. In his first months at United he tried, as he did at Ajax, to bring about a total change of mentality, creating a culture of absolute dedication. No excuses. No justifications. No egos. No complacency. Anyone who did not want to engage and contribute would irrevocably get dropped. His message would now be even stronger, and players were aware that anyone who didn't absorb that message would be out the door sooner or later, no matter their status, reputation or price tag. With the media fracas over, the manager could gain greater control over the dressing room, fostering a style of play that everyone in the squad and the stadium believes in and loves.

16

THE TEACHER

'The deepest principle in human nature
is the craving to be appreciated.'
WILLIAM JAMES

When people talk about discipline, they often think of someone cracking the whip, meting out just penalties for insubordination. But negative discipline is only part of a larger picture. Positive reinforcement is a more important dimension. The real test of quality for a parent, teacher, boss or manager is whether he or she can get his or her children, students, employees or players to internalise discipline. He or she must inspire the members on the team – of whatever type – to believe that they are worthy of being taken care of by themselves, to invest in and make high demands of themselves. They must understand and believe in their own value, learn the art of adequate self-care and cultivate self-discipline. In sporting terms, this means that the manager has to make a positive, personal investment in his players. Although professional football is not commonly associated with emotional sensitivity and a timely human touch, these qualities are an essential part of good team management. Coaches do not necessarily inspire the best performances of their teams by being exacting taskmasters. Steely resolve is a necessary asset for the manager of a top team, but empathetic understanding, on and off the pitch, is just as important.

Emotional intelligence is usually defined as the ability to correctly perceive, understand and manage emotions. The concept became widely known with the publication of Daniel Goleman's 1995 book *Emotional Intelligence – Why it Can Matter More Than IQ*. But the idea is not necessarily new. 'Know thyself,' said Socrates – and he wasn't speaking about getting a high score on an IQ test. Knowing one's emotions, recognising a feeling as it happens, is the keystone of emotional intelligence. Being emotional is not the same thing as being emotionally intelligent. Road rage and soap operas are examples of how people are manipulated by emotions, their own or those of others. People with greater certainty about their authentic feelings are better pilots of their lives. Marshalling emotions in service of a goal is essential for self-motivation, mastery and creativity.

People with high emotional intelligence recognise their own emotions and those of others, and use that understanding to guide thinking and behaviour. Empathy, the ability that builds on emotional self-awareness, is a fundamental 'people skill'. People who are empathetic are more attuned to the feelings, needs and wants of others. Empathy makes good spouses and parents, and good team leaders, while being emotionally tone deaf has a high cost in human relationships. The art of relationships is, in large part, skill in managing emotions in others. Empathy is dismissed by some football managers as the 'soft side'. But practising empathy is actually very hard, especially when things run counter to expectation. Players and fans become frustrated and impatient, and tempers flare. Judgment comes easily. As one coach said, 'A three-year-old can criticise.' Putting yourself in the shoes of another person to better understand their mindset, their circumstances and their worldview is a different story. Understanding alone is not enough: the manager must also demonstrate his awareness of the player's situation through clear, well-timed and appropriate acknowledgement. There are few things as powerful as when someone knows they are being understood.

Top football clubs are massive structures, with many people and departments. Even though there are other people in the organisation who have more power, such as the owner or the CEO, the manager is at the heart of what counts: the team and the football. He is the hub of what matters to the fans, the media and the sponsors, and the whole club is affected by his thinking and actions. The manager is not just a football technician. In many ways, he sets the tone and determines the culture of the entire organisation. If he is successful, everyone wants a piece of him, and he is a father, brother and friend to everyone at the club. If he is not, he is the first one to get the blame for whatever is going wrong. In the volatile environment of a top club, the manager is the most vulnerable – managers get fired at the drop of a hat. The average tenure of a manager in the Premier League is about 18 months. Most players last longer. Most executives last a lot longer. If the manager wants to play his part in creating stability in the team and at the club, he needs to be credible. People will follow his lead if they feel he can be trusted. Leadership is rarely a matter of the heroism of the man at the top. It is more about inspiring everyone around them. The essential components of this are inspiring confidence, trust and commitment, and bringing joy and excitement.

The pictures of Erik ten Hag at Carrington show that this man – despite his generally stern demeanour on match days – has a canny sense for the right word or touch at the right moment. He combines keen professionalism with astute man-management. Nico Dijkshoorn usually serves up scathing commentaries in his *Voetbal International* column. But his write-up on Erik ten Hag exudes warmth and admiration, and hits the nail on the head. 'All winning coaches, all legendary coaches understand and achieve success by growing a squad of friends. Erik ten Hag immediately saw what Manchester United needed: love and understanding. Anyone who thinks that Erik's discipline or his tactical insight have brought him so much is wrong. It is his ability to keep coming across as a human being and not as a miracle coach. He's a strange fellow. Too common for Ajax and too common for Manchester United. Too provincial. On various occasions, I too have made fun of Erik's ordinary presence in this column. In retrospect, I am deeply ashamed of my lack of insight. I understood too late that Erik ten Hag has been saving football from certain death in recent years. He is a believer in "doing together". Erik ten Hag – and this is perhaps his greatest strength – enjoys it when other people enjoy their work. You only get that when you feel a bond with the people who are on the field with you every day.'

The life of a football player does not suddenly stop when he walks out of the stadium or off the training ground. If a player wants to make a career at a big club, he has to be capable of believing in his abilities and keeping them in perspective off the field as well as on. Everything matters in daily life too, and that brings considerable pressure. There are players who have great talent, but if they cannot keep their minds clear, their feet on the ground and work to continuously improve, they will be eliminated. Only the ones who can withstand the unrelenting pressure of performing at the very top will make it. It must be a top priority. There is no partial commitment. All players make errors or experience a drop in performance at times, but what brings them back is that love and joy in playing the game and the deep motivation to be the best they can be. That has to be an intrinsic motivation. One of the things a good manager does is redirect a player when he loses his way and shorten the time taken for his recovery.

The manager must understand the player and focus on his strengths. The faith of the coach inspires the self-confidence of the player. As a consequence, the player may become greater than he himself believed possible. Conversely, there are players with incredible talent and great skill whose careers take an unexpected nosedive at some point. Stars from top clubs make a reappearance at the lower tiers not because they suddenly became incompetent. Almost invariably, there is a crisis of confidence or a lack of commitment. Usually it is both, with the latter following the former, as the cart follows the horse. Good managers can get players who are in internal turmoil back on track.

A good measure of the quality of a manager is the number of players who improve themselves. A great coach can change the perspectives and lives of his players. Ten Hag's toughness is interlaced with softness, as demonstrated by his treatment of Jadon Sancho. His handling of the winger showed a rare emotional acuity. Sancho was clearly struggling with some aspects of his life in Manchester. Ten Hag helped the young man to rediscover his focus and love of the game. Sancho now looks like what he is: talent and promise. Marcus Rashford, Diogo Dalot and Fred are examples of transformation. At one point, they were considered to have reached their Manchester United expiry date. During Ten Hag's tenure, they have come back to life. Luke Shaw became a reliable ever-present. He looks fit, sharp and happy. Full-back Aaron Wan-Bissaka was written off, until Ten Hag revitalised him and instilled confidence. He impressed when he replaced Diogo Dalot after injury.

Midfielder Scott McTominay is one of the players who has greatly benefitted from Ten Hag's guidance. He put in a masterful performance that helped Scotland secure a famous 2–0 victory over Spain in the Euro 2024 qualification campaign. Making headlines the week before with two goals against Cyprus, he was at the heart of both of Scotland's wins. McTominay values the personal touch brought by Ten Hag and said it's unlike anything he's experienced before. 'Obviously, you have conversations which are kept in-house. On tour [in Thailand and Australia], he asked me about my family and how they were and how they're getting on. That was a really good touch because I felt like I could then trust him, want to play for him and be in a team where he's pushing me. I want to make sure I'm doing my best for him because he's got a real understanding about my personal life as well, which is massive for a player. I've never really properly had that before. I've had bits from other coaches, but I feel like he's really, really good in that aspect.'

Speaking about the work that goes on behind the scenes, McTominay said it's a real team effort. 'It always is the collective as a staff. In terms of man-management as well, with the other staff – Mitchell van der Gaag, Darren Fletcher, the manager himself – we've got a real good group there. Steve McClaren is literally one of the best guys you can have in football because he keeps everybody alive, he keeps everyone together and that is so good for players in boosting their confidence. I feel like some players needed that at the end of last season. They needed lifting, and that energy brought into the group – and they've most definitely done that.' Ten Hag won the Premier League's Manager of the Month prize for September – the first United boss to do so since January 2019. He was keen to be pictured with his coaches and analysts when collecting the award, saying, 'It's never one in football; there are a lot of people.'

When Marcus Rashford made his Manchester United debut under Louis van Gaal in 2016, he was seen as a striking stopgap. He was never allowed to grow into the role of a number 9, hindered by the continuous changes in managers and styles at United. He had lost his confidence after a season in which he had fewer goals and fewer playing minutes than ever before. He was a football player who was mentally entangled with himself. Now, for the first time in almost three years, Rashford was completely free of injury, after time spent wrestling with a stress fracture in his back, shoulder problems that required surgery the year before and ankle ligament damage. While naturally slim and athletic, he has filled out and is a more muscular, powerful forward. Stability is essential for growth because it takes time to work out where and how players can flourish. Erik ten Hag understands that. One of his key words is 'patience'. Ten Hag had faith in his striker. He alleviated the pressure Rashford felt, and helped him enjoy football again.

Ten Hag told Rashford that it was important to smile on the training pitch. 'We want the players to enjoy the training sessions. If you are happy, you get energy from it. On the first day we met, I told him, "I want to see your smile, I want to see your teeth." We see it often, and I think he is in a happy place. The whole dressing room is in a happy place, and I think it is good. You notice that his game without the ball has improved enormously. When he is in behind the last line, in my opinion there is hardly a better player in the world. At the moment you have a similar type with Mbappé. Rashford is great when he shows up in that position.' Rashford emerged as the top scorer and talisman of a team that has new life. He scored for the ninth consecutive home game against Manchester City, equalling the record set by 'Busby Babe' Dennis Viollet in 1959. Now, Rashford is someone who looks happy and comfortable in his role, and altogether in his element.

Ten Hag was able to rebuild Rashford's shattered mental state while honing his game. Rashford started scoring relentlessly, and his goal celebration features him pointing his finger at his temple, demonstrating that his 'head is in the game' now. 'Football is probably

95 per cent your mentality,' Rashford said. 'That gives you the baseline to perform. There are a lot of players that have ability – that's why they play at the top level. But what sets them apart is the mentality. I've been on both sides of it. I understand the strength of it and the value. I'm concentrating a lot more on keeping myself in that headspace, and it's needed in order to win games and trophies. I struggled at times last season – more mental things, not my own performance. It was other things off the pitch. Too often last season I wasn't in the right headspace. It's a completely different energy around the club and the training ground and that puts me in a better headspace. That's the biggest difference from last season.'

Ten Hag said, 'I see the technical class every day with Marcus Rashford. He made a big impression from the first training. In the penalty area, everything really hits the target – hard and straight. Such high quality, and everything at pace. Of course, you also get to work with such a player to see where the biggest improvements can be made. With Marcus, for example, that is his headers, which weren't really top yet. Those are details, but the higher you go, the more it's about the details. We touched on that and started working on it, in this case especially assistant coach Benni McCarthy. Then it is nice to see that he scores against West Ham United with a header. He is a true lover of the game. After every training he always wants to do a series of shots on goal. With the right, with the left, from different angles, from crosses. And then also those headers. That's what gave us the three points against West Ham United.'

Ten Hag instantly surmised that Rashford needed a transfusion of confidence. 'From the first moment I was convinced. I was really excited to work with him, I thought I could get more out of him. I think the most important thing, of course, is the way of play that gives him the base, gives him structure, gives the team structure. The way of play is in his favour because I knew his skills. Then you also bring staff around who can make him better, who can make him progress or motivate him. I thought we needed one in the staff who was specific and responsible for strikers, and Benni's doing a good job.' McCarthy is fluent in English, Dutch, Spanish and Portuguese. The South African not only provides group sessions, but also does personal coaching with Rashford. The 25-year-old has clearly been reaping the dividends. Ten Hag said, 'In our coaching staff we had a lot of expertise in the field of defenders and midfielders. I wanted to find a good balance. Benni knows about attacking because he is a former striker. This is a very specific task in the team. I've never played in front positions, so I'm lucky to have someone on my staff who has. Football is ultimately about scoring. You have a goalkeeper coach, but you also need offensive specialists.'

Rashford has become much smarter in using the weapons he has. In Ten Hag he has found a manager who can translate the qualities of players to the field. Ten Hag was modest when quizzed on how he got the best out of Rashford. 'I'm not Harry Potter! It's confidence – every player has to get their own confidence. He fought for it. With my coaching staff we brought structure, especially in the way he plays. We gave him some routines for what he needed to get in the right position, but then finally it's up to him. I remember at the start of the season, I was questioning, "Can he score 20 goals?" Now he has reached that marker, he has scored 20 goals, but now it's about getting more. He has to challenge himself to get 30 or 35, but the focus has to be on the next goal.' Rashford now has a maxim – that the only shot you will regret is the one you don't take – and he is taking more shots, hitting the target more and creating more chances than at any point in his United career. He has Wayne Rooney's club record of 253 goals in his sights and believes it is an attainable target if he sees out his career at Old Trafford. 'I'm enjoying it. Every forward always has a number they want to try to reach, and mine is to score more than I ever have before in a season – that's 22.' Against Chelsea at home, he reached the magic 30, the first player to do so since Robin van Persie a decade earlier.

Jadon Sancho didn't play for United for a while from 22 October 2022. He returned after spending eight weeks away from the club on an individual training programme, which included working at the Dutch amateur club OJC Rosmalen, with coaches who are trusted by Ten Hag. The manager had noticed a sharp drop in Sancho's form and confidence and, after a series of talks with the player, felt a total 'reset' away from the day-to-day training environment was the best course of action. Sancho turned off all his social media accounts and would not return until he was physically and mentally ready. That also meant missing United's winter training camp in Spain. Ten Hag explained, 'Sometimes they need motivation, sometimes they need a push, sometimes they need interaction, sometimes they need inspiration and a plan. That makes the job so exciting. It's wonderful to work with young people to get the best out of them, but they have to do it by themselves.'

'Most of the time, the drop off comes slowly. He started the season really well, but after the international break his performance was lower. First you observe it but then the stats also back it up. At the start of the season he had goals and assists, and his key moments and key actions, but it became less and less. I can't force the process. I have to show patience, although I don't have patience because we have a lack of options in the front line – players who are capable of contributing in the Premier League. Jadon is one – when he is fit – who can contribute, and then we have an extra option, so we will have more chances of winning a lot of games. I think for many top athletes, in football and other sports, it's sometimes good to go away from the place where you are every day to get a new vibe and experience. This can give you the right push to get back on track. Football players aren't robots. No one is the same. For everyone, you need an individual approach. We thought that, in co-operation with Jadon, it was the best choice.'

There was genuine appreciation in the dressing room for the way Ten Hag dealt with Sancho. The forward was given a rousing reception when he was introduced as a second-half substitute in the second leg of the League Cup final against Nottingham Forest. Ten Hag said, 'I thought it was great that the fans gave him love. I think he enjoyed being back on the pitch. He has been smiling in the last few weeks in Carrington. I hope he can keep this process going and, of course, that he has a huge contribution to the season.'

Roy Keane identified Luke Shaw, Aaron Wan-Bissaka, Fred and Scott McTominay as players who 'need to be phased out' because Manchester United needed to 'move on from their problems of the past'. But Shaw is the compelling proof of Ten Hag's coaching skills, and today is very much a part of the team's future. José Mourinho portrayed the left back as a dim-witted force who, as a young player, had to be constantly controlled. 'I made every decision for him,' the Portuguese sneered in his period at Old Trafford. After being dragged off at half-time against Brentford in August, it would be another eight weeks before Shaw started a game. There was no self-pity, no sulking – just hard work. He spent more time in the gym than ever before. Ten Hag sees him as a multifunctional technician, a tactically intelligent player and a leader. 'I like that he's so honest. From the first day in training at pre-season he was working really hard. You could see when he has the right approach. He's a top player. I don't mean only as a team player – he's shown a lot of leadership capacities, and with his skills and his physical power he brings a lot. He's an example of how to win big games. I'm really happy with his development. He's a great player and a great personality for the dressing room.'

In an interview with the Welsh newspaper the *National*, Luke Shaw expressed his satisfaction with his manager and the impact he had on his game. He suggested that standards had not always been consistently applied at Manchester United. 'The good thing about this coach is: if you don't play well, you don't play. That was not the case in the past. I think the good thing about this manager is that he's keeping everyone on their toes. He makes sure that everyone is 100 per cent every day. If you're not at it then you won't play. That's a positive thing. We all know that. I didn't really need him to say anything to me. I knew the first two games were nowhere near good enough. I completely understood that it was my time to come out of the team. I could only keep training so that the manager could see that I was working hard. I waited for my chance and was patient, because the team performed well. Then you can't complain. I am always involved with the team, whether on the bench or in the starting 11. It is clear what the manager wants. He wants to see intensity, he wants aggression, he wants us to play high up the pitch and put pressure. He also wants to see a lot of movement between the lines. We are in transition and it takes some time, but there are positive signs. As players, we see those signs every day in training with him. We had good conversations. This is the start of something new.'

Ten Hag's decision to start Shaw in central defence with Varane against Manchester City was the clearest demonstration of the manager's faith in the defender, and his new thinking. Ten Hag said, 'It was a big decision, but I think when you analyse the profile of Haaland and the combination with De Bruyne, it was also the right decision. Luke has the physical power to compete with them and also has the tactical view to make the right decision and technical skills to play in that position. We can see from game to game what we need. I think we have more players in our squad who also have the capacity to be multifunctional, and we can use that as a weapon in games.' Sky Sports commentator Gary Neville said, 'Playing Luke Shaw at centre back ahead of Lisandro Martínez: they're brave decisions. I thought Martínez would play, I thought Shaw would be left back. But Ten Hag knows what he wants to do. He's willing to take risks, he's his own man. He's done a very, very, very good job. An outstanding job.'

Erik ten Hag said, 'Manchester United didn't exactly have charisma last season. The team appeared apathetic to the public. There was no spirit; I didn't see any team dynamics in the squad. The fighting spirit, for each other, prioritising the team – that wasn't really there in this squad. I was appointed to do it differently. They said, "We want you to be the new manager because you play proactively, you can bring dynamism to the team, you play attack and you are flexible." Those were the four points that I received from the owners and the management to bring to the club. I really looked at the culture. How did Manchester United get its stature? That was very clear to me. Take Sir Alex Ferguson. His teams excelled in togetherness and spirit. Those teams were all hard to beat; you couldn't defeat them. And they always had top strikers: Cantona, Cole, Sheringham, Yorke, Van Nistelrooy, Van Persie; and top keepers: Schmeichel, Van der Sar, De Gea; in the centre, great personalities: Jaap Stam, Vidić, Rio Ferdinand; and always a midfield strategist: Roy Keane, the boss, Paul Scholes, magnificent footballer and personality. And think of players like Ryan Giggs or David Beckham. That is the culture of Manchester United. I thought, if we get players, then you look positionally, at quality, at technical skills, but certainly also at the mental quality of players. We had to bring back that resilience.'

Ten Hag's seriousness, his moral framework and non-negotiable commitment to following the right way have been catalysts for profound changes at United. It is a reminder that essential human virtue has a transformative effect, even in the tumult of a top football club. 'When you go to the recruitment in the summer, it was not only about signing players. We were looking for players with character, with personality. A lot of players in the world have great technical skills, or they can run really fast, but we were looking for players who have leadership, who take responsibility, who are resilient. That is the type of player I was looking for after I analysed the squad. Casemiro has not surprised me – absolutely not. I knew what a magnificent player he was. Just look at his profile, at all the cups he's won. He has won five Champions Leagues, that's not a coincidence. If you want to win something, you also have to have older players. They can influence the culture in the dressing room. For me it's always the same: you have players who win, and who win always, and players who lose and are always losing. You have to do your research and find the type who are cooperative and humble in the dressing room, but who take responsibility on the pitch.'

Casemiro has had a dramatic impact on the midfield. United's midfield was the problem for many years, and that's actually the strongest component of their current makeup. The Brazilian rapidly acquired the same key role at United as he played at Real Madrid. A powerhouse between midfield and defence, Casemiro covers huge spaces and is particularly resolute when he makes an intervention. Wherever he plays, the team invariably perform better tactically. The midfielder said, 'Ten Hag is a hard-working manager who asks a lot of his players, but that's how we are always at our best – and that's important. I also see him as a manager who has the desire to develop and make Manchester United bigger. In fact, I think that's his best feature. He is very intelligent. He knows what to ask of everyone. I do whatever he tells me to do.'

'After being in football for quite a while even though I'm only 30, his obsession for winning is what surprised me the most. We want to win, and Ten Hag is obsessed with teaching us and making us better to the millimetre. That obsession with winning is something I've only seen with a few managers. I've worked with Ancelotti and Zidane: they are managers who want to win, which is the most important thing. Hard work and dedication, being intensely dedicated to the club – that's what is most important.' Casemiro saw first-hand how, under Ten Hag, Ajax pulled off one of the most stunning Champions League results with a 4–1 win at the Bernabeu in 2019. 'I believe Manchester United have a great manager. I was there to see at Ajax, I think he's doing a good job here. I believe it's his desire to win, his ambition, his hard work. We are still a club under construction. We're on a good path. This is the way to win titles, but we need to keep growing.'

Ten Hag has very precise ideas about how his team should play, but he does not micromanage his players. 'I will give players trust. When they work hard, when they give their best in training sessions, when they take responsibility on the pitch, I will back them.' Winger Antony entertained United home fans by producing a 720-degree spin with the ball stuck to his left foot. The Brazilian performed the skill, which consists of a double swivel, while controlling the ball during the 3–0 Europa League win over Sheriff Tiraspol. It drew scathing commentary from some pundits. He responded to criticism of his 'showboating' by stating he would not stop the 'art' that made him successful. In an Instagram post, Antony said, 'We [Brazilians] are known for our art and I will not stop doing what got me where I am.' Ten Hag refused to criticise the young player and said that, if it was functional, he could just keep doing what he has been doing.

Antony has great pace and technical dribbling ability, enabling him to break through the lines, and he is willing and able to press with high intensity. Ten Hag likened him to former Bayern Munich winger, Dutchman Arjen Robben, because he is a left-footed right winger who cuts inside and threatens the goal with shots from his left foot. 'First, I know he can also use his right, he has to do it more. Second, he can also go outside. But he is so good on the inside. I've seen it, for instance, with Arjen Robben a lot. They say he has only one trick, but that one trick is so brilliant no one can stop it. Of course, if you can go both ways you have more variations, you are more difficult to stop. But improve the trick you are really good at. His first yards with the ball as he dribbles are outstanding. I think they're so difficult to defend against, so he has to keep doing that. I think he is growing. We also want him to be more dynamic, more variable and more direct. We are happy with his improvement in this moment, but there is still more to come. There is a big potential in him, and he has to develop it every day.'

Alejandro Garnacho made his first United start at the age of 18. Garnacho has the 'X factor', according to Ten Hag. 'I am happy with him – he's got a better attitude, more resilience, more determination – and you see he is a talent. To deal with the ball in tight areas, to run behind and especially also his tempo dribbles, he can take players on and that's a good capability in football nowadays, especially against opponents who are defending compact.' Garnacho overtook George Best as the club's youngest non-English goalscorer in a major European competition. He opened his United account with an excellent goal in San Sebastián, scoring the only goal in the Europa League away match against Real Sociedad.

With most of his first team away at the Qatar World Cup, Ten Hag took an unconventional Manchester United squad to Spain for some warm-weather training ahead of domestic football's restart in late December. In Andalusia, he wanted to look ahead after the dramatic departure of Cristiano Ronaldo, and cultivate new potential. Only 11 players who made the trip could be considered regular first-teamers; three of them were goalkeepers and one was the newly promoted Garnacho. The rest of the 29-man strong group was made up of the club's gifted prospects, only six of whom had any senior minutes. In a video released from the first training session in Cadiz, it was clear that Ten Hag gave the teenagers just as much attention, as he relayed a series of instructions during a passing drill. 'The normal objective for every training camp is to get back into the rhythm of the game. So first, fitness levels, and then second, the way of playing. But we are here with a mixed team, so I have to talk about several objectives. We have a lot of young players with us. They can show us what they have to offer, what their capabilities are and what their potential is. I think it's a great opportunity for them. Normally we don't have this break. Many players are at the World Cup, so there are positions available and the young players can be used in these positions. They can showcase themselves and they can challenge players who play in the Premier League, so it's fantastic for them. This is an important objective: to close that gap so that we are better after the winter, in the restart.'

United ended a 38-day absence from competitive action with the 2–0 Carabao Cup fourth-round victory over Burnley, and resumed their Premier League campaign against Nottingham Forest at Old Trafford on 27 December. 'We all knew the restart was five or six days after the World Cup final,' said Ten Hag. 'Everyone has to be ready and accept it – the manager and coaching staff, but also the players. The World Cup doesn't help, of course. Many players have been out for weeks, in a different team, with a different way of playing. And we don't have any preparation time, because we are playing matches immediately. We had a plan for how to do it, how to manage. It is all based on the individual. No one is the same and no one has the same programme or the same minutes. They are all playing in different positions, and they are all at different ages. We are really trying to cater to everyone. You see, in this World Cup many nations are playing passively, waiting and playing in reaction. We want to be dominant and proactive. Players come back and they have been playing for six weeks in a different environment with a different style of play, and then they have to get back to our style and system and our rules and principles. It's a team sport, so all 11 have to be on the same page.'

By March of the season, Bruno Fernandes had played more minutes than any other player in the top five leagues. Despite some calls for him to be rested, Ten Hag kept him in his starting line-up. He wore the captain's armband in place of Harry Maguire during the season. Fernandes is not afraid to speak his mind. He had a few choice words for his teammate Antony playing against Crystal Palace at Selhurst Park when an attack broke down. But Ten Hag almost relished the flashpoint: 'I think they are really OK with that. So much is about brains, but there is emotion too, when the heart rules the head. Those two, and there are others, when they bring that emotion to the game, it makes their performance better. Sometimes they cross the line with each other, but in the same minute, they are best friends again.'

The main reason behind the upturn in Fernandes's form was obvious. Ronaldo's exit during the World Cup lifted a weight off the other forwards in the squad. Suddenly, United were playing with the freedom that Ten Hag and the supporters craved. It's no coincidence that the two players who benefitted most from Ronaldo's departure were Rashford and Fernandes, who both had to play support roles when Ronaldo was on the field. Rashford's superb goalscoring after the World Cup overshadowed just how impressive Fernandes has been. With a more mobile set of attackers in front of him, Fernandes has the ideal outlets to maximise his creative qualities. He hit double figures for assists, with Rashford very grateful. 'He's so tough,' Ten Hag said. 'He's such a strong leader. He gives so much energy to the team. His determination, passion, resilience – we need players like him if we want to win games and get trophies.'

Fernandes explained the change in dynamic. 'The manager brought his ideas, the discipline during the training sessions, during the week, during the games. I think the most important change is that the results and confidence are much higher now. We believe that the process that we are going through is the right one. I think every-one has the right belief. Everyone is following the ideas the coach has brought to the club, to the team. He demands a lot from us. He knows what we are capable of doing and that's why he demands it. So, I think everyone understood that you have to be in his line. You have to follow his rules. If not, it will not be good for you. I think everyone understood that straight from the pre-season. He was really strong with his words. In Thailand and Australia there were really tough training sessions. No one could quit running, no one could stop. I think everyone understood the standards that are set for us. And from there on, we have to follow that. Straight away in the pre-season he showed us the direction he wants to go, the rules he wants us to follow, the ideas of football.'

Sir Alex Ferguson was known for his fiery temper during his time in the United dugout. No one escaped his wrath. Even the fixture list planner was berated for the number of games United had to play. 'I've been saying this for a few months, but our programme didn't do us any favours, and I think we have been handicapped by the Premier League in the fixture list.' In his time, Louis van Gaal went on record as complaining about Manchester United's 'crazy' Christmas schedule. Ten Hag is different. He said he and his team wanted to remain in as many competitions as possible. 'I think all the players prefer games to training, so when we have a game every three days, we are happy. There is a lot of work, that is clear, but it is worth it. You get some kind of energy from it, and it is about getting that rhythm to play the game and move forward. We want to stay in all of those competitions as long as possible, so we have to fight for that. That's good for the development of this squad. I think games are good for the process. We have a game plan, we give the players feedback, and in the feedback, there are often development points. Games are a very good tool to develop the way of play. Every game is an exam, as a team and as an individual. The more we are tested, the better. In the coming period we will often play three times a week: that can help us to improve faster.'

The Old Trafford record was almost faultless in the 2022–3 season. United did not lose a league game at Old Trafford after being beaten 2–1 by Brighton on the opening day of the season. They remained undefeated on their own patch in any competition after 8 September. Ten Hag well recognises the importance of deliberately involving the fans in his team's changing fortunes. He singled out the support at home for praise. 'No team likes to come to Old Trafford. I think that cooperation between the fans, the players and the team is so strong. But you have to prove it every time. It is a new test, and you have to start from zero. We really feel that the fans are behind us. We have to focus to be successful, because that is what the fans expect. I'm sure when we give performances like we do all season, the fans are behind us and there is a lot of energy. There's a really strong bond between the fans and the players.'

In 2021–2 United won just 13 games in M16, just half of the 26 fixtures played at the Theatre of Dreams. It created a dour, doom-laden feel among the Red Army – a sense that what could go wrong probably would. Erik ten Hag rebuilt confidence at Old Trafford, describing the stadium and its huge, ever-present 70,000-plus crowd as a 'weapon' that United could utilise to intimidate opponents. Now, fans are turning up to Old Trafford expecting United to win again. Supporters are responding to the not-on-my-patch mentality of Martínez; the commanding authority of Varane and Casemiro in defence and midfield; the tireless running and splendid finishing of Rashford. The latter's song, 'Rashford is Red', continues to swell on each match day. The confidence and conviction of the Red Army is returning. There is burgeoning faith in Ten Hag. It's a happy, hopeful time to be a Manchester United fan.

By now, Ten Hag is extremely popular in Manchester, not only among the fans but among the media as well. Journalists have come to appreciate his straightforwardness and the gentle charm of his unscripted public appearances. In the press room of the AON Training Centre in Carrington, they can recite in their sleep the Ten Hag vocabulary: 'focus', 'mentality', 'process', 'intensity'. These words are part of the Ten Hag mantra, and the manager uses them constantly in short, measured sentences. During his first press conference, Jürgen Klopp dubbed himself 'The Normal One', in a parody of José Mourinho's famous 'The Special One' proclamation of 2004. The Liverpool manager's self-appellation would be eminently applicable to Ten Hag. There is simple honesty, directness and a complete absence of pretentiousness. Samuel Luckhurst wrote in the *Manchester Evening News*, 'Appointing Ten Hag is arguably the best decision United have made since Ferguson changed Robin van Persie's course from City to United in 2012 … When eight of us lunched with Ten

Hag at United's hotel in Jerez in December, it was a throwback to an era when managers socialised with journalists. For someone who can appear gruff, Ten Hag has a deadpan, Dutch sense of humour, and that luncheon reaffirmed that United have a concise communicator in the dugout.'

There is this combination of pure love of the game and striving for excellence. This is the mindset of the manager, and that is what he looks for and naturally brings out of his players: having the desire and drive to be as good as one can be, refusing to be average. 'As manager you set the standard and then intervene and adjust at the right times. That standard of mine can be captured in a few words: good is not good enough; it has to get better every day; and satisfaction leads to laziness. To get that into the dressing room, you need personalities. The United shirt is heavy. Only real personalities, who can perform under great pressure, can be used here. Players we bring to Manchester United must meet the highest standards. We have to give the best every day and also give the best version of ourselves. If everyone is doing that and cooperates well, then you can achieve a lot. That is the way we want to go.'

17

THE STRATEGIST

'Finally, United are coming back.'
PEP GUARDIOLA

In football, almost all managers are appointed during some kind of crisis or need for turnaround. The new manager often arrives on a wave of hope and expectation. What he typically inherits is low confidence and stretched resources. His primary goal is to deal with the crisis and put the team back on track to long-term success. In *The Manager*, Mike Carson compares the challenge of bringing a poorly functioning team to full health during the football season to building an airplane when it is airborne. 'It is ludicrous to imagine building an airplane in the air. Two things would be going on simultaneously: the minute-to-minute operational challenge of keeping the aircraft flying, with all the challenges of navigation, communication, technology, engineering, safety and passenger comfort; and the foundational work of design, sourcing and manufacturing of components, heavy engineering, assembly, testing and the rest. These are clearly incompatible. And yet when the manager is asked to take on the failing or underperforming team in crisis, this is effectively what he is being asked to do.'

A leader's philosophy is so important that, if he departs from it, he abandons his true self. Having a coherent philosophy is the starting point for all sound management. Football managers need to have a clear philosophy guiding their strategy and tactics. They must have clear reasons underpinning their decisions. Most do not share these reasons in detail with their team, assuming that, by doing so, they will invite endless debate because everyone – coaches and players – has an opinion of how the game should be played. But he must share enough to convince his players that he has a distinct system as the foundation for his directions to his team. At the same time, a coach must have a skill set that ensures that he is capable of handling everything that is thrown at him during the season's competition. This technical know-how and the ability to get it across give him the credibility among a group of ambitious professionals. Deep understanding of the game is the bedrock during moments of high pressure.

The manager must have the ability to clearly communicate his ideas to his team. These principles have to become so self-evident through practice on the training ground that they become second nature to the players. When the team encounters a common situation during game time, it then becomes 'an issue we have dealt with before', a question to which there is a clear-cut answer. The reaction comes from a repertoire of well-tried methods, almost as in a set piece. The situation can be 'managed', and the coach and his team roll out a routine that they have successfully used before. Even when the problem is complex, requiring several steps, there is a predictable solution. At other times, the manager and team face a challenge that is completely new and requires a creative response: an injury of a key player or playing an opponent who is superior in just about every way.

The stereotype of the British 'stiff upper lip' – remaining resolute and calm in the face of adversity – was arguably put to its greatest test during the Second World War. In the new millennium, it appears to have lost some of its lustre, and the British generations X, Y and Z are more open with their emotions than their parents were. But there still is something in the English mindset that appreciates the person who displays stoic calm in high-pressure settings. Those commenting on the behaviours of Erik ten Hag frequently express appreciation for how the Dutchman remains unruffled even under the most challenging conditions. Ten Hag is a calm and dignified man, and that is one of the things people find admirable about him. It also lends him an aura of authority. It is easy to fear someone who is shouting and ranting all the time, but harder to truly respect them. Ten Hag projects the compelling image of a leader who remains centred in all circumstances, radiating a steadiness to his people that they can depend on. No one can claim to have that mindset all the time but, in the turmoil of Premier League football, Ten Hag's stoic reserve and resilience are notable assets.

Senior members of the Manchester United squad have singled out Ten Hag's confidence in his philosophy and methods as a core driver behind their team's ascent. He appears to be in complete control of himself and of the situation on the pitch. The system is unambiguously clear, and all the players know exactly what they are required to do. There is no need for drama on the touchline – the histrionics that some of Ten Hag's less sophisticated colleagues are given to. When a crisis develops, he engages with his signature calm and professionalism. In the heat of the moment, he thinks clearly and drives the tactical changes that very often make the difference: withdrawing one team member and introducing another, switching positions or roles and refining responsibilities.

At the same time, Ten Hag readily admits that he does not know everything and is always learning. He is able to distinguish what he knows and understands from what he doesn't. This requires wisdom and flexibility. Confidence needs to be paired with humility. Knowing what one knows and what one does not – psychologists call it 'metacognition' – leads to self-awareness. It comes from having a fairly objective understanding of one's own abilities. This, in turn, is the foundation for self-belief, the confidence of being able to make the required judgments and decisions. The heightened tension that comes from inflated fan expectations can all too easily knock a manager off balance. With self-belief, he can be what his players need him to be – self-assured and lucid while under pressure. The manager needs to have an unshakable belief in his ability to achieve competition goals. Part of that is understanding the unique qualities that make his team better than the opponents. Ten Hag is an expert at this: if he does not know it yet, he'll figure it out soon enough, either in the second half or in the next match.

On 2 October 2022, there was no device in Ten Hag's toolkit that could make up for the sheer difference in quality at the Etihad Stadium. Player inexperience played a factor. Tyrell Malacia, for example, didn't know what to do with Phil Foden. For the young defender, the meeting clearly came too soon after his transfer from Rotterdam. At half-time, Ten Hag took him to the side and replaced him with Luke Shaw. By then, Foden had already scored a brace, as had Erling Haaland. With their team trailing 4–0, many United fans left. With their backs to the pitch and arms on their neighbours' shoulders, Manchester City fans jumped up and down to celebrate the dismantling of United. The Poznan, as the wild dance is called, only gets going on special occasions. At full-time, there had been some redemption, with the score at 6–3. Ten Hag concluded, 'First, I had to change the attitude of the team. I think that was the reaction in the second half. We were braver, we came into their half, we created chances and we scored three goals.'

The humiliation in the most goal-rich Manchester derby ever reemphasised the scope of Ten Hag's task. He did not let his players complete a disciplinary training, as after the implosion at Brentford. 'That punishment was because they outran us and we didn't work hard enough. It's not always about punishment. This was more of a mental issue. You have to step onto the field with the belief that you can get a result. We did put that attitude on the pitch in the five previous matches. In those games, our team was confident; there was a good spirit, there was a good vibe, but today we didn't bring it on the pitch from the first minute. We made many wrong decisions in and out of possession, we didn't get on the front foot. If you don't fight, then you have a problem against a team like City. I criticised them, and myself as well, because I didn't get the message through. With this lack of confidence, we cannot win games. I don't think this attitude is Manchester United. We didn't follow the rules of the way we play and then you get hammered.'

A slump after the initial post-crisis success does not spell disaster. The challenge for a leader is to remain grounded in reality. He must show the confidence that he is going to get through it and that he is going to take the team with him. Staff close to Ten Hag at Carrington believe his greatest strength is how he reacts in dark moments. He refuses to blame or to complain. He takes ownership of his failures and successes. He believes in setting and modelling high standards of behaviour, and in the inherent goodwill and abilities of his staff and players. His custom of taking responsibility enables him to deal equably with all triumphs and disasters. United are obviously in need of more transfers, but Ten Hag refused to make excuses. 'It's not about the players who are missing. It's about the players who are on the pitch. They have to perform. I believe in them, trust them, and they have to show it.'

Erik ten Hag thanked Manchester City for the instructive experience. 'We got a reality check with City, and we know we have to step up. We came out of the international break and in that game, we just forgot our rules, principles and beliefs. So, thank you for the lesson, Pep and City. We will take it. We've got to understand we have to do things much better. It's physical, it's mental. It's also sustainability. It's like a routine, a way of life, and you have to bring it every training, in your system as a squad and as an individual player. There has been a lack of it in the last years. It's not something that you build or progress in a week or a month. It has to be consistent; it is a demand in top football nowadays. It's quite clear City sets the standard, but I think we also can deliver that. We have seen it against Liverpool, we have seen it against Arsenal, but now we have to do it on a consistent basis. We have learned some lessons for the future; we have to improve a lot to face opponents of the level of City.'

Saturday 14 January 2023 saw a rousing comeback derby win over Manchester City at Old Trafford. United responded to Jack Grealish's 60th-minute opener with goals from Bruno Fernandes and Marcus Rashford. Ten Hag calmly analysed, 'One of the main jobs for a manager is to work on the mentality, and this has a lot of elements. One is resilience. The determination of this team is progressing a lot, dealing with suffering in painful moments, and the ability to keep going after setbacks like a goal against. We have experienced players on the pitch who know that in one moment a game can change. We are much better able to deal with such situations than a couple of months ago'. Apparently, there are sound experts at Manchester United who measure the decibel (dB) levels around Old Trafford during every home fixture. The stats prove that fans turned up the volume when it mattered. The loudest match was the 2–1 triumph over Liverpool in August 2022 (95.9 dB), followed by September's important 3–1 victory over Arsenal (94.9 dB). The dramatic 2–1 win over Manchester City was the third loudest game (94.3 dB). The volume of a passing freight train is about 80 dB.

Arsenal, Liverpool and Tottenham had already been beaten at Old Trafford, but victory over Manchester City was the most powerful statement of Ten Hag's tenure so far. United are some distance from playing like City, but they found a solution for playing against City. Fred was an unwanted shadow for Kevin De Bruyne. On average in the Premier League this season, De Bruyne completed 42 passes per 90 minutes. At Old Trafford, he completed just 31. He completed only 13 of 22 passes in the attacking third, and none to Erling Haaland. Despite City enjoying 71 per cent of possession, they got only one shot on target. United had much less of the ball but four attempts on Ederson's goal. After an hour, City were one goal up and seemingly in control. Within three minutes they were hit with two classic United goals: furious breakaways, capitalising on defensive mistakes of the opponents. Under past managers, going a goal behind might have meant capitulation. But with Ten Hag in charge players believe in their own abilities.

With Manchester United up for sale and significant expenditures in the transfer market the previous summer, the American owners had no intention to substantially invest in new player acquisitions in winter. The transfer market closed the night of 31 January with United having added only three new members to their squad on loan deals. Goalkeeper Jack Butland and striker Wout Weghorst joined. Midfielder Marcel Sabitzer came from Bayern Munich at the last minute, when it was clear that Christian Eriksen would be out with an injury for most of the remaining season. Sabitzer is a midfielder who had consistently provided goals and assists throughout his career. He is versatile, having operated in a multitude of roles, including attacking midfielder, second striker, winger and deep-lying midfielder. The second half of United's season showed that getting him on board just in time had been a shrewd move. Ten

Hag demonstrated that he was capable of successfully improving his team even with these very modest additions.

Ten Hag gradually turned United into a team that operates as a sort of boa constrictor, trapping the opponent in its own half with a game of dominance and intensity. In the last quarter of the match, United eliminate the paralysed opponent – piling on pressure when the spaces on the pitch are getting larger. This so-called provocative pressing means that opponents have to capitalise on one or two moments in a match. Average teams barely get to test David de Gea. The 2–1 win over Crystal Palace marked United's thirteenth home win in a row. With Lisandro Martínez and Casemiro, Ten Hag very purposefully added *grinta*, Latin grit, to his team. This was clear when former Ajax player Antony was shoved over the sideline by Jeffrey Schlupp shortly after the second goal, and virtually the entire United team jumped into the breach for the winger. Ten Hag was pleased to witness the team spirit. 'I've seen the incident, where the Crystal Palace player risked causing a serious injury to Antony, and then emotions got really high for several players. Our players have to behave, they have to control their emotions, but I'm happy that we have the spirit, and we stand up for each other. That is great.'

Lisandro Martínez had rebuffed Arsenal's advances to reunite with Ten Hag at United. He sees a kindred spirit in the manager. 'I know him well, his mentality, we are almost the same in that way. For sure, we want to win everything.' With Martínez, Ten Hag brought in a quality player who added something special to the team: spirit, poison, character. Yet, Martínez, who has been sent off just once in his career, has learned not to cross the line. 'I try to do my best but you have to work very hard. You have to be very clever on the pitch. You have to be sharp in every situation, because if you're smart you can win the duels. You have to be clever. I can do it, otherwise, I will be suspended every game. It is hard. Sometimes I want to kill, but you have to control yourself as well.' At Ajax, Ten Hag experienced how the team spirit was strengthened by players who really connect with their teammates. Martínez is such a type. With him, something fundamentally changed in defence compared to the season before. Now there is someone who is constantly pointing and directing traffic; the friendly slap he deals to David de Gea after a fantastic reflex save on the goal line; the clenched fists after a crucial tackle; the high-fives with teammates after a good defensive play; the compliments to attackers who track back.

Martínez is among the stand-out performers in the Premier League. The fee and the faith have been justified. 'He is a warrior, and I think the fans will admire him', Ten Hag predicted. It took Martínez less than seven months to achieve something close to cult status at Old Trafford. Martínez was amazed to hear the chants of 'Ar-gen-tina' regularly rolling off the terraces. 'It's been a surprise to hear that but, in the end, you give everything that you have and the people recognise that. It's very important to have that connection. Football is always physical. You always have to train hard. You have to be ready. I always try to give 100 per cent.' It is the sort of attitude that supporters are drawn to. Soon after the defender's arrival at United a record number of people took the trouble to choose their favourite player. With 84 per cent of the vote, Lisandro Martínez was named August 2022's Player of the Month.

Ten Hag has given the Manchester United backline a solidity that wasn't there before. United have two World Cup winners anchoring central defence, and it shows. The change from Harry Maguire to Lisandro Martínez in the defensive heart of Manchester United has worked wonders. Raphaël Varane developed a season of understated brilliance. He exudes calm and authority and revels in playing along-side Martínez. The two have developed quite the partnership. They celebrate every block and tackle together, communicate in Spanish and are unafraid to hold teammates to account. 'We understand each other very well,' Martínez said. 'We are talking almost all of the time about everything.' Varane's importance is obvious to Martínez. The Argentinian has dubbed Varane *leyenda* – legend – and 'awesome' in comments on his Instagram posts.

In the age of computer algorithms and big data, the inflow of information is enormous, and football is not immune. Organisations such as Opta Sports extract a mass of data from the beautiful game, which is gleefully regurgitated by the media for consumption by football fans. But much of this is trivia: curious tidbits, sometimes fascinating morsels, but useless to the manager and his staff. A massive quantity of data is not going to help; it is going to overwhelm and confuse. A manager can only make good decisions if he has facts. He needs meaningful information that can help him to make wise choices. The information has to be useful: stuff that makes a difference for the team on the pitch. Less is more. It takes practice, experience and wisdom to sort the wheat from the chaff. Access to the right data doesn't make management any easier, but it does help the man in charge to come to higher-quality decisions.

Manchester United and Barcelona played out a scintillating 2–2 draw in the first leg of their Europa League knockout play-off at the iconic Camp Nou. United had suffered a 3–0 defeat on their last visit to Barcelona under Ole Gunnar Solskjær in 2019. To make sure there was no repeat of that, Ten Hag used a group of expert analysts to help his team. A photo showed eight Manchester United staff with laptops watching from a location in the stadium's rafters during the match. Technical director Darren Fletcher sat alongside goalkeeper coach Richard Hartis and analyst Kevin Keij, who previously worked with Ten Hag at Ajax. The team collated video material and data during the game to relay to the dugout. It was also fed into a central database at the Carrington headquarters to be scrutinised by the club's head of first-team analysis, Paul Brand, so it could be used by Ten Hag to prepare his players for future games.

As is his custom, Ten Hag went out onto the pitch at Camp Nou prior to the match. This ritual is also part of the – more intuitive – Erik ten Hag data collection apparatus. 'I usually do it. Whenever I come to an away stadium – Premier League or Europe – I always go to the pitch. I want to see the quality of the pitch and I take it into my preparation. You get a certain feeling from every stadium. It's just about imagination and how you want to prepare your team, so that they are ready. All the small details can make the difference.' Ten Hag subscribes to the specifics, from the measurement of training cone distances to how long a player has been in the ice bath. He believes every action counts, and there is an edge to the smallest habits – like his pitch inspections.

It was a Europa League tie of Champions League proportions. It was billed in Catalonia as the 'Battle of the Champions'. There were 35 attempts at goal, 18 to Barcelona and 17 for United, which is no small feat for an away team at Camp Nou. United continued to demonstrate an ability to play the game on their own terms under Ten Hag. It was a thrilling match and a warning shot from two of Europe's historic football superpowers on their way back to the top. United came from behind against a team that had taken La Liga by storm during the season. Ten Hag injected a fearlessness into his players that was personified by the man at the top end of the pitch. Rashford scored magnificently and superbly forced the second, an own goal by central defender Jules Koundé. Ten Hag nonetheless criticised his team's finishing. 'We dictated the game, we outplayed them and created so many chances. We should have scored four goals.' But for Barcelona goalkeeper Marc-André ter Stegen, Ten Hag would have become the first United manager to beat Barcelona at the massive old stadium.

Loanee Wout Weghorst became the fifteenth Dutchman enlisted by Manchester United, following big names such as Jaap Stam, Ruud van Nistelrooy, Edwin van der Sar and Robin van Persie. Like Ten Hag, he is a Tukker, hailing from Borne, a village close to Ten Hag's hometown. They literally speak the same language. Weghorst never was a finely cut artist, but coaches like Louis van Gaal love him because of his almost unrestrained fanaticism, even in training sessions. In England, he may have been lampooned as a 6ft 6in hulk, but he was the perfect fit for Ten Hag's United setup. He could not have been more of a polar opposite to Ronaldo: the work rate, the utility, the altruism. The way Weghorst surrenders himself for the greater good is in exact contrast to Ronaldo's need to be the perennial centre of attention. The seamlessness with which Ten Hag switched from one to the other shows the master tactician at work. Weghorst rarely scores, but at this point in United's development it's not about the goals for him.

More innovative coaching from Ten Hag: Wout Weghorst led the midfield press against Barcelona. The manager redeployed him as a number 10 in order to create space for Rashford. The *Daily Mail* was taken aback by the strategy. 'Erik ten Tag surpassed Pep Guardiola with a weird move to play Wout Weghorst in midfield.' The manager explained, 'It's more tactical, but also to get some other players in good positions in the whole front three; Bruno, Rashy and Jadon. I think the plan worked well. In the end, it doesn't matter who scores.' He keenly identified how the attributes of the maligned striker would benefit the collective. Ten Hag wants to press from the front, and Weghorst does that uncompromisingly. Ten Hag observed, 'I am very pleased with him, he is doing extremely well. We've scored more as a team since he arrived. He knows his role very well and he fills it very well.' Ten Hag got the most out of the towering Dutchman's enormous running ability. Weghorst engaged in one defensive duel after another and ended the game with the most tackles – eight – of all the players on the field.

One of the most important ways in which a manager's craft is judged is by the substitutions he makes during a game. Some will be in reaction to an injury or a red card and a mandatory change in formation. The most interesting, dramatic and telling ones are the tactical substitutions: the ones a manager makes when he recognises that something needs changing. Something or someone isn't quite working out. His team needs a new impulse. Erik ten Hag does not wait if he sees a problem in his team; he acts without hesitation. Until the return match against Barcelona in England, 19 Manchester United goals were scored by substitutes in all competitions, more than any side in Europe's five big leagues. Ten Hag has an uncanny success rate.

On a rousing evening at Old Trafford, Robert Lewandowski's penalty opened the scoring. At the interval Ten Hag withdrew Weghorst and introduced Antony. The positional changes enhanced United's attack. United equalised via Fred two minutes into the second half before Antony's winner knocked Barça out of the Europa League play-off. It was a match that will live long in the memory of the United supporters. By the final whistle, United were celebrating a great night: 1984, 2008 and now 2023. Manchester United beat Barcelona for the first time since April 2008, ending their five-game winless run against the Spanish side. It was a triumph made more special by the fact they had to achieve victory from behind. For Barcelona, it was the first time they have been eliminated from European competition without reaching the last 16 since 1998–9. It was also Barcelona's first defeat since October and ended an unbeaten 18-match run.

Interim coach Ralf Rangnick had predicted that Manchester United would need six years to close the gap with the top clubs in the Premier League. Ten Hag managed to do that in six months. He did this by defining very specific roles for his players. He played Fred to his strengths, where previous United managers made him struggle by demanding a too technical role from him. After the great victory over Barcelona, Ten Hag praised his midfielder, and not primarily because of his important goal. 'It was Fred's job to stop Frenkie de Jong. He had to hang around him like a mosquito. And he did.' From an offensive point of view, Fred's willingness to do the running played a key role. Ten Hag knew how to convert Fred's industriousness and tactical insight into more freedom for others. Under Ten Hag, the Brazilian box-to-box player has an important supporting role. Both defensively and offensively, Fred lets others excel as he does the dirty work.

A delighted Ten Hag said, 'In the end, it was a great win because we had the belief to get that win. We got it by getting forward and, in the right moments, we strike. When you can beat Barcelona, one of the best teams at this moment in Europe, then your belief can be really strong that you are able to beat anyone. When you [as Barça] are eight points ahead of Real Madrid in La Liga and you beat Real Madrid in the Super Cup 1–3 and we have seen Real Madrid playing against Liverpool this week [winning 5–2] and you beat a really good opponent, we have the potential to beat all good teams. Liverpool and Arsenal at home were really good wins, but I think this tie over two legs against Barcelona is a big win. We have great personalities, starting with David, Raphaël Varane, Lisandro Martínez, Casemiro, Bruno – winning types. Everyone has such a strong belief in this team and fights. When you concede a penalty, you have to go on, and you can turn around such a game. But you have to get the evidence. And when you win a big game like this, from 1–0 down in a difficult situation, you know you can do it. This win is a good motivation in the season.'

'Having a beginner's mind' means looking at the world through a new learner's eyes. *Shoshin* is a Japanese word used in Zen Buddhism practice. It means you approach every situation as if it's the first time you are seeing it. Ten Hag's refreshing enthusiasm and genuine love of the game captures the essence of this idea. Before the Carabao Cup final he said, 'Every match gives excitement. To get experience of a different culture and different stadiums is great to have in your life, and it makes life exciting. I'm really looking forward to going to the stadium [Wembley]. It's so well known, but I only know it from television. On Sunday, I will experience it for myself, and I'm really looking forward to it.'

It may have been only the League Cup, essentially the fourth most important competition, but it looked like a lift-off for United. They claimed their first trophy under Ten Hag. When he left his post-match press conference, he forgot to take the trophy with the three ears with him, before being reminded. 'I'm already on to the next cup. This one is in,' he said with a smile. It is a success Manchester United have been craving for almost six years. Ten Hag said, 'You have to win the first one and that is what we did today. You can take inspiration from this, but also more confidence. We showed the right spirit – we fought and gave everything, as a team. It wasn't always the best football, but it was effective. There is a hunger and desire for trophies. The players are really good collectively. Also, they challenge each other, which needs to happen. It's a good dressing room. When it's difficult they help each other out. It's great to see, and I think it's the best a manager can get. Some champagne for the staff. The players have a game on Wednesday!'

Steering United to Carabao Cup glory should not be underestimated. It's possible that this final could stand – like Manchester

City's victory in the FA Cup final in 2011, like Chelsea's victory in the 2005 League Cup final, like United's own victory in the 1990 FA Cup final – as a major landmark. Roberto Mancini's learned the importance of winning a first prize when he was managing Manchester City. 'I think we changed our mentality after the FA Cup. We started to believe in ourselves. When you arrive at a club that has not been winning, you need to win one title. It's not important if it's the FA Cup or [then] Carling Cup – it's important to start. When you start to win, the mentality changes. The players are human beings – if every day you work hard and you still don't achieve your goals after one or two years, the players can go down. If instead you work hard and, in the end, you win a title, your job becomes easier. It is never easy to do this job, but when you win your car is full, everybody is with you. When you lose you are alone.'

Players and supporters have reconnected. Erik ten Hag's open letter to Manchester United supporters, 27 February 2023, affirmed that. 'When I arrived at the club, we spoke about the challenge and importance of reuniting this group of players with our amazing fans. Believe me, this squad knows exactly how important you are. The bond between the supporters and the team is there for everyone to see, and what we experienced together yesterday will only further strengthen that bond. The atmosphere generated by those of you at Wembley was incredible. From the first minute until the last you were there with us, driving the team on, supporting and encouraging them to get over the line to bring the trophy back to Manchester. For those of you who couldn't be there, we felt your support before, during and after the game. We set ourselves high standards every day. At Wembley we met those demands and got the reward of our first trophy together. We are so happy to bring the trophy back to Old Trafford, but we are by no means satisfied and we will not stop here. We have experienced the feeling of what it means to win together for Manchester United. Please know that you are vital to what we want to achieve, and take yesterday as proof of what can happen when we are all United together. Thank you for your support and dedication – Erik ten Hag.'

Football stirs strong emotions for everyone involved. Players, staff and fans all feel deep pride and despair, strong attachment and over-whelming joy. Football is a territorial business and clubs are like tribes that require real commitment. The club defines the fans, and the fans define the club. When a player or coach joins the club he becomes 'one of us'. He takes up the mantle of the club, wears the club colours and badge. Managers and players are well-paid professionals, but the club and the fans expect not just skill but also loyalty. 'Man U Religion' is not just chutzpah. Restoring faith and building a good and close relationship with the fans is something that Ten Hag has deliberately set out to do. His devotion to the club and passion to get the best out of each moment has been recognised by the supporters. 'I am sharp and always busy with the club, the team and the players, but I also enjoy every day. I thoroughly enjoy Old Trafford. Sometimes we really don't play well, but the supporters are behind us. In the Netherlands, at many clubs, cynicism quickly takes over when the game is bad. In England they keep supporting you, they keep urging you on. It's beautiful.'

Ten Hag told his players to embrace the hostile environment of Anfield, where United have not won since 2016, scoring only once in the past eight trips. Seven days after winning the League Cup, there was widespread indignation over the 'disgrace', 'shambles' and 'embarrassment'. The 7–0 thrashing by Liverpool was United's joint-heaviest competitive defeat – matching those by the same score against Blackburn Rovers in April 1926, Aston Villa in December 1930 and Wolves on Boxing Day 1931. Six of the goals came in a stunning second-half Liverpool display, with their opponents simply unable or even unwilling to cope. There was an aghast Sir Alex Ferguson, a delighted Sir Kenny Dalglish and the sight of streams of United fans heading for the exits early. Ten Hag stood almost motionless for the final 15 minutes to 'analyse the performance of my team, their approach, their character, their mentality, how they deal with setbacks. I looked at their body language.'

Roy Keane gave voice to collective United shame by suggesting that, 'I would go into hiding.' That is exactly what Ten Hag did not do. A leader shows his mettle by being unchanging in changing circumstances. 'What happened doesn't destroy all the good work we have done this season', was the message from the boss. He told his team to be hungry to put things right. He believed they would benefit from sessions with Rainier Koers, the Dutch sports psychologist he brought to the club, whose website suggests that people can 'make headway by standing still for a moment.' There was no replay of the entire game, but Ten Hag did show his players select video clips 'to make them angry', just as he had tried to rile them at Anfield by demanding silence in the away dressing room so they could listen to Liverpool's celebrations.

The exertions of ousting Barcelona to progress in Europe, securing the first piece of silverware at Newcastle's expense and reaching the FA Cup quarter-finals had their impact: 21 fixtures in 75 days with a stretched squad is not ideal. The 99.01km they ran at Anfield was the lowest since the 95.6km at Brentford, but there were mitigating circumstances. The two days of training leading up to Liverpool were below par, and Ten Hag knew his players were feeling the strain. There was no point flogging them this time. It had been a gruelling schedule. Ten Hag said, 'We win together, we lose together, we made a mess on Sunday and we have to deal with it. But also it is only one game. This team is strong enough and we will reset and bounce back. If you do the right things, if you react with the right measures as a manager and as a team, you can learn a lot from it and can strengthen your mentality.'

Bruno Fernandes was savaged for his role in the debacle. There were calls for Ten Hag to strip him of the captain's armband. But belief and loyalty are twins, and Ten Hag is a man of faith, in the broader sense of the word. Asked if Fernandes would remain as captain, the United manager said, 'Yes, definitely. He's playing a brilliant season, he's had a really important role getting us to the position we are because he's giving energy to the team, not only running a lot at the highest intensity, but also in the right way and right direction. He's pointing and coaching players, he's an inspiration to the whole team. No one is perfect. Everyone makes their mistakes, and everyone has to learn. I have to learn. He will learn as well because he's intelligent. I'm really happy to have Bruno Fernandes in the team, and that he's captain when Harry is not on the pitch.'

Ten Hag is a manager who does not believe in 'home' and 'away' games. 'For me, it's no different – the pitch is the same size everywhere, there are three referees, there's a fourth official, the ball is round, there's air in the ball. So, we have to play and to make it our game, and [winning away at a top-four rival] is the next step we have to make. Developing a team takes time. You can't go from zero to 100 – you have to construct it with the fundamentals before you go to the top, to the roof. Unfortunately, it takes time, and I'm really impatient. But I have to wait. Our build-up is improving game to game. So now we have to develop our attacking game more, but it's the most difficult part, so it takes even more time. You can't increase the tempo of that process.'

Against Sevilla, United capitulated after going behind inside eight minutes to Youssef En-Nesyri's goal in the Estadio Ramón Sánchez-Pizjuán. The ghastly errors by David de Gea and Harry

Maguire tell only part of the story of the surrender that spelled the end of the Europa League campaign. Ten Hag drew his own conclusions. 'I think there were some traumatic experiences this group had in previous years. Sevilla was a good learning moment for us. We need to think about that and learn from those moments to avoid letting the opponent back into the game. The biggest teams always show composure in those moments and stick to the plan, staying in the game and finding a way to bounce back. We are capable of bouncing back between games, now the next step is to bounce back in the game. That's what we have to improve. I have to teach the players to do better in such circumstances. The demands on this team are high because we are Manchester United. So I have to teach the players, and the players have to step up.'

Manchester United reached the FA Cup final after beating Brighton on penalties at Wembley, following a tense 120 minutes where either side could have felt they deserved to face Manchester City in the final. Each of the first 12 penalties in the shoot-out were converted successfully, until Solly March's miss left Victor Lindelof to score the winning spot-kick. Substitute Wout Weghorst was allowed to grab the ball after calmly converting his penalty before handing it over to March. Weghorst pressed the ball to his lips before saying something to the Brighton forward. Manchester United supporters were hailing Wout Weghorst's 'kiss of death' as the reason behind their FA Cup semi-final victory.

United set up the first all-Manchester FA Cup final in the 151-year history of the competition. Rarely was a final so eagerly anticipated. City took the lead 12 seconds into the game through Ilkay Gündoğan, the fastest-ever goal in a FA Cup final. United battled back into the game and were level after half an hour through a Bruno Fernandes penalty. A second Gündoğan shot in the second half secured the victory for City. Ten Hag said after the match, 'We conceded two soft and unnecessary goals. But we kept ourselves in the game. There was a great spirit and very good organisation. We were hard to beat and didn't allow much open play against the best team in the world at that moment. We maybe are the only team in the world who are capable of fighting back against City. It's hard when you concede a goal so quickly, but you see once again, the mentality and character of this team is very good. We stayed calm. I think in the end we could have got an equaliser. On another day maybe we could have won this game. You can tell we played a fantastic season. We have qualified for the Champions League, won a trophy and got to another final, so I am very happy with the performance from my team.'

Knowing the boundaries of one's control is important for all people, but it is vital for those in a leadership position. The manager in the Premier League can easily get distracted by all the noise in and around the club and lose his focus. As someone who has been in the sporting limelight for a good number of years, Ten Hag understands this well. The controversies over Manchester United's ownership are a case in point. Asked how important it was that the United take-over process was resolved swiftly so he would know what the future holds, Ten Hag said, 'I think it's clear what I want, but it's not up to me. It's about others in this club. The [Glazer] family are the owners, they make the decisions … So I do everything I can and I influence the processes I'm in charge of, but that [the ownership] is not my job or responsibility. I don't have the power to influence that. I have to make sure the team is progressing and I'm focusing on that.' Ten Hag was spotted picking up a green and gold scarf – a symbol of the anti-Glazer movement – at the match against Aston Villa, but he said, 'I know what's going around, what symbol it is, but this matter was just [being] polite.'

Liverpool manager Jürgen Klopp suggested that his club could not keep up with Manchester City and Newcastle due to their financial backing, but Ten Hag believes Manchester United can compete with state-owned clubs. 'I look at the competition around the Premier League, they all have the opportunity to invest. It's a tough competition between seven or eight clubs. That's a change in circumstances when you compare that to five or 10 years ago, so the competition is much tougher. Newcastle are coming, even West Ham, maybe not now in the table, but they have huge investment. Quickly count seven or eight clubs that can compete in the league, and it's clear that when you don't have the right players and the quality players, you will not be successful and achieve the targets you set. The competition is really tough, so you need the right players. We are able to compete with City and Newcastle. I think it's also about strategy, not just money.'

Whether in football or in business, a truly motivated person is able to transcend himself when he is doing something that he loves. Then he can accomplish something that is difficult to achieve. Excellence becomes a motivation for the manager and his team. Once the team wins, they want more, and then again and again. Thus, a spiral of high performance kicks in. When the team wins, there is an atmosphere: people work hard, they enjoy their work and they stimulate each other. They work for the team, and they work for each other. Cynics say that, in the end, it all boils down to money: when a player sees a bigger wallet appear somewhere else, he is off to different hunting grounds. Money matters, of course. But in the end, a player wants to bring his capabilities and art to the big stage. It is about the joy of playing the game and the desire to win. These are the real motivators for the true professionals. The same applies to the manager. Being successful begins with the love of the game. The spirit and enthusiasm of the manager will resonate with that of the players. If that connection is made, the beginning of a good and successful cooperation has been established. Without that precondition, nothing else matters.

In December 2022, the supercomputer at Bonus CodeBets – Big Blue – ran the numbers and concluded that, unfortunately, United would not be able to reach the top four in the 2022–3 season, and instead would finish sixth. A spokesperson said, 'Tottenham are set to finish fourth and it might come with a bit of a shock that Newcastle are predicted to finish fifth, ahead of Manchester United in sixth and Chelsea in seventh.' The team expected to join Tottenham finishing in the top four was given as Liverpool by the computer. Big Blue's prediction: 1. Manchester City 2. Arsenal 3. Liverpool 4. Tottenham Hotspur 5. Newcastle United 6. Manchester United 7. Chelsea. The reality: 1. Manchester City 2. Arsenal 3. Manchester United 4. Newcastle United 5. Liverpool 6. Brighton 7. Aston Villa 8. Tottenham 12. Chelsea. What this demonstrates, other than the relative uselessness of computer algorithms for predicting football competition outcomes, is the excellent performance of Manchester United under Erik ten Hag. He won 40 out of 60 games, a higher win ratio than any of his predecessors in a debut season. Pundits were as surprised as computer programmers.

United secured a Champions League return with an emphatic 4–1 victory over Chelsea, with goals from Casemiro, Anthony Martial, Bruno Fernandes and Marcus Rashford. When Arsène Wenger was Arsenal's manager, he said a top-four finish was akin to claiming silverware. Ten Hag agreed it is a very big deal. 'This club belongs in the Champions League. It's not easy in the Premier League, as a lot [of teams] compete for that. It's massive when you get it done. We're still not where we want to be, but we're back in the Champions League and I think that was a really important step.' This is also vital to guarantee quality transfers for the next season.

Ten Hag is tasked with sculpting a future where Manchester United not only compete consistently in the Premier League but consistently win it. For those ambitions to be realised, a prolific striker must be acquired. 'Everyone is different, obviously, but for a striker the main thing is to score goals by any method, that is so far ahead of anything else. We need a striker who scores goals because we have ability in the team to put balls in the box, so we need a striker to finish. We have to build a new future, and we need a striker who not only scores goals but contributes by linking up play very well and pressing, which is very important.' Ten Hag claims there are not the same 'reservations' among potential recruits that existed the previous summer, when the club had concluded their worst Premier League season. 'I see a big difference in comparison with last year. There were a lot of reservations last year when I spoke with players, and now many players see the project, what's going on, the dynamic and the ambition in this project, the quality especially. They are really keen to come, I've noticed that.'

How does the manager respond to all the excitement of the 2022–3 Manchester United season? He is his unperturbed self. The plan does not change. Ten Hag focuses calmly, intelligently and consistently on changing attitudes and ethics, at every level. United have needed this kind of manager for years. Earlier in the season, he said, 'In every country, I have had my favourite club, and in England that has been Manchester United. The beginning is always difficult. You don't know the club yet. Before you introduce your ideas to the squad, and they accept them – that takes time. A coach can't perform magic, although the media often expect them to. I must say I have a strong belief in myself. This is a big challenge, but everywhere I've been, I've got the maximum out of my teams. This is my most difficult project, but I am convinced I can do it.'

ERIK TEN HAG CURRICULUM VITAE

Born on 2 February 1970 in Haaksbergen, the Netherlands

Career as player:
SV Bon Boys youth, 1977–85
FC Twente youth, 1985–9
FC Twente, 1989–90
De Graafschap, 1990–2
FC Twente, 1992–4
RKC Waalwijk, 1994–5
FC Utrecht, 1995–6
FC Twente, 1996–2002

Career as manager:
FC Twente U17 coach, 2002–3
FC Twente U19 coach, 2003–6
FC Twente assistant manager, 2006–9
PSV Eindhoven assistant manager, 2009–12
Go Ahead Eagles manager, 2012–13
Bayern Munich II manager, 2013–15
FC Utrecht manager, 2015–17
Ajax manager, 2017–22
Manchester United manager, 2022–present

Achievements as player:

De Graafschap, Eerste Divisie title, 1990–1

FC Twente, KNVB Cup, 2000–1

Achievements as manager:

Go Ahead Eagles, promotion to the Eredivisie, 2012–13

Bayern Munich II, Regionalliga Bayern title, 2013–14

Ajax, Eredivisie title 2018–19, 2020–1, 2021–2; KNVB Cup 2018–19, 2020–21; Champions League semi-finals, 2018–19; Johan Cruyff Shield, 2019

Manchester United, Carabao Cup 2022–3

Special honors:

Rinus Michels Award, Eredivisie Manager of the Year, 2015–16, 2018–19, 2020–1

ABOUT THE AUTHOR

Maarten Meijer spent his childhood and youth in the rural Netherlands. He hitch-hiked across southern Europe, from Spain to Italy to Greece, and sailed across the north, from Ireland to Denmark to Finland. When Europe became too small, he sailed a two-mast yacht with friends across the Atlantic Ocean to Central America. After touring Martinique, Guadeloupe and a handful of other Caribbean islands, he ended up in the USA. He enrolled at the State University of New York, receiving a bachelor's degree in science and a master's degree in philosophy. In 1982, he met his beautiful Latina wife Myra, a Manhattan native.

In 1991, thirst for new adventure led the family, which by then included two children, to Russia. Maarten taught philosophy in post-Communist Moscow, and again traveled widely, from Riga and Crimea in the west to Lake Baikal and Vladivostok in the east. He received his Ph.D. in Russian literature from Moscow State University, writing a dissertation on *The Family in the Works of Leo Tolstoy*. He is fluent in English, German, Russian and Dutch, and gets by in French and Korean. Living in a Moscow student dormitory with many friendly Korean families inspired a move to South Korea in 2000.

Maarten taught writing at Seoul Women's University for several years and began to publish. He is the author of *What's So Good about Korea, Maarten?* (South Korea, 2005), *Guus Hiddink – Going Dutch* (Australia, 2006), *The Korean Education Code* (South Korea, 2011),

Dick Advocaat – Biografie (Netherlands, 2013), *Louis van Gaal – the Biography* (UK, 2014), *How to Create Top Education – Finland and Korea* (South Korea, 2015, co-authored with daughter Renée), *The Marriage Blessing* (US, 2020) and *Smarter than Covid – How South Koreans Beat the Virus* (US, 2021). Since March 2006, he has been teaching writing and philosophy at an international school in the Korean mountains, while doubling as social critic and football commentator.

Maarten and Myra have a daughter, who was born in Montana, and three sons, born in New York, Moscow and Seoul, respectively.

IMAGE CREDITS

ZJJ / Shutterstock (Image 1)

ANP / Alamy Stock Photo (Images 2, 3)

Robert Hoetink / Shutterstock (Images 4, 5)

PA Images / Alamy Stock Photo (Image 6)

REUTERS / Alamy Stock Photo (Image 7, 8, 23)

Cristiano Barni / Shutterstock (Image 9)

Pro Shots / Alamy Stock Photo (Images 10, 11, 13)

Soccrates Images / Getty Images Europe (Images 12, 18)

Sipa US / Alamy Stock Photo (Image 14, 17)

Orange Pics BV / Alamy Stock Photo (Images 15, 16)

ANP / Getty Images Europe (Image 19)

Ash Donelon / Manchester United / Getty Images (Image 20)

Wason Wanichakorn / AP /Shutterstock (Image 21)

News Images LTD / Alamy Stock Photo (Image 22)

Mark Pain / Alamy Stock Photo (Image 23)

SOURCES

Burt, Jason. 'Solly March misses as Brighton lose FA Cup semi-final on penalties to Manchester United'. The *Telegraph*, 23 April 2023.

Draper, Rob. 'The day 13-year-old Erik ten Hag gave his idol Johan Cruyff a real grilling …' The *Mail on Sunday*, 23 July 2022.

Ducker, James. 'How Erik ten Hag faith and "new man" body hauled Marcus Rashford out of slump'. The *Telegraph*, 1 October 2022.

Ducker, James. 'Erik ten Hag: I will not push Jadon Sancho into early Manchester United return'. The *Telegraph*, 5 January 2023.

Flintham, Jack. 'Erik ten Hag's Manchester United tactics explained ahead of manager appointment'. *Manchester Evening News*, 14 April 2022.

Hamilton, Tom. 'Man United manager Erik ten Hag: The "tactically brilliant" coach who became a winner at Ajax'. ESPN, 21 April 2022.

Hunter, Andy. 'Shaw claims Manchester United team has not always been picked on merit'. The *Guardian*, 17 October 2022.

Jackson, Jamie. '"Thank you for the lesson": Erik ten Hag to use derby rout as guide for future'. The *Guardian*, 5 October 2022.

Janssen, Willem. 'Erik ten Hag is the best coach I have played under – these are the reasons why'. The *Guardian*, 22 April 2022.

Jones, Rich. 'Uncovering Erik ten Hag: Early years of next Man Utd manager – "Even as a kid, a winner"'. The *Mirror*, 3 May 2022.

King, Dominic. 'Pep Guardiola's apprentice is primed to rescue Man United, he demands high standards and has no time limits on training …' The *Daily Mail*, 1 April 2022.

Liew, Jonathan. 'Traits that made Cristiano Ronaldo great now hasten his painful decline'. The *Guardian*, 21 October 2022.

Luckhurst, Samuel. 'Cristiano Ronaldo has underestimated Erik ten Hag too many times at Manchester United'. *Manchester Evening News*, 20 October 2022.

Marshall, Tyrone. 'Cristiano Ronaldo has accidentally done Erik ten Hag a favour at Manchester United'. *Manchester Evening News*, 25 October 2022.

Marshall, Tyrone. 'Why Erik ten Hag is the biggest winner from Cristiano Ronaldo leaving Manchester United'. *Manchester Evening News*, 22 November 2022.

McGrath, Mike. 'Erik ten Hag and Sir Alex Ferguson parallels becoming harder to ignore'. The *Telegraph*, 29 January 2023.

Mullock, Simon. 'Man Utd bound Erik ten Hag opens up on tragic air crash which still haunts him'. The *Irish Mirror*, 26 March 2022.

Mullock, Simon. 'Who is Mitchell van der Gaag? Erik ten Hag's new Man Utd assistant to play pivotal role'. The *Mirror*, 16 April 2022.

Pitt-Brooke, Jack. 'Juventus vs Ajax result: Giant-killers turn history on its head to knock out Cristiano Ronaldo's Italian champions'. The *Independent*, 16 April 2019.

Renard, Arthur. '"Erik ten Hag is a genuine person – you are willing to go through fire for somebody like him"'. The *Times*, 13 April 2022.

Unwin, Will. 'Marcus Rashford the best striking solution for Ten Hag in short term'. The *Guardian*, 29 October 2022.

Van Gaal, Louis, *LvG: De trainer en de totale mens*. Nieuw Amsterdam, 2020.

Wallace, Sam. 'The making of Erik ten Hag: "Only one coach could analyse games like him – and that was Fergie"'. The *Telegraph*, 21 April 2022.

Wallace, Sam. 'Narcissistic Cristiano Ronaldo interview plays into Erik ten Hag's hands'. The *Telegraph*, 14 November 2022.

Wheeler, Chris. 'Manchester United 3–1 Arsenal: Erik ten Hag's resurgent Red Devils make it FOUR wins in a row …' The *Daily Mail*, 4 September 2022.

Wheeler, Chris, 'Erik ten Hag's eyes in the sky: Who are Manchester United's team of analysts and what do they do?'. The *Daily Mail*, 22 February 2023.

Whitwell, Laurie and Hay, Anthony. 'Antony must improve consistency to become a top-class player – Erik ten Hag'. The *Athletic*, 17 April 2023.

Wilson, Jonathan. 'The devil and José Mourinho'. The *Guardian*, 22 December 2015.

With additional thanks to the following rightsholders: AFC Ajax, Ajax Showtime, Ajax TV, Algemeen Dagblad, BBC, Coaches Betaald Voetbal, Dutch Soccer Site, ELFvoetbal, ESPN, EW magazine, FC Bayern München, FC Utrecht, Financial Focus, Jan's Dutch Soccer Site, Knack Sportmagazine, Manchester United FC, KNVB, Nu.nl, NOS Sport, NOVA Sport, NRC, PSV, De Stentor, Sport/Voetbalmagazine, Sky Sports, De Telegraaf, Tubantia, Trouw, Twente Fans, Twente Insite, TwenteVisie, Utrecht Business, Voetbal International, Voetbal Primeur, Voetbalzone, De VoetbalTrainer, de Volkskrant.